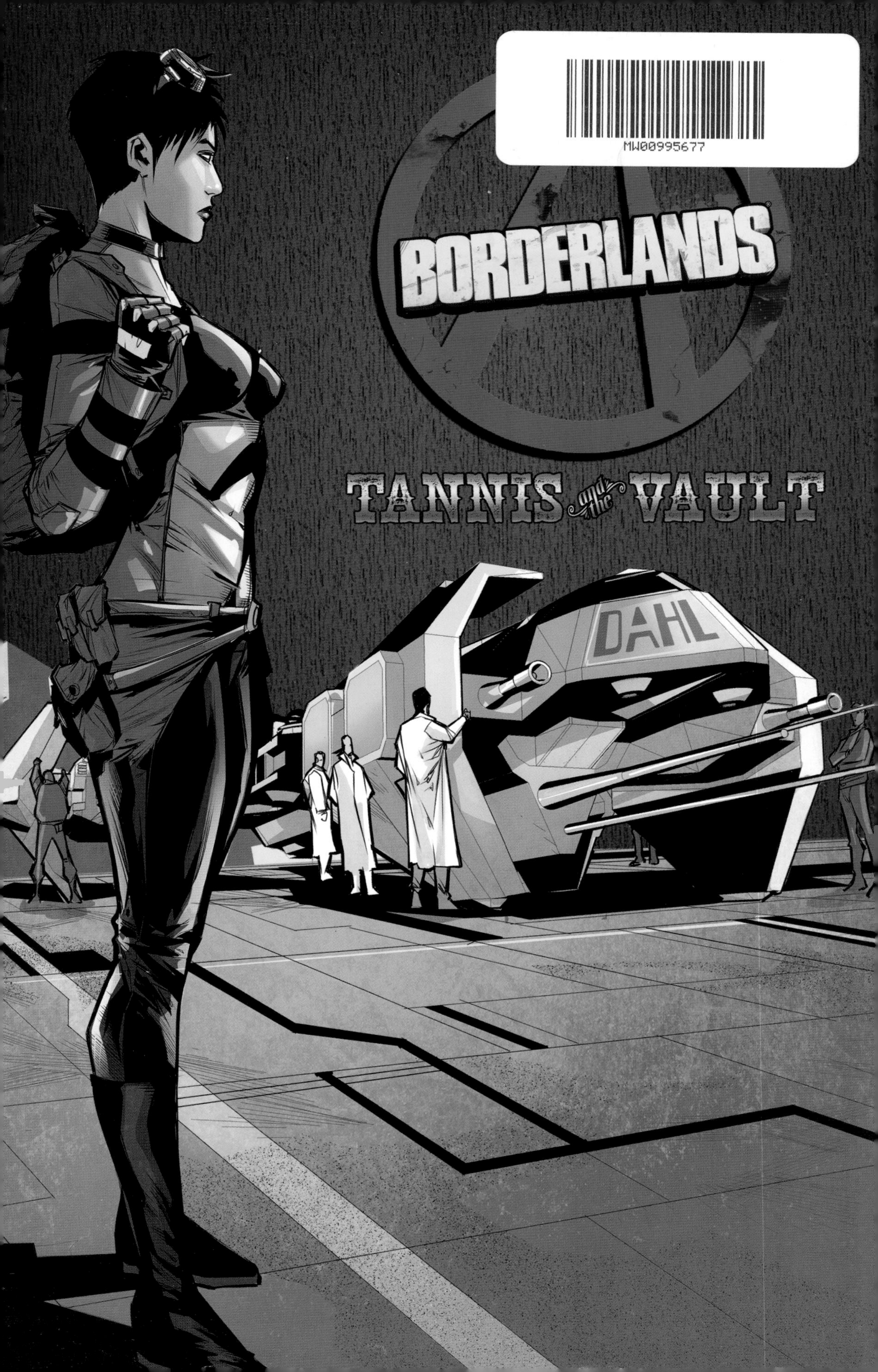
BORDERLANDS
TANNIS and the VAULT
DAHL

written by MIKEY NEUMANN
art by AGUSTIN PADILLA
colors by ESTHER SANZ
letters by NEIL UYETAKE
series edits by TOM WALTZ

cover by AGUSTIN PADILLA
cover colors by ESTHER SANZ
collection edits by JUSTIN EISINGER
and ALONZO SIMON
collection design by CHRIS MOWRY
and NEIL UYETAKE

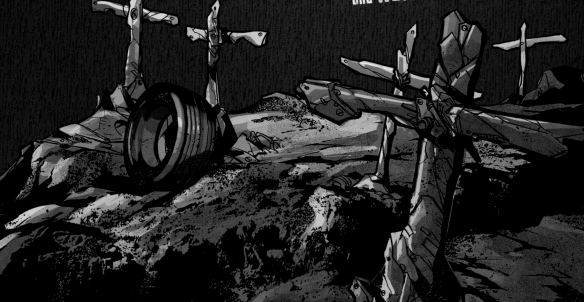

Special thanks to Randy Pitchford, Brian Martel, David Eddings, Scott Kester, and Eduardo Alpuente.

ISBN: 978-1-63140-271-5

18 17 16 15   1 2 3 4

www.IDWPUBLISHING.com
IDW founded by Ted Adams, Alex Garner, Kris Oprisko, and Robbie Robbins

Facebook: facebook.com/idwpublishing
Twitter: @idwpublishing
YouTube: youtube.com/idwpublishing
Instagram: instagram.com/idwpublishing
deviantART: idwpublishing.deviantart.com
Pinterest: pinterest.com/idwpublishing/idw-staff-faves

BORDERLANDS

TANNIS and the VAULT

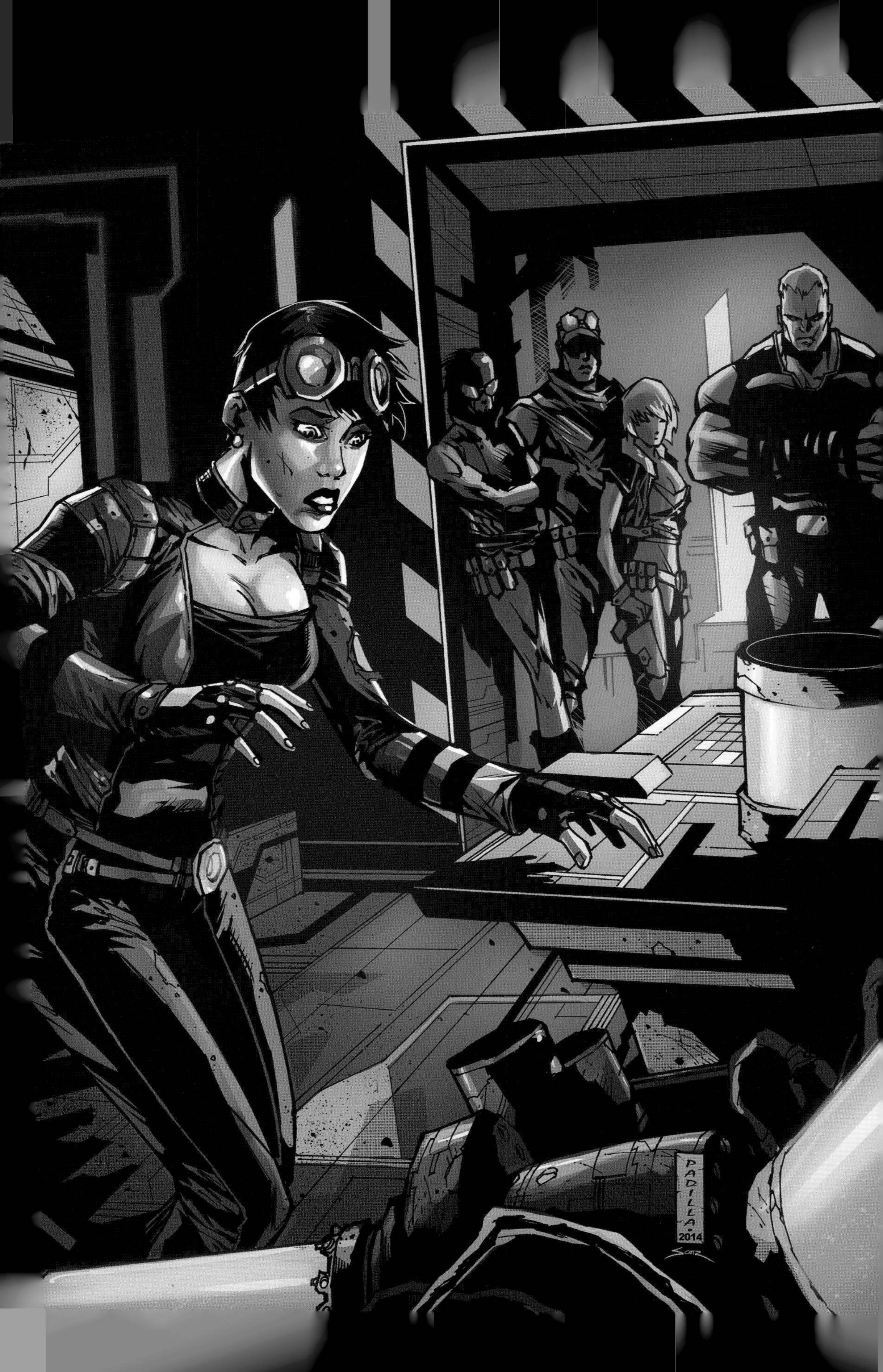
PADILLA 2014

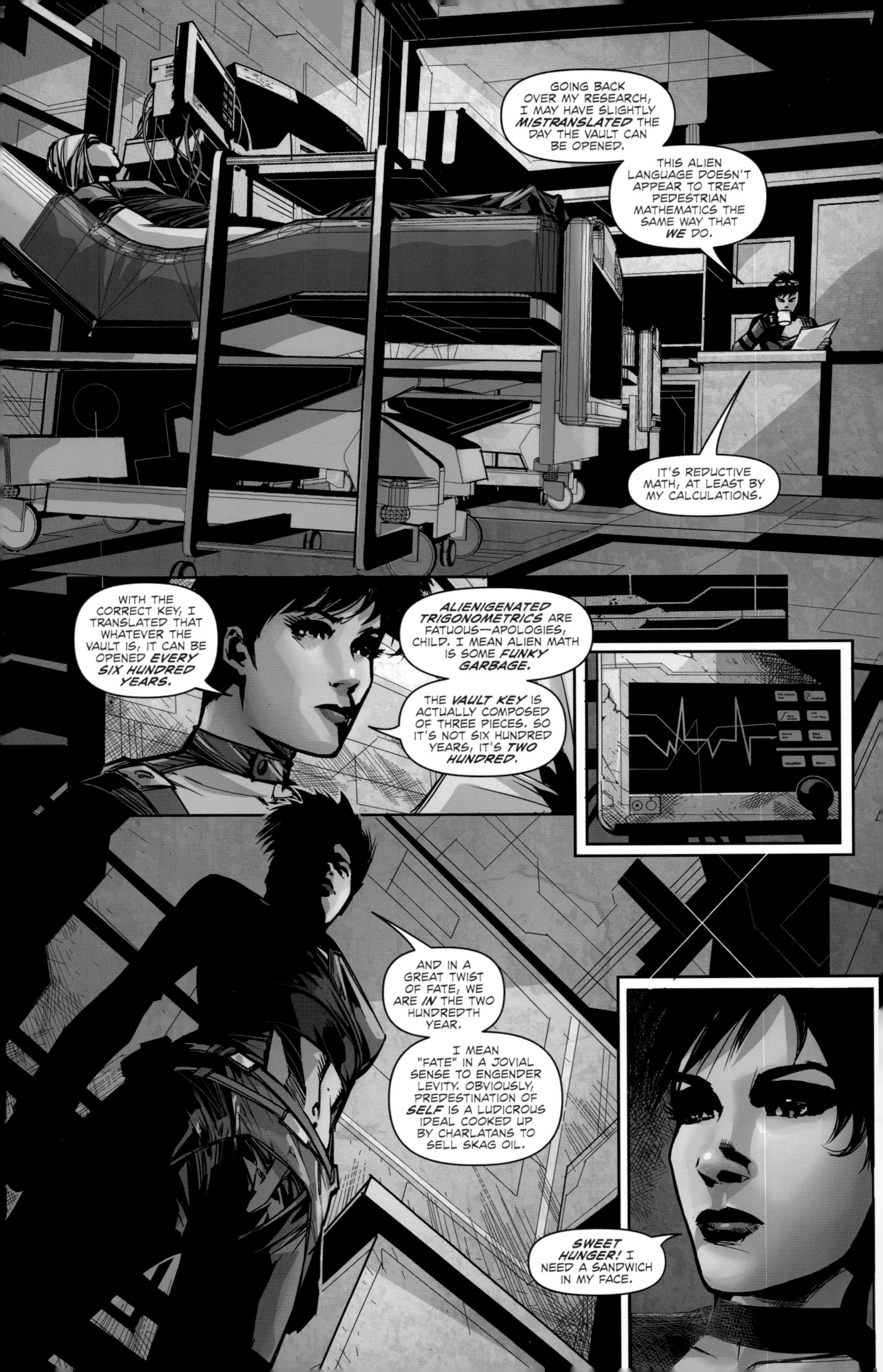
GOING BACK OVER MY RESEARCH, I MAY HAVE SLIGHTLY MISTRANSLATED THE DAY THE VAULT CAN BE OPENED.
THIS ALIEN LANGUAGE DOESN'T APPEAR TO TREAT PEDESTRIAN MATHEMATICS THE SAME WAY THAT WE DO.
IT'S REDUCTIVE MATH, AT LEAST BY MY CALCULATIONS.
WITH THE CORRECT KEY, I TRANSLATED THAT WHATEVER THE VAULT IS, IT CAN BE OPENED EVERY SIX HUNDRED YEARS.
ALIENIGENATED TRIGONOMETRICS ARE FATUOUS—APOLOGIES, CHILD. I MEAN ALIEN MATH IS SOME FUNKY GARBAGE.
THE VAULT KEY IS ACTUALLY COMPOSED OF THREE PIECES. SO IT'S NOT SIX HUNDRED YEARS, IT'S TWO HUNDRED.
AND IN A GREAT TWIST OF FATE, WE ARE IN THE TWO HUNDREDTH YEAR.
I MEAN "FATE" IN A JOVIAL SENSE TO ENGENDER LEVITY. OBVIOUSLY, PREDESTINATION OF SELF IS A LUDICROUS IDEAL COOKED UP BY CHARLATANS TO SELL SKAG OIL.
SWEET HUNGER! I NEED A SANDWICH IN MY FACE.

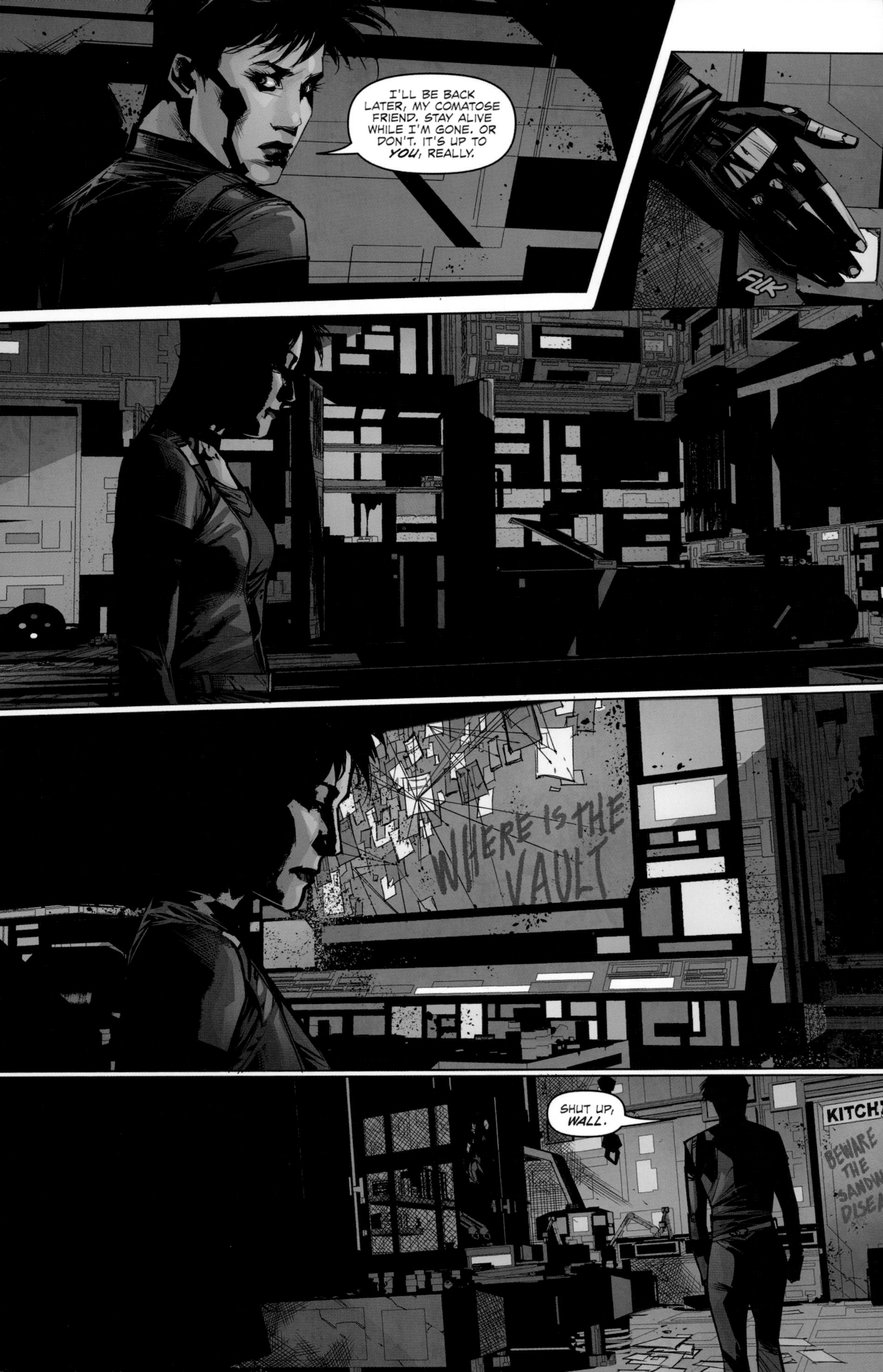
I'LL BE BACK LATER, MY COMATOSE FRIEND. STAY ALIVE WHILE I'M GONE. OR DON'T. IT'S UP TO YOU, REALLY.
FLIK
WHERE IS THE VAULT
SHUT UP, WALL.
KITCH
BEWARE THE

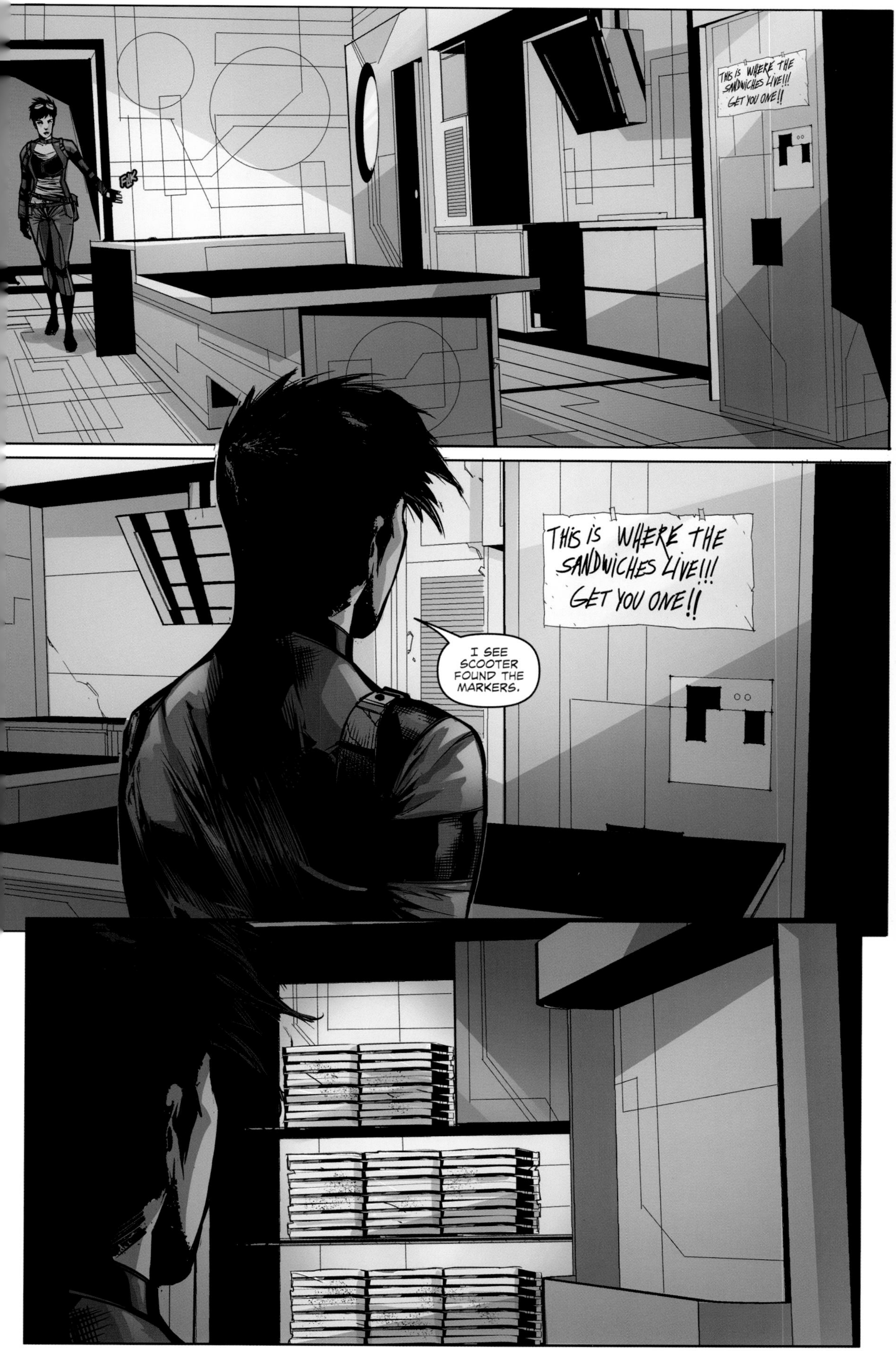
FLIK
THIS is WHERE THE SANDWICHES LIVE!!! GET YOU ONE!!
THIS is WHERE THE SANDWICHES LIVE!!! GET YOU ONE!!
I SEE SCOOTER FOUND THE MARKERS.

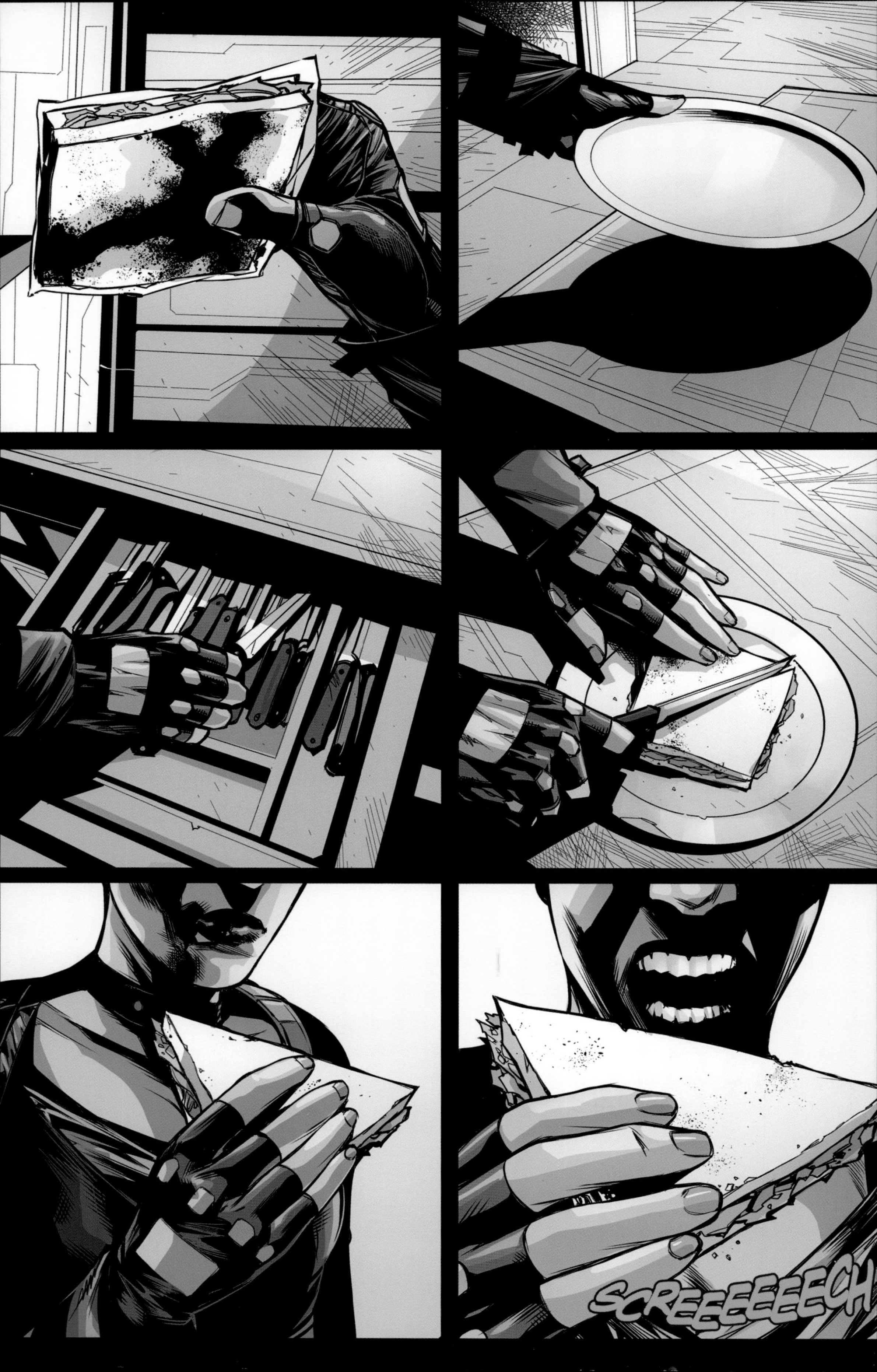
SCREEEEEEEECH

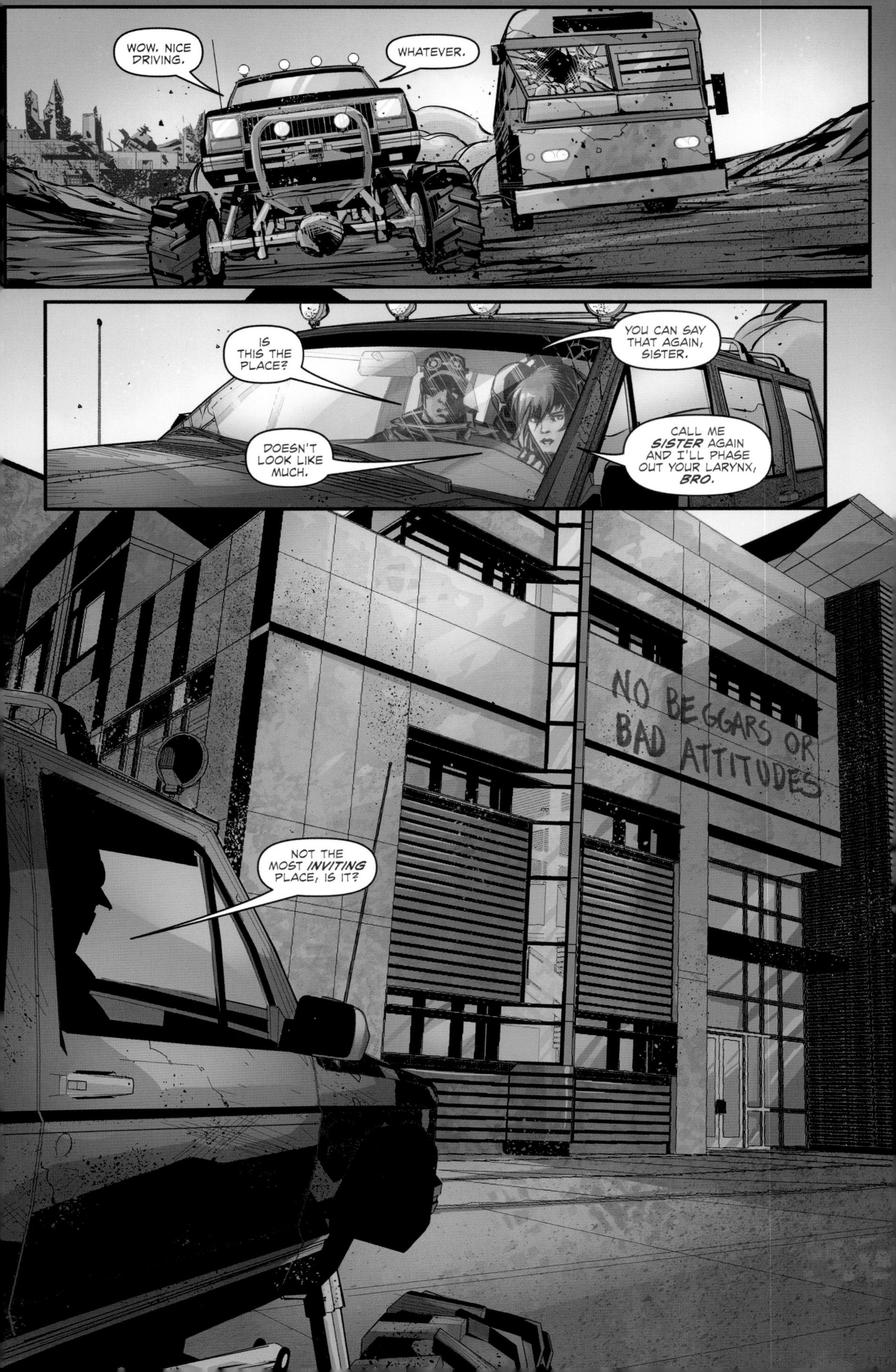
WOW. NICE DRIVING.
WHATEVER.
IS THIS THE PLACE?
DOESN'T LOOK LIKE MUCH.
YOU CAN SAY THAT AGAIN, SISTER.
CALL ME SISTER AGAIN AND I'LL PHASE OUT YOUR LARYNX, BRO.
NO BEGGARS OR BAD ATTITUDES
NOT THE MOST INVITING PLACE, IS IT?

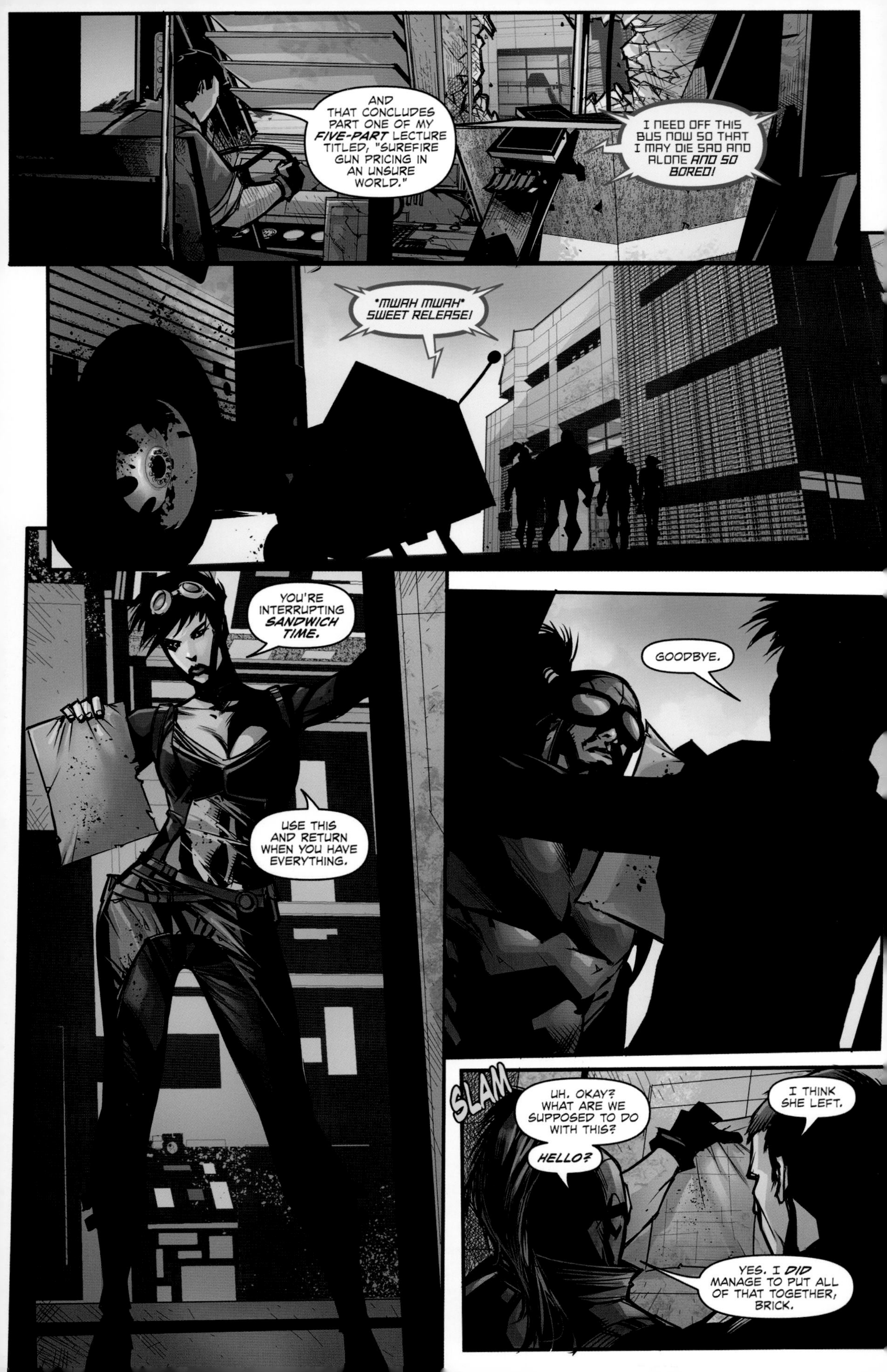
AND THAT CONCLUDES PART ONE OF MY FIVE-PART LECTURE TITLED, "SUREFIRE GUN PRICING IN AN UNSURE WORLD."
I NEED OFF THIS BUS NOW SO THAT I MAY DIE SAD AND ALONE AND SO BORED!
MWAH MWAH SWEET RELEASE!
YOU'RE INTERRUPTING SANDWICH TIME.
USE THIS AND RETURN WHEN YOU HAVE EVERYTHING.
GOODBYE.
SLAM
UH. OKAY? WHAT ARE WE SUPPOSED TO DO WITH THIS?
HELLO?
I THINK SHE LEFT.
YES. I DID MANAGE TO PUT ALL OF THAT TOGETHER, BRICK.

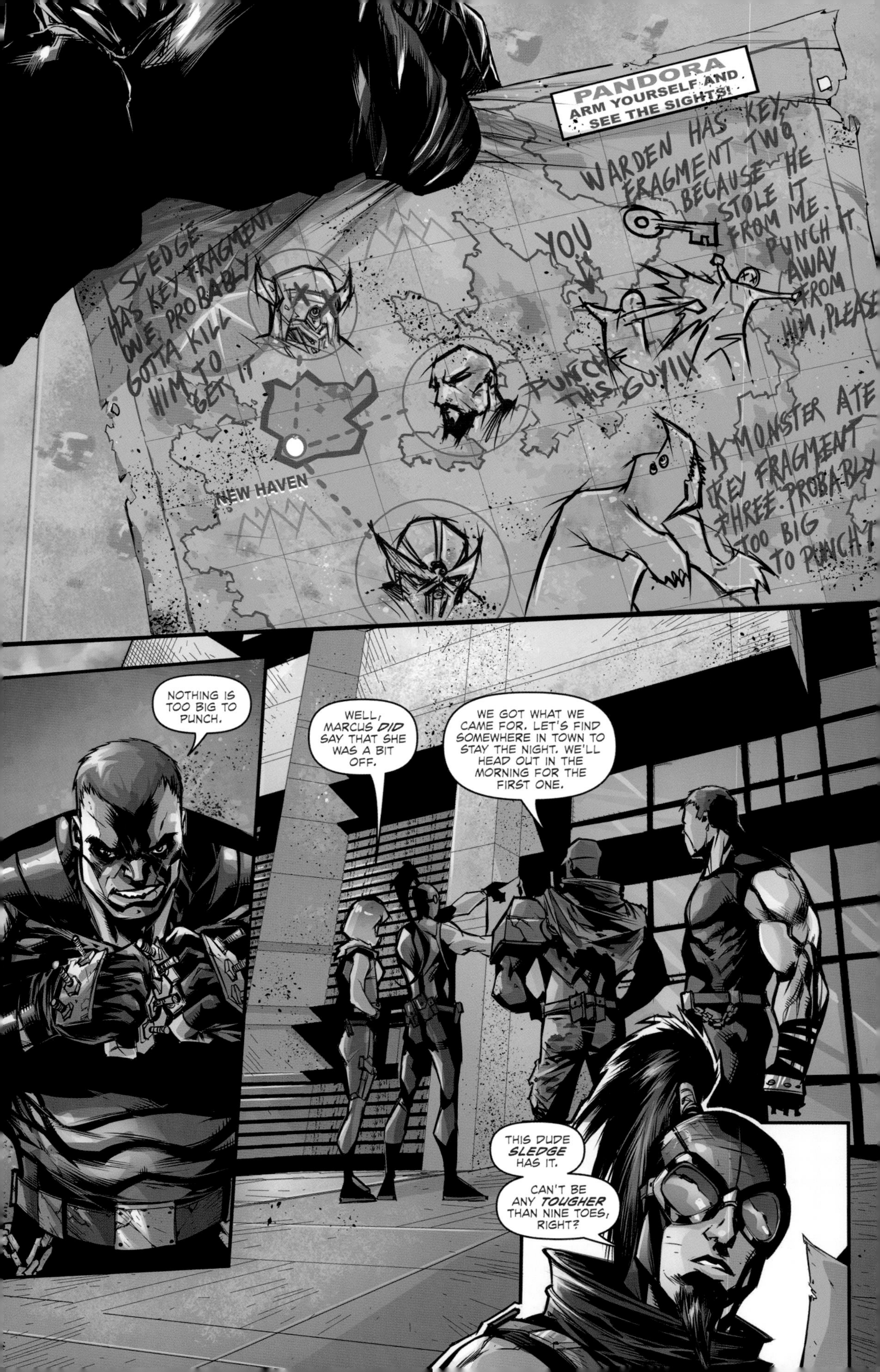
PANDORA
ARM YOURSELF AND SEE THE SIGHTS!
WARDEN HAS KEY FRAGMENT TWO BECAUSE HE STOLE IT FROM ME. PUNCH IT AWAY FROM HIM, PLEASE
YOU
SLEDGE HAS KEY FRAGMENT ONE PROBABLY GOTTA KILL HIM TO GET IT
PUNCH THIS GUY!!!
A MONSTER ATE KEY FRAGMENT THREE. PROBABLY TOO BIG TO PUNCH?
NEW HAVEN
NOTHING IS TOO BIG TO PUNCH.
WELL, MARCUS *DID* SAY THAT SHE WAS A BIT OFF.
WE GOT WHAT WE CAME FOR. LET'S FIND SOMEWHERE IN TOWN TO STAY THE NIGHT. WE'LL HEAD OUT IN THE MORNING FOR THE FIRST ONE.
THIS DUDE *SLEDGE* HAS IT.
CAN'T BE ANY *TOUGHER* THAN NINE TOES, RIGHT?

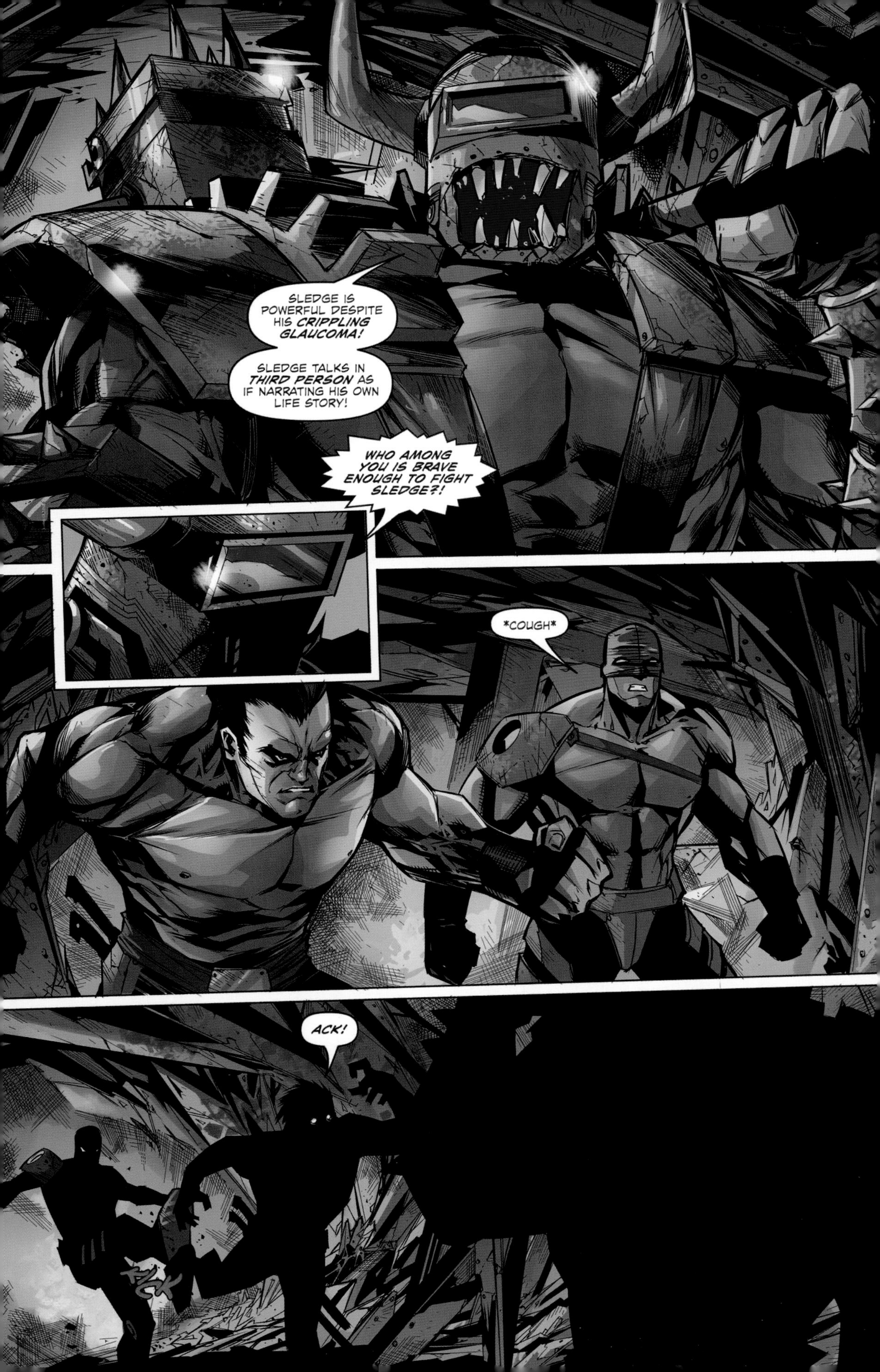
SLEDGE IS POWERFUL DESPITE HIS CRIPPLING GLAUCOMA!
SLEDGE TALKS IN THIRD PERSON AS IF NARRATING HIS OWN LIFE STORY!
WHO AMONG YOU IS BRAVE ENOUGH TO FIGHT SLEDGE?!
COUGH
ACK!

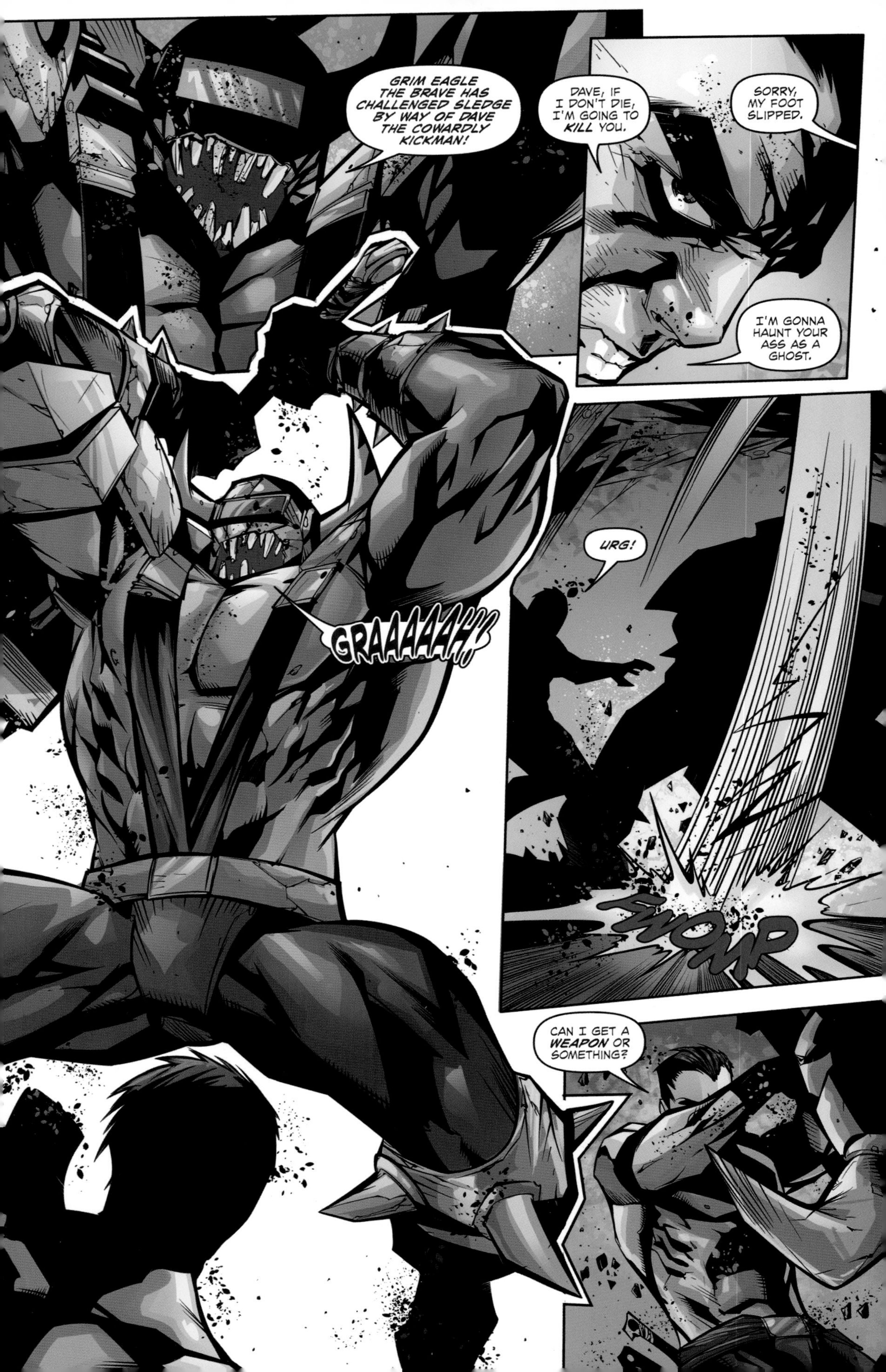
GRIM EAGLE THE BRAVE HAS CHALLENGED SLEDGE BY WAY OF DAVE THE COWARDLY KICKMAN!
DAVE, IF I DON'T DIE, I'M GOING TO KILL YOU.
SORRY, MY FOOT SLIPPED.
I'M GONNA HAUNT YOUR ASS AS A GHOST.
GRAAAAAH!
URG!
FWOMP
CAN I GET A WEAPON OR SOMETHING?

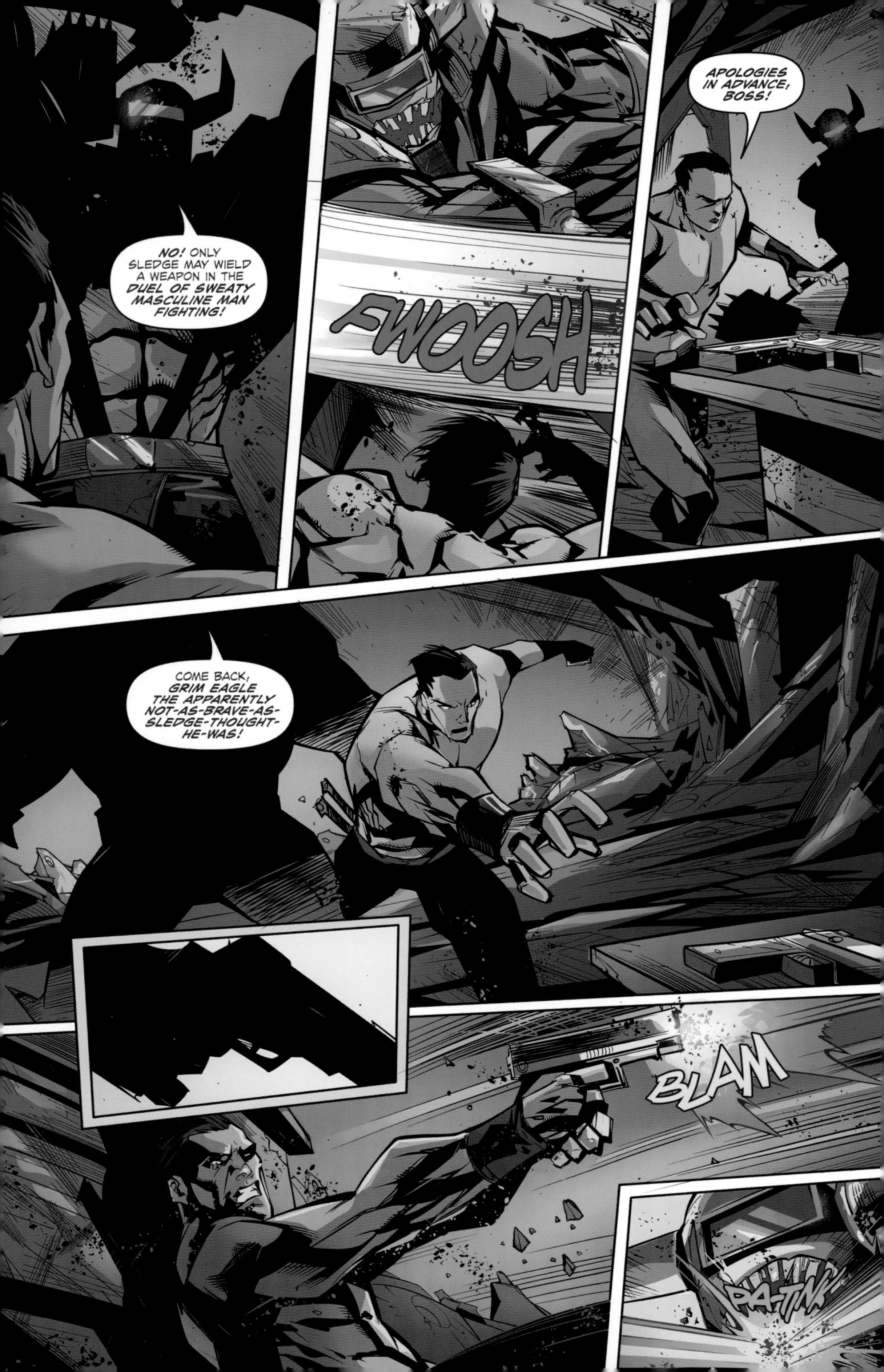
NO! ONLY SLEDGE MAY WIELD A WEAPON IN THE DUEL OF SWEATY MASCULINE MAN FIGHTING!
FWOOSH
APOLOGIES IN ADVANCE, BOSS!
COME BACK, GRIM EAGLE THE APPARENTLY NOT-AS-BRAVE-AS-SLEDGE-THOUGHT-HE-WAS!
BLAM
PA-TNK

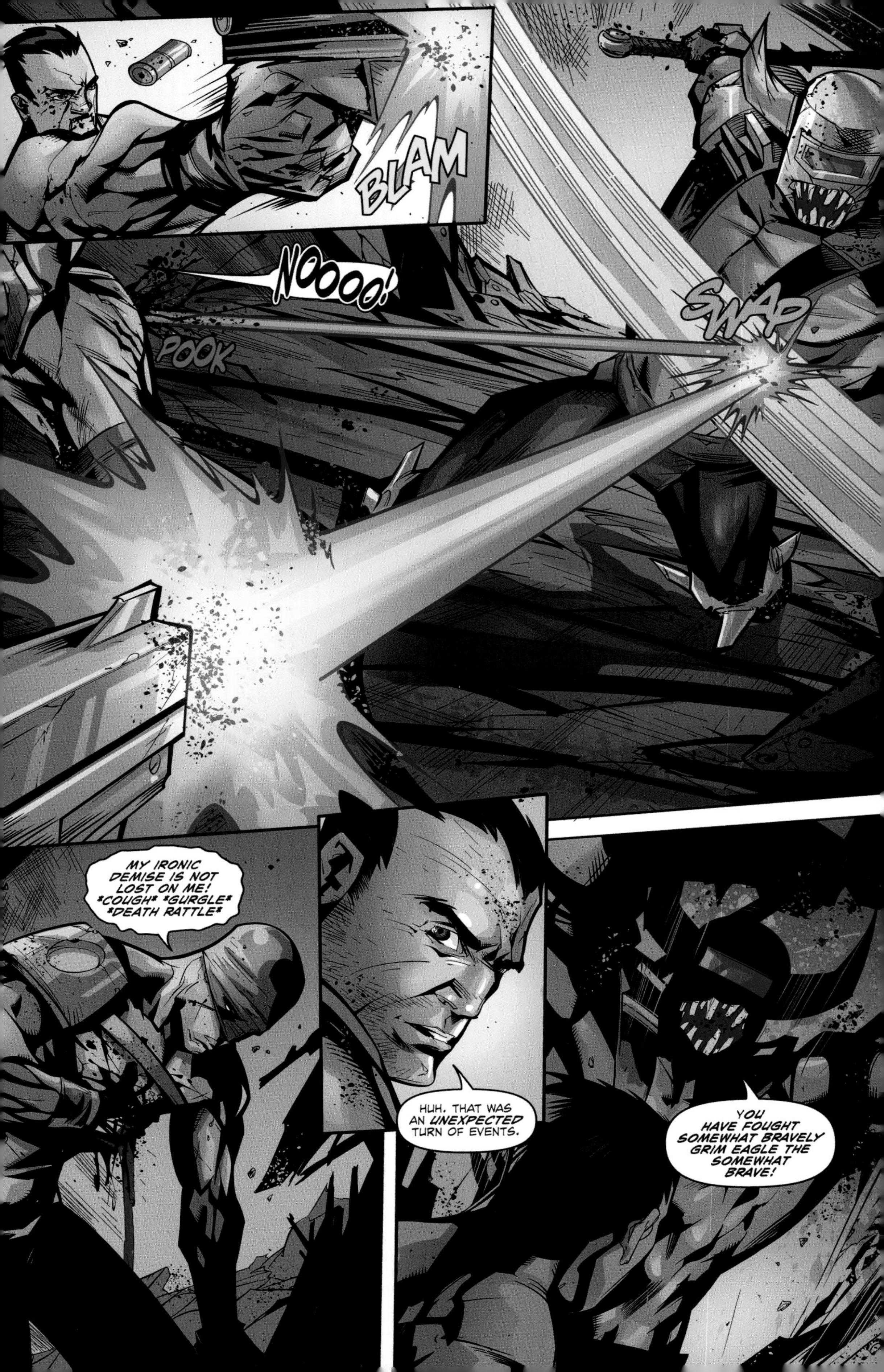
BLAM
NOOOO!
SWAP
POOK
MY IRONIC DEMISE IS NOT LOST ON ME! *COUGH* *GURGLE* *DEATH RATTLE*
HUH. THAT WAS AN UNEXPECTED TURN OF EVENTS.
YOU HAVE FOUGHT SOMEWHAT BRAVELY GRIM EAGLE THE SOMEWHAT BRAVE!

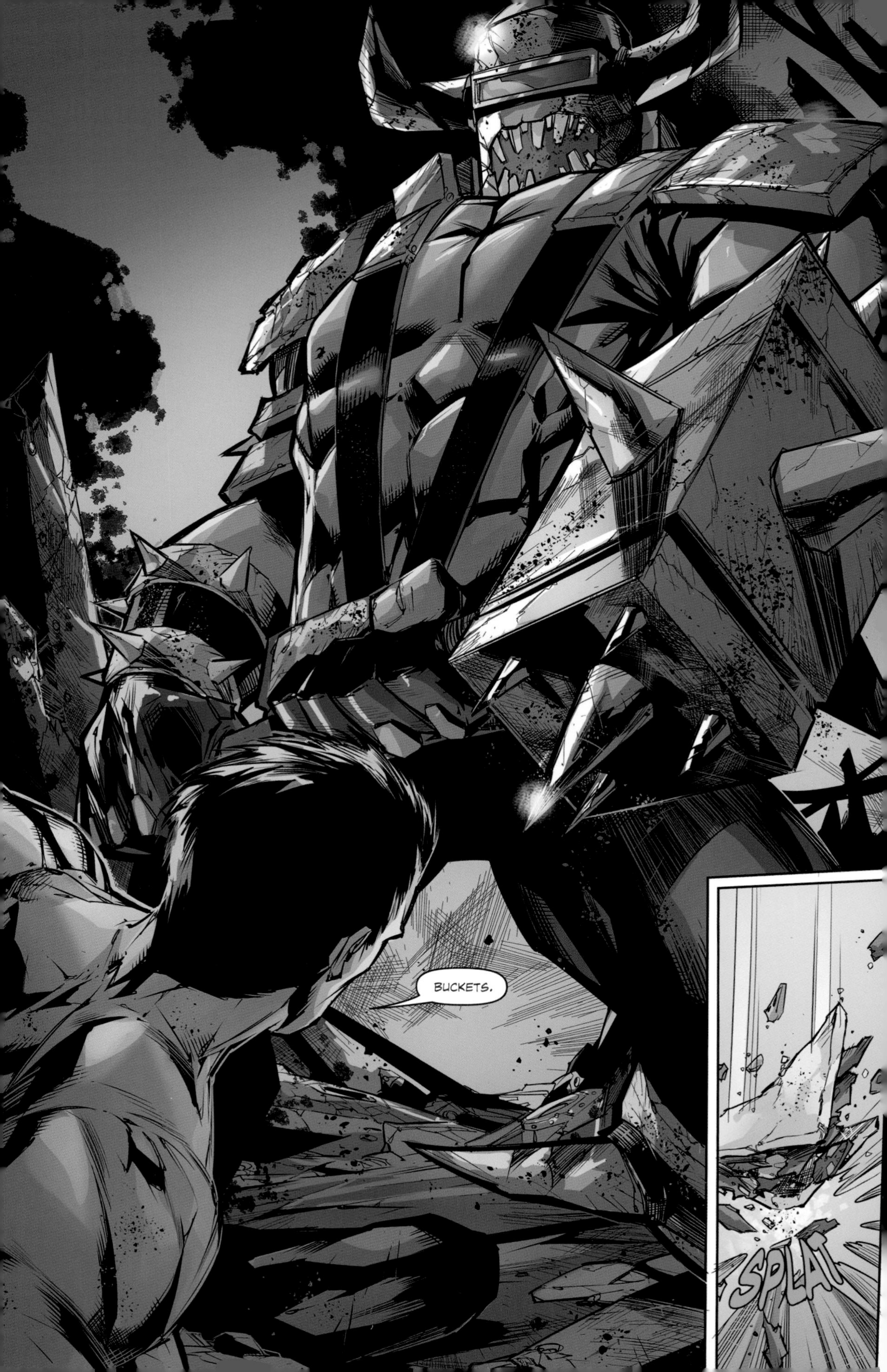
BUCKETS.
SPLAT

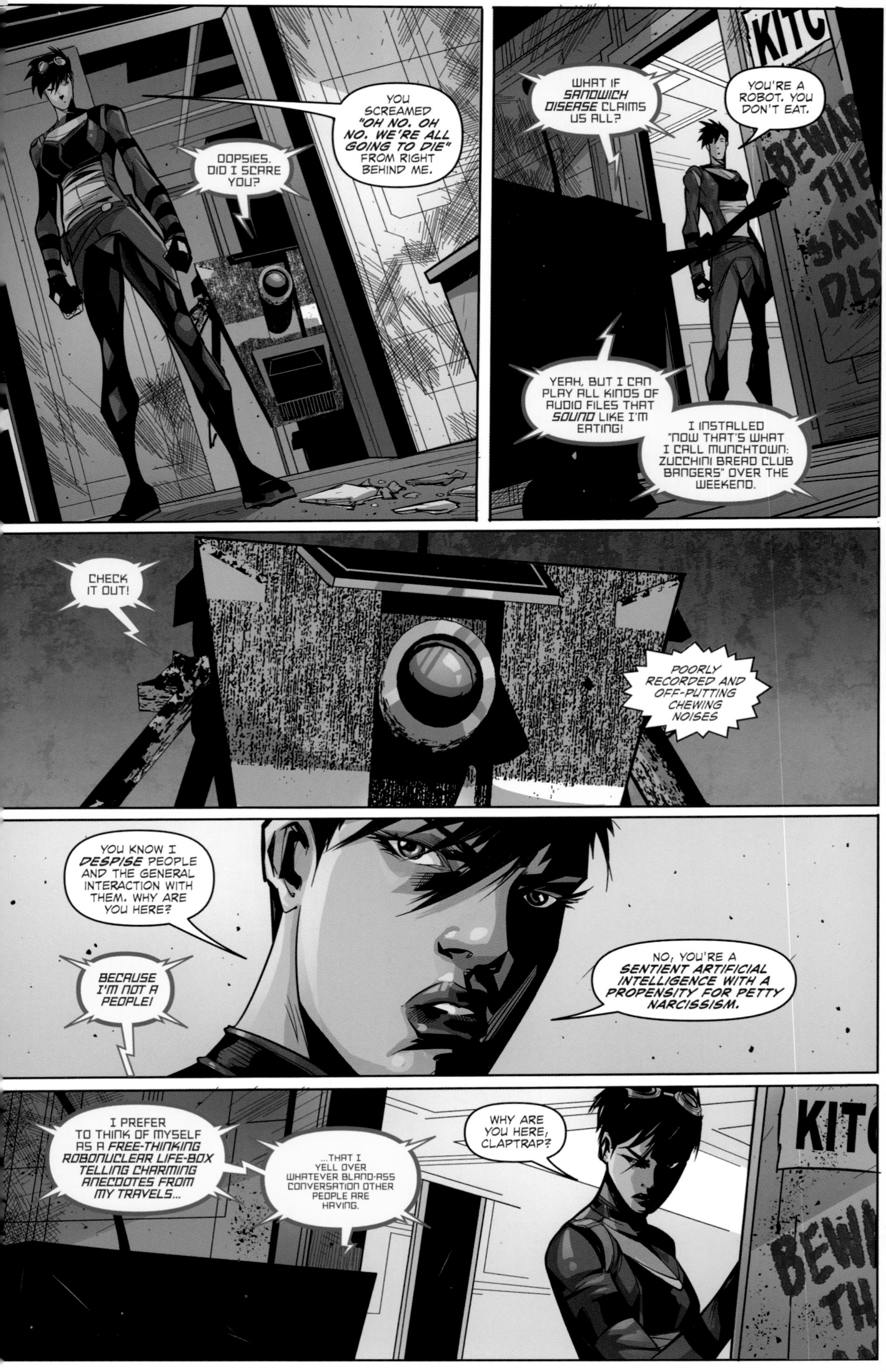

YOU SCREAMED "OH NO. OH NO. WE'RE ALL GOING TO DIE" FROM RIGHT BEHIND ME.
OOPSIES. DID I SCARE YOU?
WHAT IF SANDWICH DISEASE CLAIMS US ALL?
YOU'RE A ROBOT. YOU DON'T EAT.
YEAH, BUT I CAN PLAY ALL KINDS OF AUDIO FILES THAT SOUND LIKE I'M EATING!
I INSTALLED "NOW THAT'S WHAT I CALL MUNCHTOWN: ZUCCHINI BREAD CLUB BANGERS" OVER THE WEEKEND.
CHECK IT OUT!
POORLY RECORDED AND OFF-PUTTING CHEWING NOISES
YOU KNOW I DESPISE PEOPLE AND THE GENERAL INTERACTION WITH THEM. WHY ARE YOU HERE?
BECAUSE I'M NOT A PEOPLE!
NO, YOU'RE A SENTIENT ARTIFICIAL INTELLIGENCE WITH A PROPENSITY FOR PETTY NARCISSISM.
I PREFER TO THINK OF MYSELF AS A FREE-THINKING ROBONUCLEAR LIFE-BOX TELLING CHARMING ANECDOTES FROM MY TRAVELS...
...THAT I YELL OVER WHATEVER BLAND-ASS CONVERSATION OTHER PEOPLE ARE HAVING.
WHY ARE YOU HERE, CLAPTRAP?

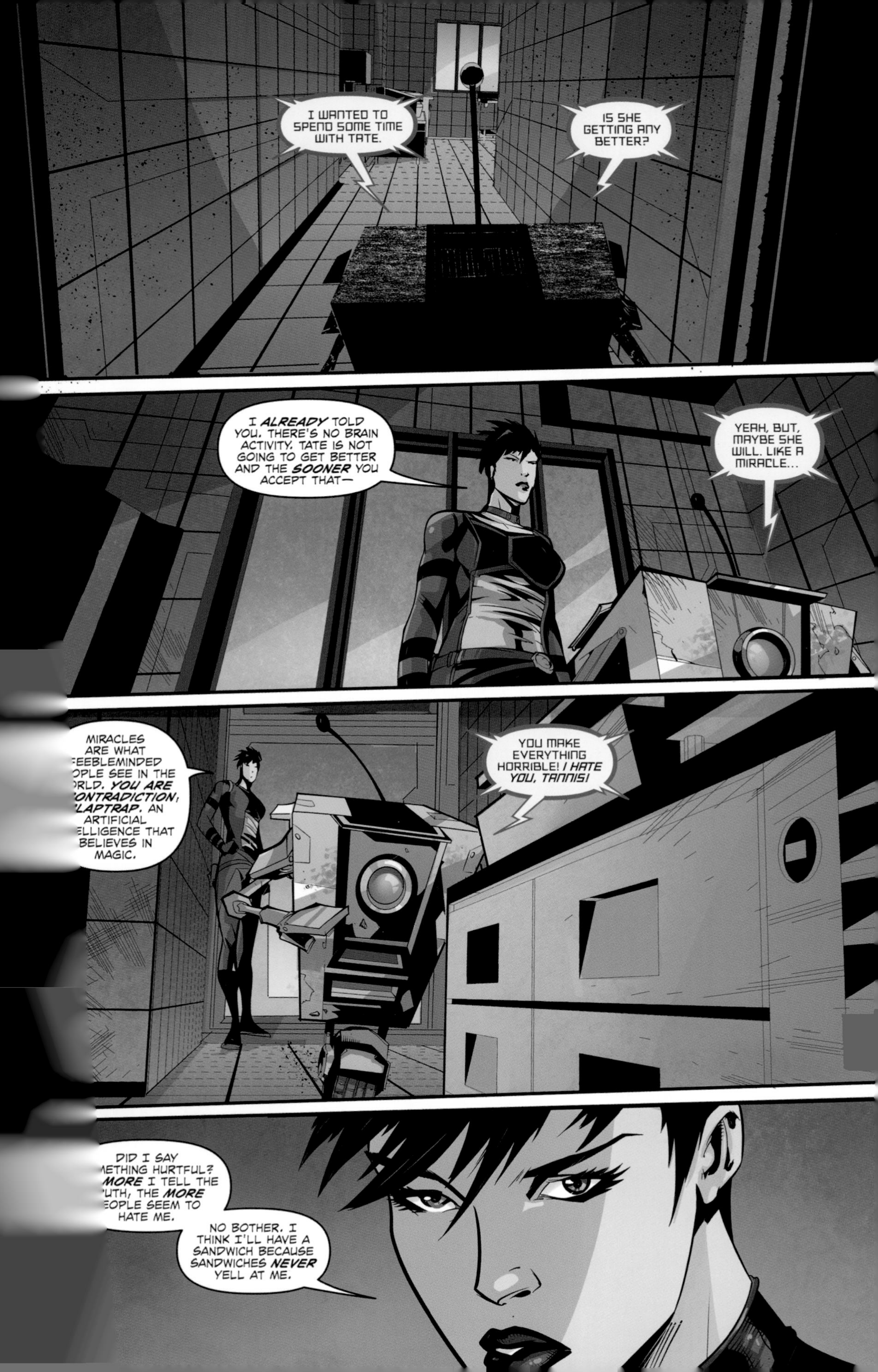
I WANTED TO SPEND SOME TIME WITH TATE.
IS SHE GETTING ANY BETTER?
I ALREADY TOLD YOU. THERE'S NO BRAIN ACTIVITY. TATE IS NOT GOING TO GET BETTER AND THE SOONER YOU ACCEPT THAT—
YEAH, BUT, MAYBE SHE WILL. LIKE A MIRACLE...
MIRACLES ARE WHAT FEEBLEMINDED OPLE SEE IN THE ORLD. YOU ARE CONTRADICTION, LAPTRAP. AN ARTIFICIAL ELLIGENCE THAT BELIEVES IN MAGIC.
YOU MAKE EVERYTHING HORRIBLE! I HATE YOU, TANNIS!
DID I SAY METHING HURTFUL? MORE I TELL THE UTH, THE MORE EOPLE SEEM TO HATE ME.
NO BOTHER. I THINK I'LL HAVE A SANDWICH BECAUSE SANDWICHES NEVER YELL AT ME.

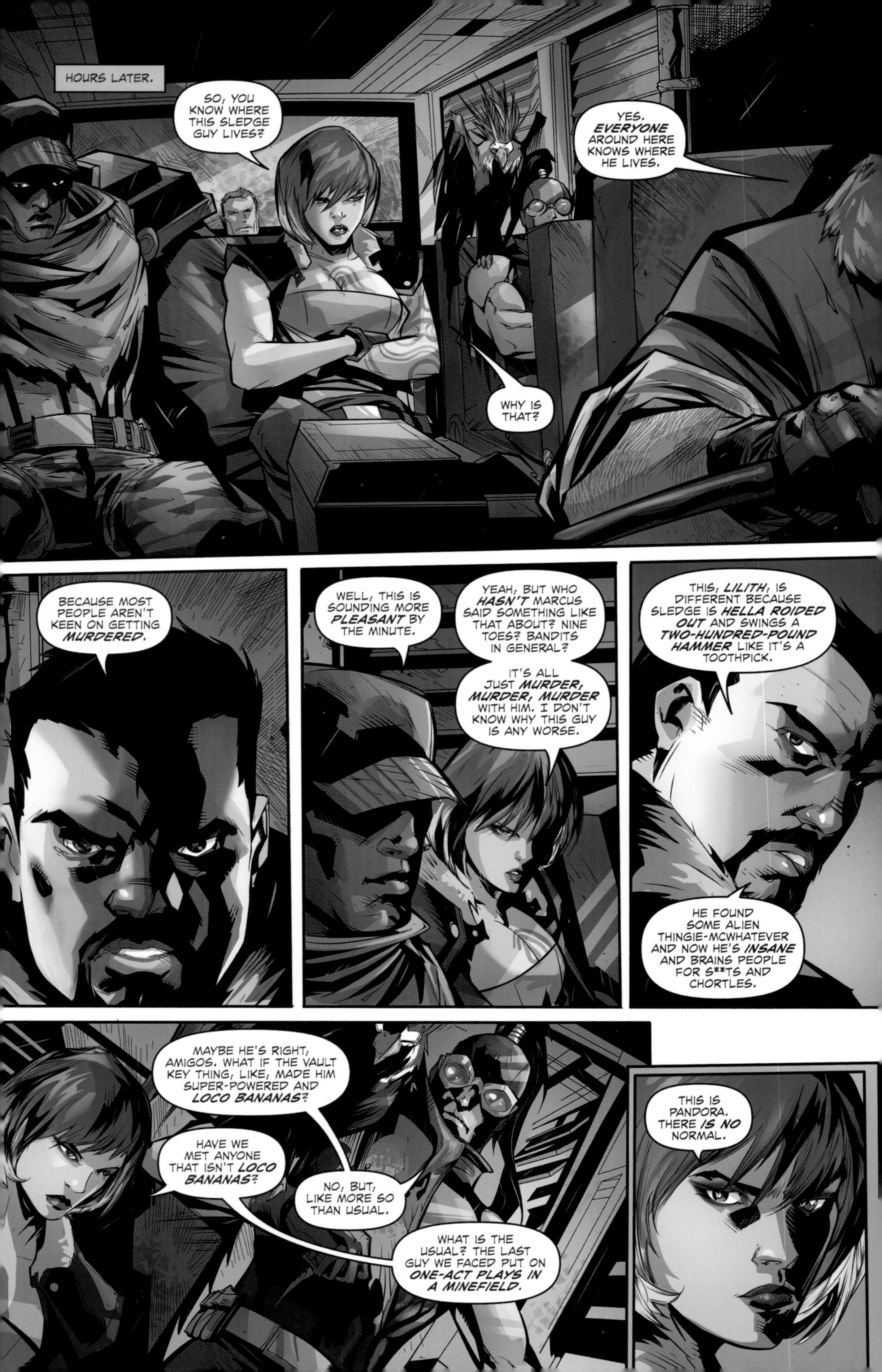
HOURS LATER.
SO, YOU KNOW WHERE THIS SLEDGE GUY LIVES?
YES. EVERYONE AROUND HERE KNOWS WHERE HE LIVES.
WHY IS THAT?
BECAUSE MOST PEOPLE AREN'T KEEN ON GETTING MURDERED.
WELL, THIS IS SOUNDING MORE PLEASANT BY THE MINUTE.
YEAH, BUT WHO HASN'T MARCUS SAID SOMETHING LIKE THAT ABOUT? NINE TOES? BANDITS IN GENERAL?
IT'S ALL JUST MURDER, MURDER, MURDER WITH HIM. I DON'T KNOW WHY THIS GUY IS ANY WORSE.
THIS, LILITH, IS DIFFERENT BECAUSE SLEDGE IS HELLA ROIDED OUT AND SWINGS A TWO-HUNDRED-POUND HAMMER LIKE IT'S A TOOTHPICK.
HE FOUND SOME ALIEN THINGIE-MCWHATEVER AND NOW HE'S INSANE AND BRAINS PEOPLE FOR S**TS AND CHORTLES.
MAYBE HE'S RIGHT, AMIGOS. WHAT IF THE VAULT KEY THING, LIKE, MADE HIM SUPER-POWERED AND LOCO BANANAS?
HAVE WE MET ANYONE THAT ISN'T LOCO BANANAS?
NO, BUT, LIKE MORE SO THAN USUAL.
WHAT IS THE USUAL? THE LAST GUY WE FACED PUT ON ONE-ACT PLAYS IN A MINEFIELD.
THIS IS PANDORA. THERE IS NO NORMAL.

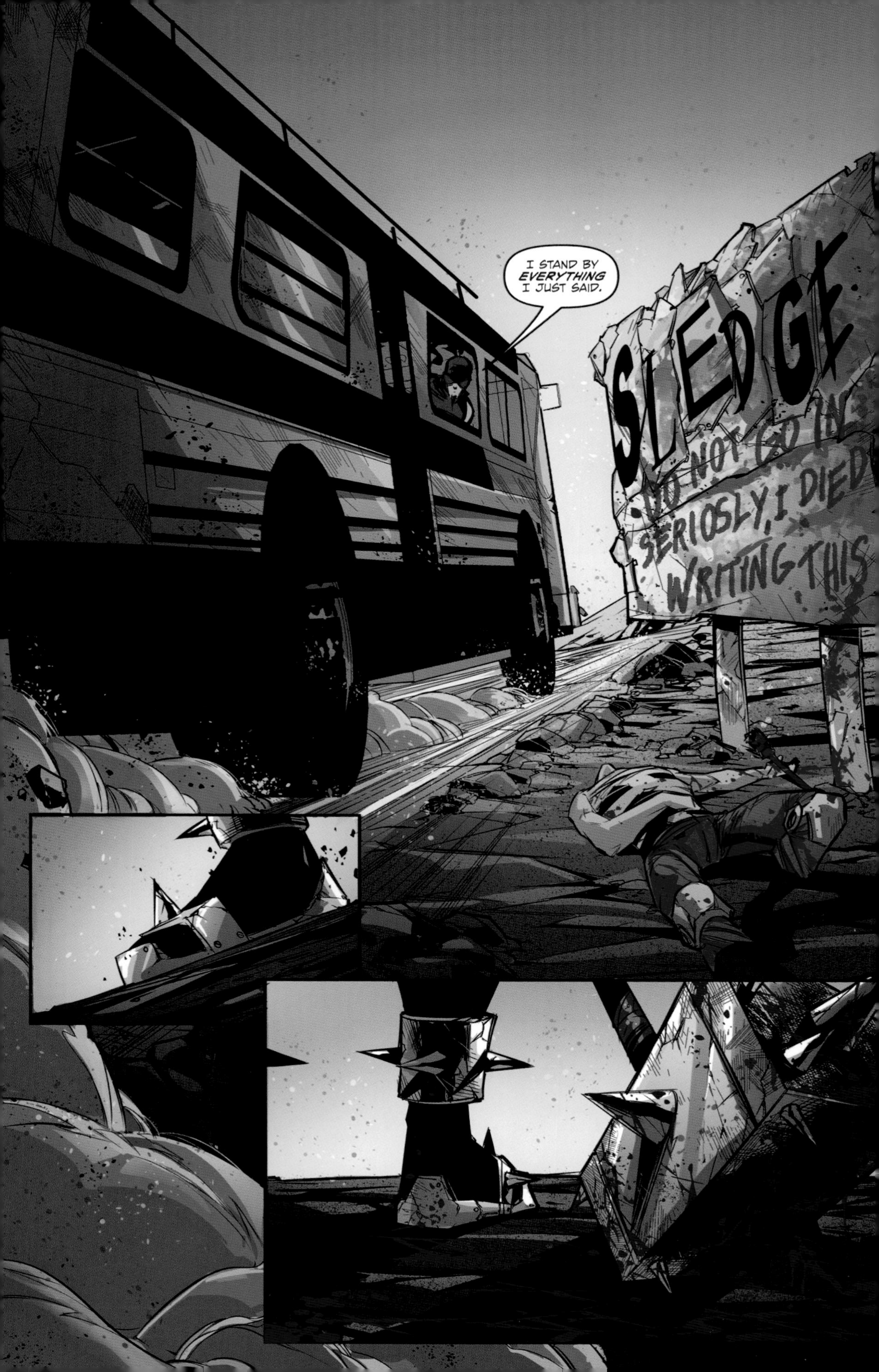
I STAND BY *EVERYTHING* I JUST SAID.
SLEDGE
SERIOSLY, I DIED
WRITING THIS

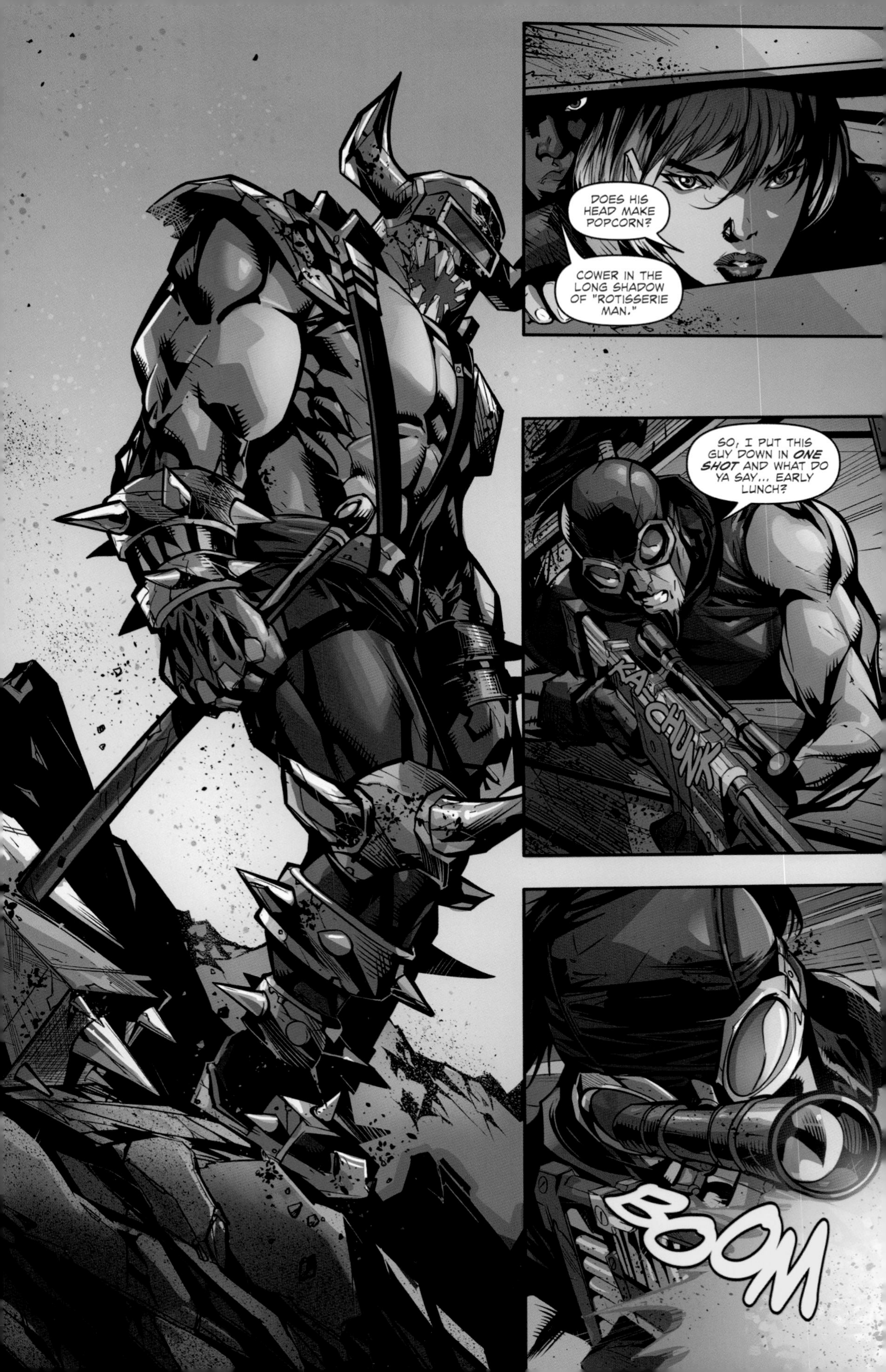

DOES HIS HEAD MAKE POPCORN?
COWER IN THE LONG SHADOW OF "ROTISSERIE MAN."
SO, I PUT THIS GUY DOWN IN *ONE SHOT* AND WHAT DO YA SAY... EARLY LUNCH?
KA-CHUNK
BOOM

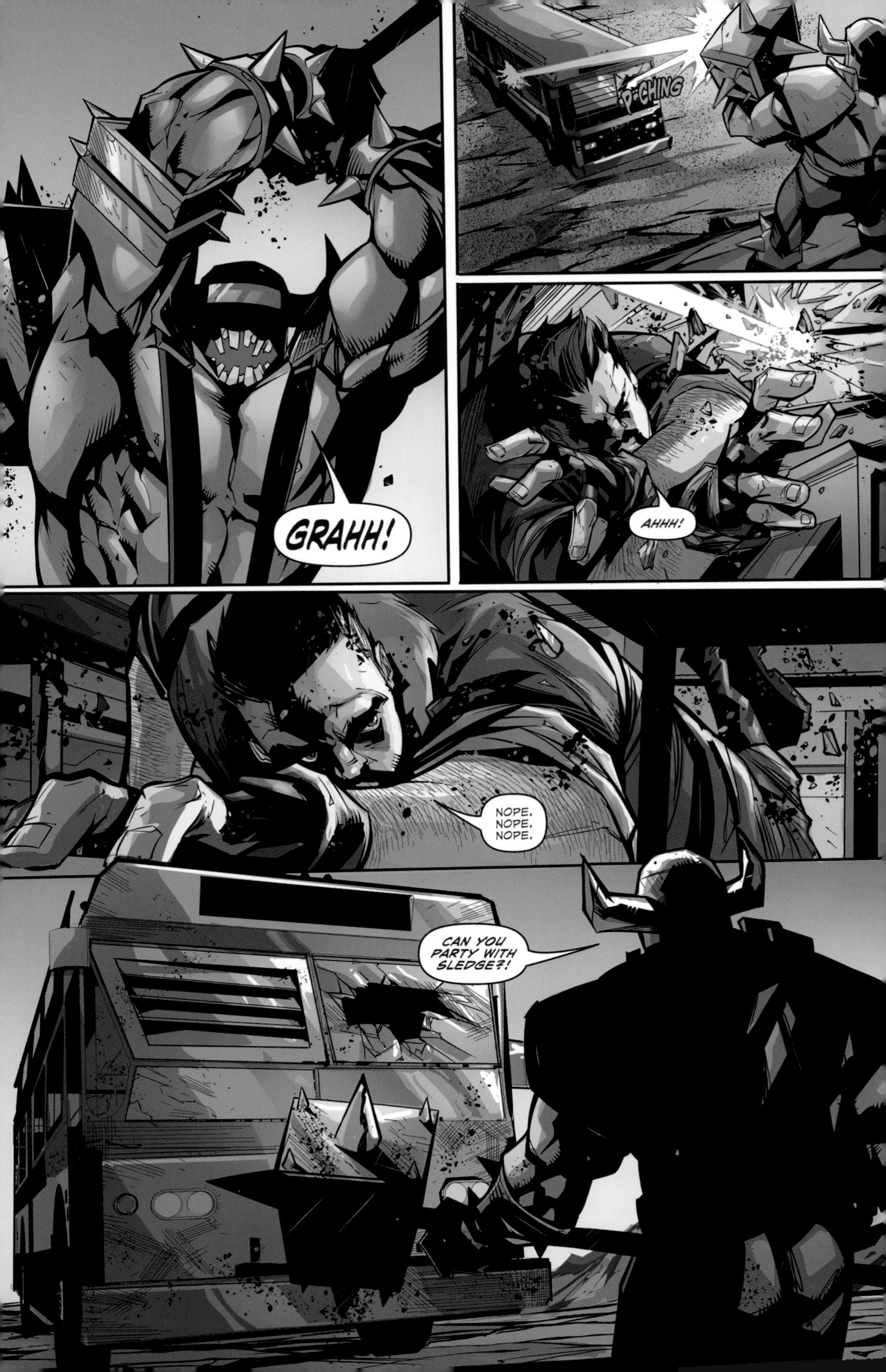
GRAHH!
P-CHING
AHHH!
NOPE. NOPE. NOPE.
CAN YOU PARTY WITH SLEDGE?!

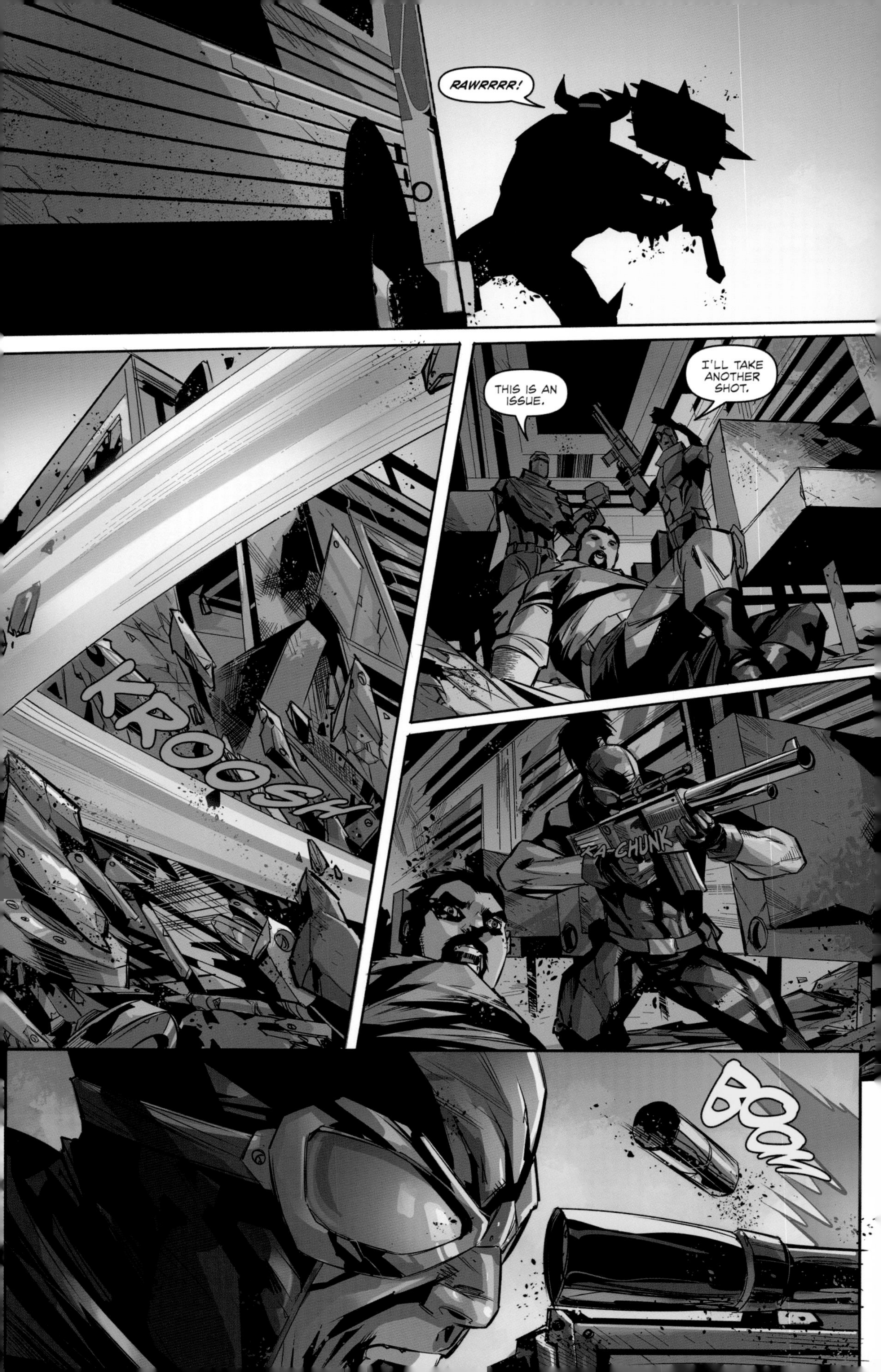
RAWRRRR!
KROOSH
THIS IS AN ISSUE.
I'LL TAKE ANOTHER SHOT.
KA-CHUNK
BOOM

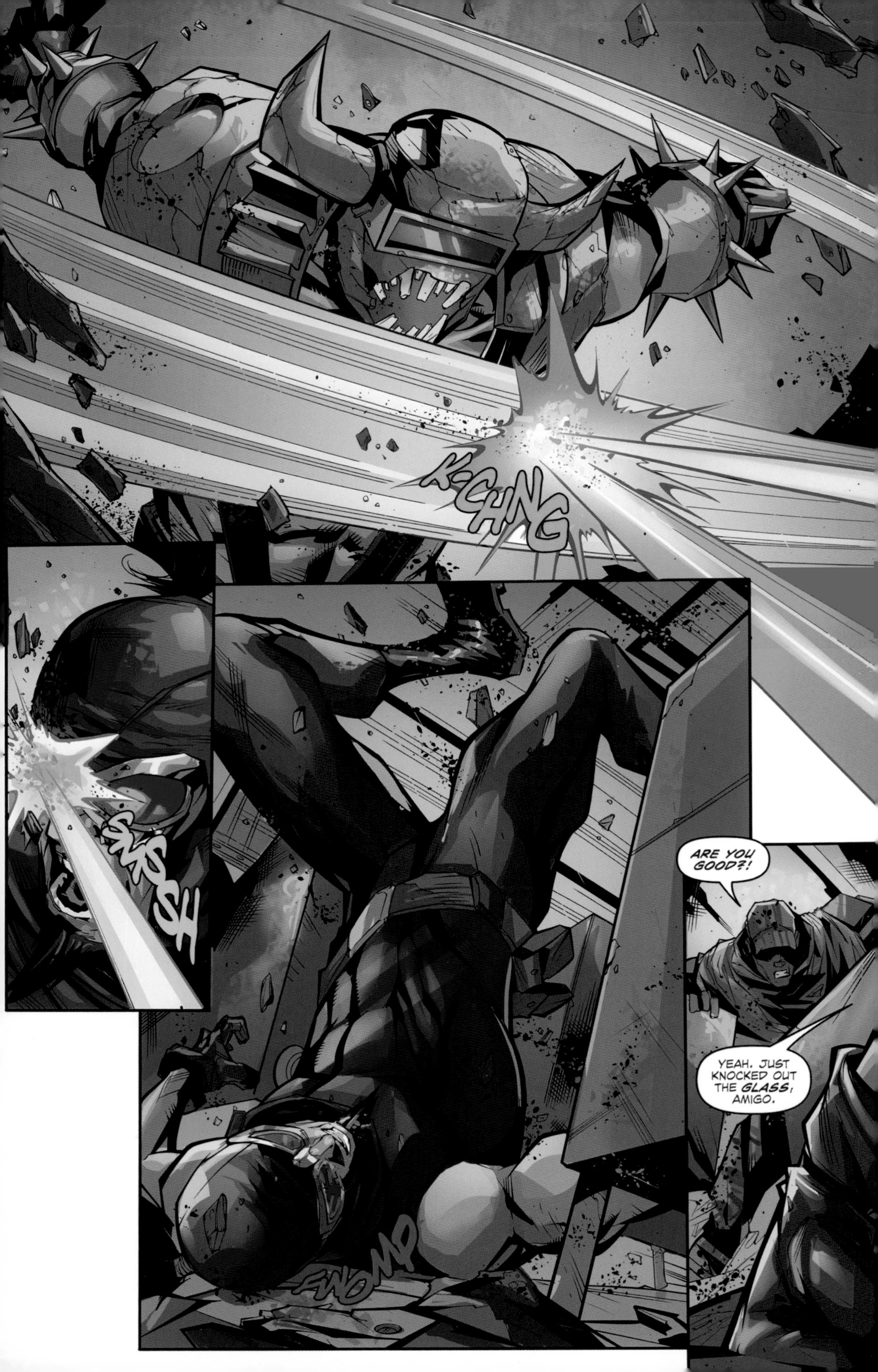
K-CHNG
SNASH
FWOMP
ARE YOU GOOD?!
YEAH. JUST KNOCKED OUT THE GLASS, AMIGO.

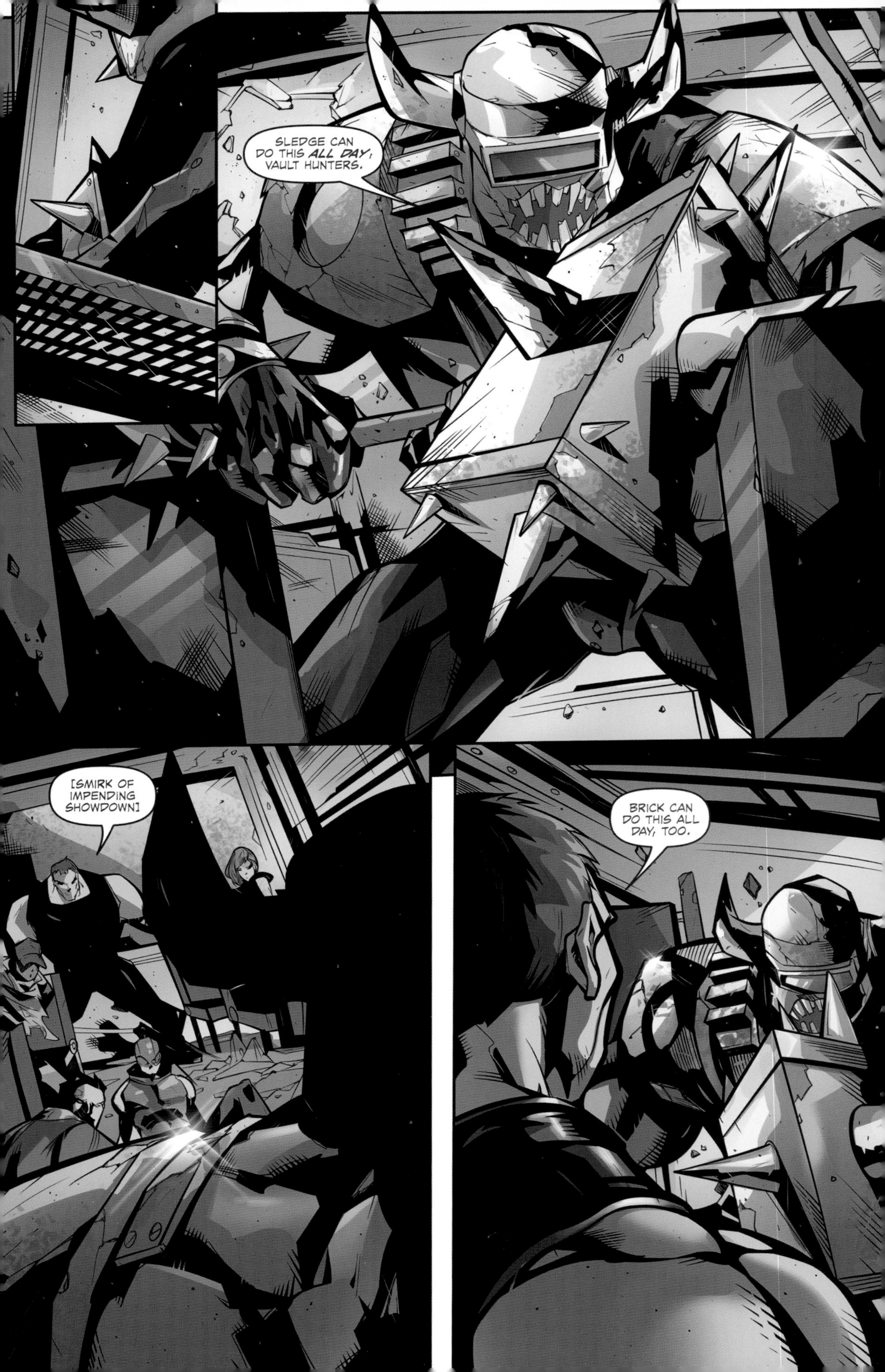
SLEDGE CAN DO THIS ALL DAY, VAULT HUNTERS.
[SMIRK OF IMPENDING SHOWDOWN]
BRICK CAN DO THIS ALL DAY, TOO.

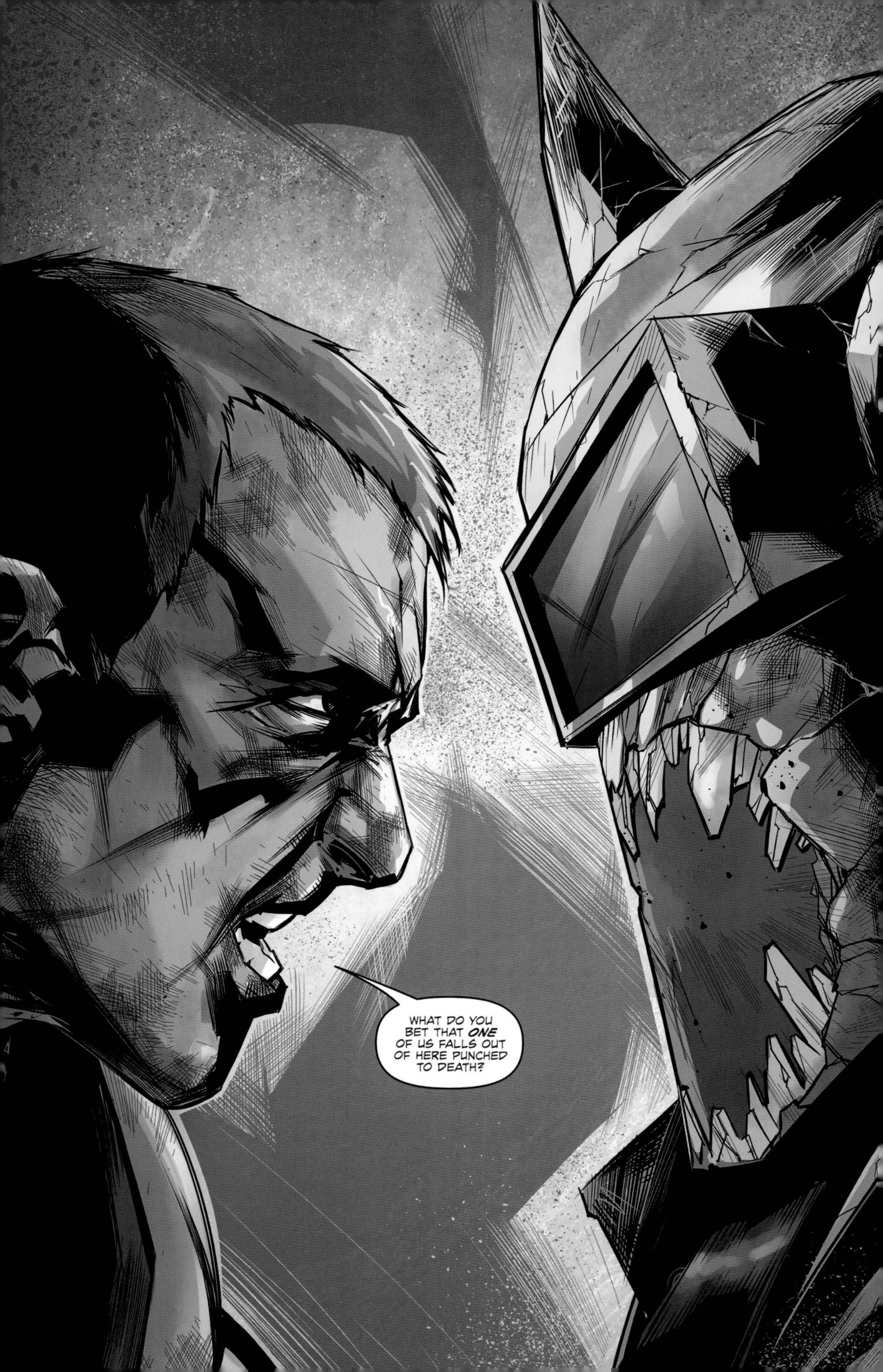
WHAT DO YOU BET THAT ONE OF US FALLS OUT OF HERE PUNCHED TO DEATH?

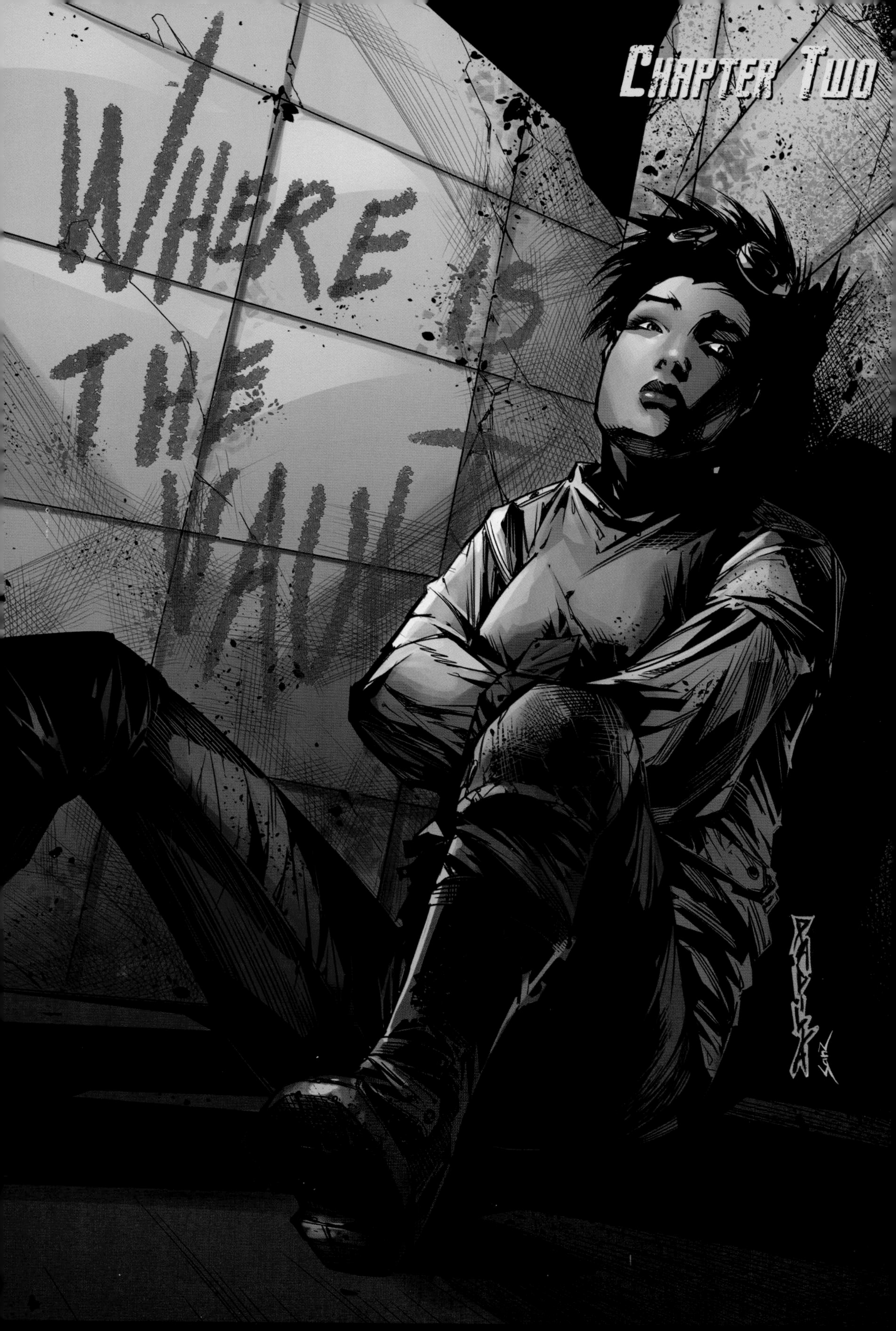
CHAPTER TWO
WHERE IS THE VAU

art by AGUSTIN PADILLA • colors by ESTHER SANZ

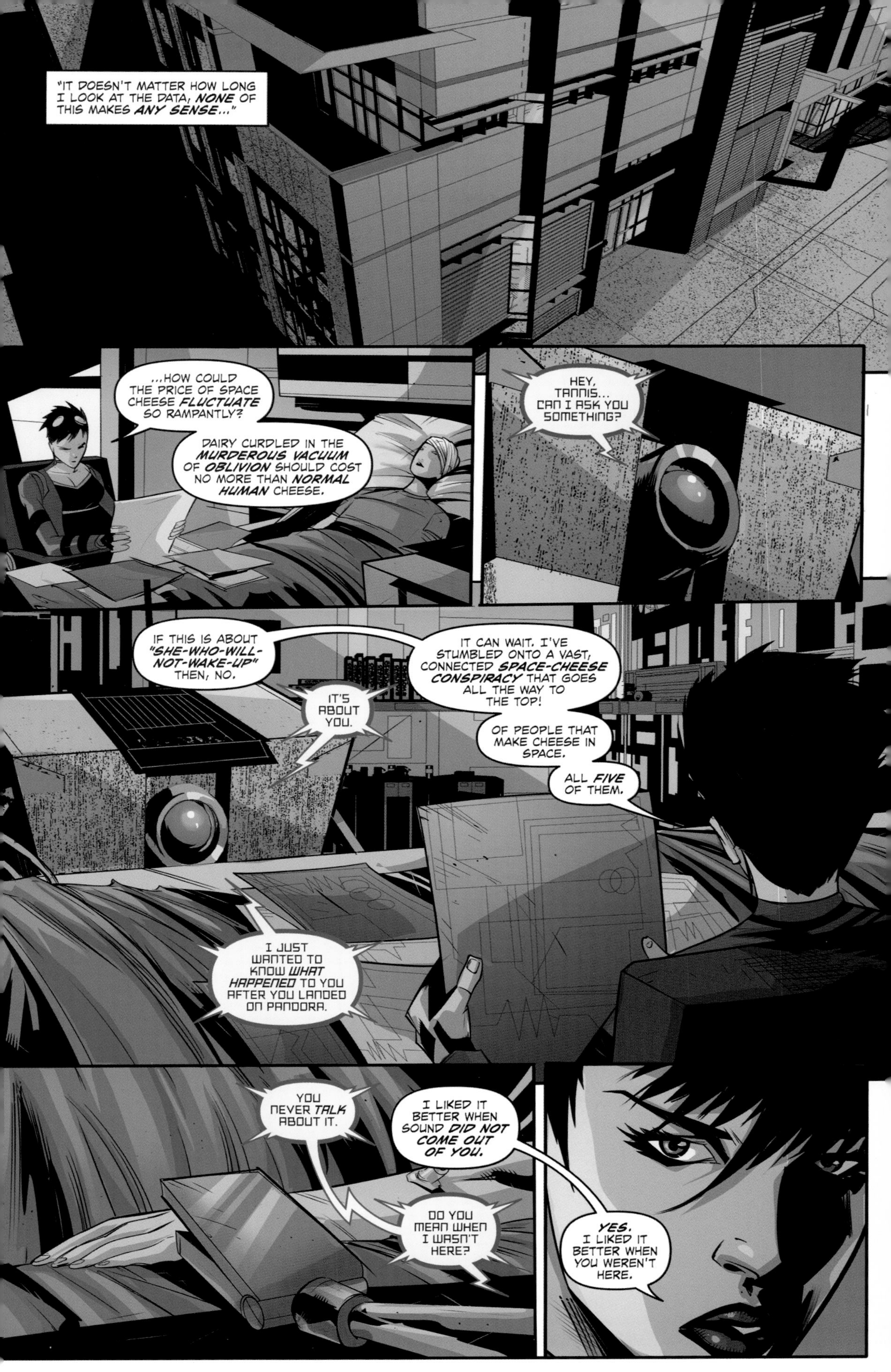
"IT DOESN'T MATTER HOW LONG I LOOK AT THE DATA, NONE OF THIS MAKES ANY SENSE..."
...HOW COULD THE PRICE OF SPACE CHEESE FLUCTUATE SO RAMPANTLY?
DAIRY CURDLED IN THE MURDEROUS VACUUM OF OBLIVION SHOULD COST NO MORE THAN NORMAL HUMAN CHEESE.
HEY, TANNIS... CAN I ASK YOU SOMETHING?
IF THIS IS ABOUT "SHE-WHO-WILL-NOT-WAKE-UP" THEN, NO.
IT'S ABOUT YOU.
IT CAN WAIT. I'VE STUMBLED ONTO A VAST, CONNECTED SPACE-CHEESE CONSPIRACY THAT GOES ALL THE WAY TO THE TOP!
OF PEOPLE THAT MAKE CHEESE IN SPACE.
ALL FIVE OF THEM.
I JUST WANTED TO KNOW WHAT HAPPENED TO YOU AFTER YOU LANDED ON PANDORA.
YOU NEVER TALK ABOUT IT.
I LIKED IT BETTER WHEN SOUND DID NOT COME OUT OF YOU.
DO YOU MEAN WHEN I WASN'T HERE?
YES. I LIKED IT BETTER WHEN YOU WEREN'T HERE.

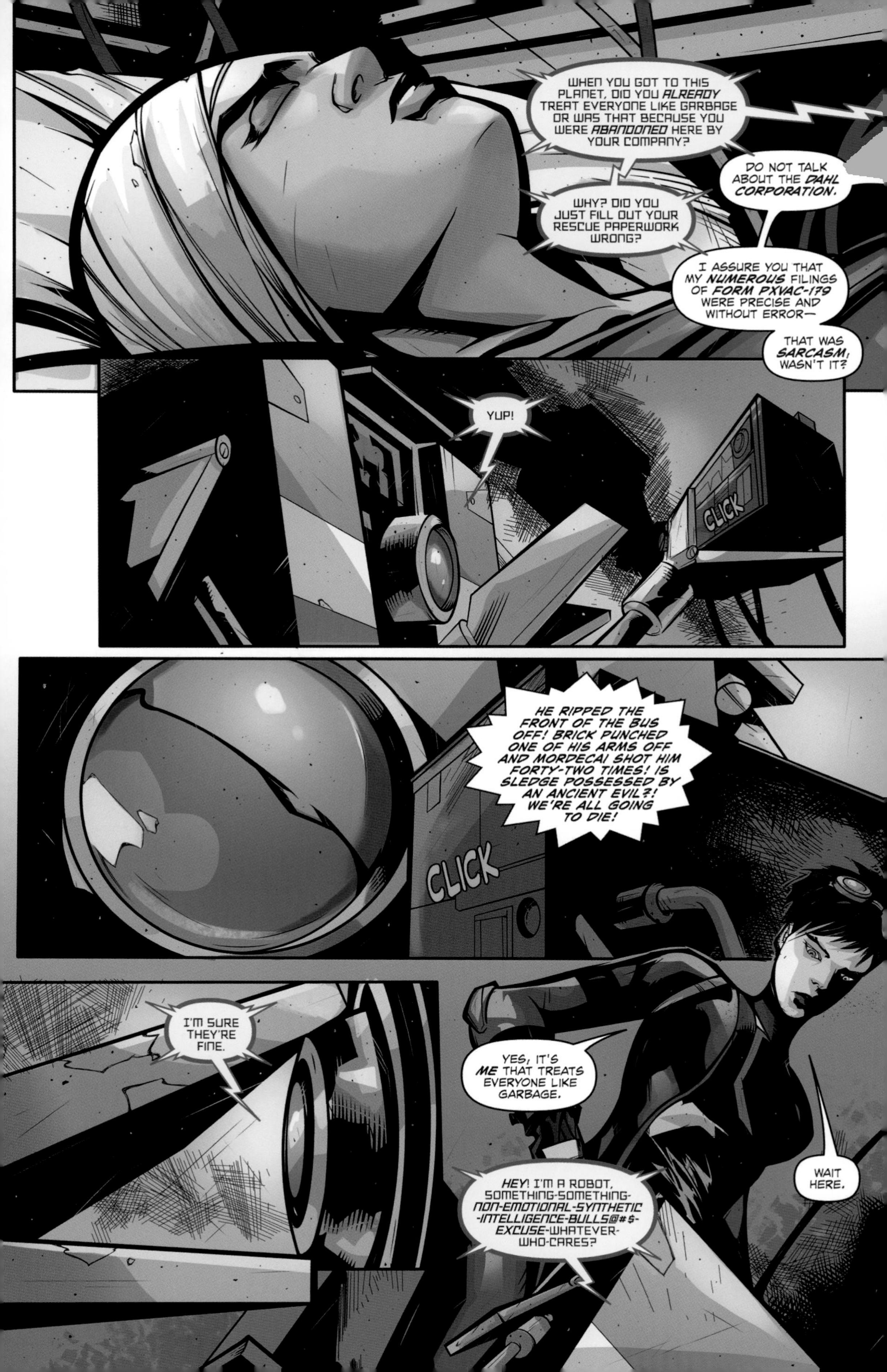
WHEN YOU GOT TO THIS PLANET, DID YOU ALREADY TREAT EVERYONE LIKE GARBAGE OR WAS THAT BECAUSE YOU WERE ABANDONED HERE BY YOUR COMPANY?
DO NOT TALK ABOUT THE DAHL CORPORATION.
WHY? DID YOU JUST FILL OUT YOUR RESCUE PAPERWORK WRONG?
I ASSURE YOU THAT MY NUMEROUS FILINGS OF FORM PXVAC-179 WERE PRECISE AND WITHOUT ERROR—
THAT WAS SARCASM, WASN'T IT?
YUP!
CLICK
HE RIPPED THE FRONT OF THE BUS OFF! BRICK PUNCHED ONE OF HIS ARMS OFF AND MORDECAI SHOT HIM FORTY-TWO TIMES! IS SLEDGE POSSESSED BY AN ANCIENT EVIL?! WE'RE ALL GOING TO DIE!
CLICK
I'M SURE THEY'RE FINE.
YES, IT'S ME THAT TREATS EVERYONE LIKE GARBAGE.
HEY! I'M A ROBOT, SOMETHING-SOMETHING-NON-EMOTIONAL-SYNTHETIC-INTELLIGENCE-BULLS@#$-EXCUSE-WHATEVER-WHO-CARES?
WAIT HERE.

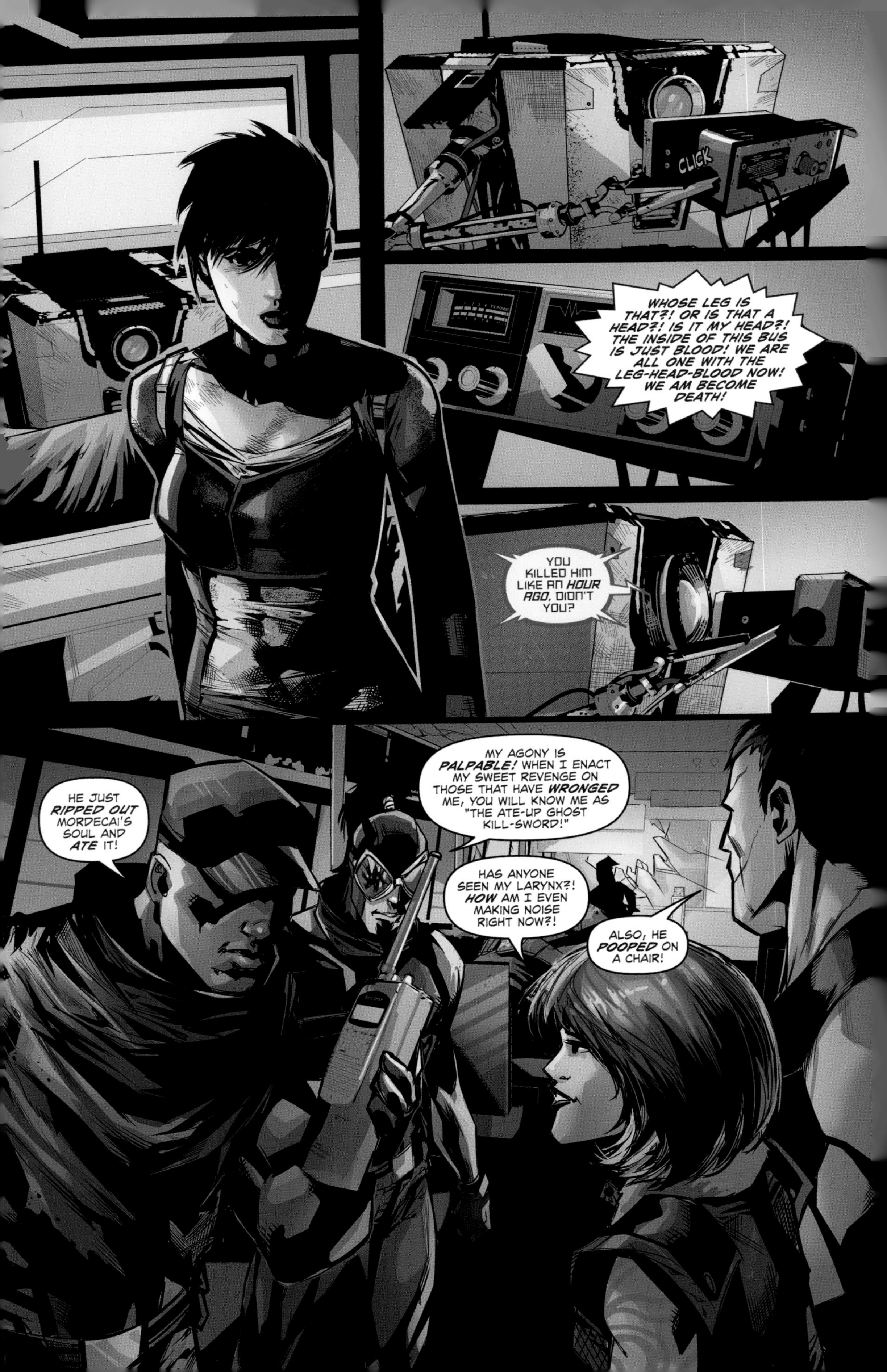
CLICK
WHOSE LEG IS THAT?! OR IS THAT A HEAD?! IS IT MY HEAD?! THE INSIDE OF THIS BUS IS JUST BLOOD! WE ARE ALL ONE WITH THE LEG-HEAD-BLOOD NOW! WE AM BECOME DEATH!
YOU KILLED HIM LIKE AN HOUR AGO, DIDN'T YOU?
HE JUST RIPPED OUT MORDECAI'S SOUL AND ATE IT!
MY AGONY IS PALPABLE! WHEN I ENACT MY SWEET REVENGE ON THOSE THAT HAVE WRONGED ME, YOU WILL KNOW ME AS "THE ATE-UP GHOST KILL-SWORD!"
HAS ANYONE SEEN MY LARYNX?! HOW AM I EVEN MAKING NOISE RIGHT NOW?!
ALSO, HE POOPED ON A CHAIR!

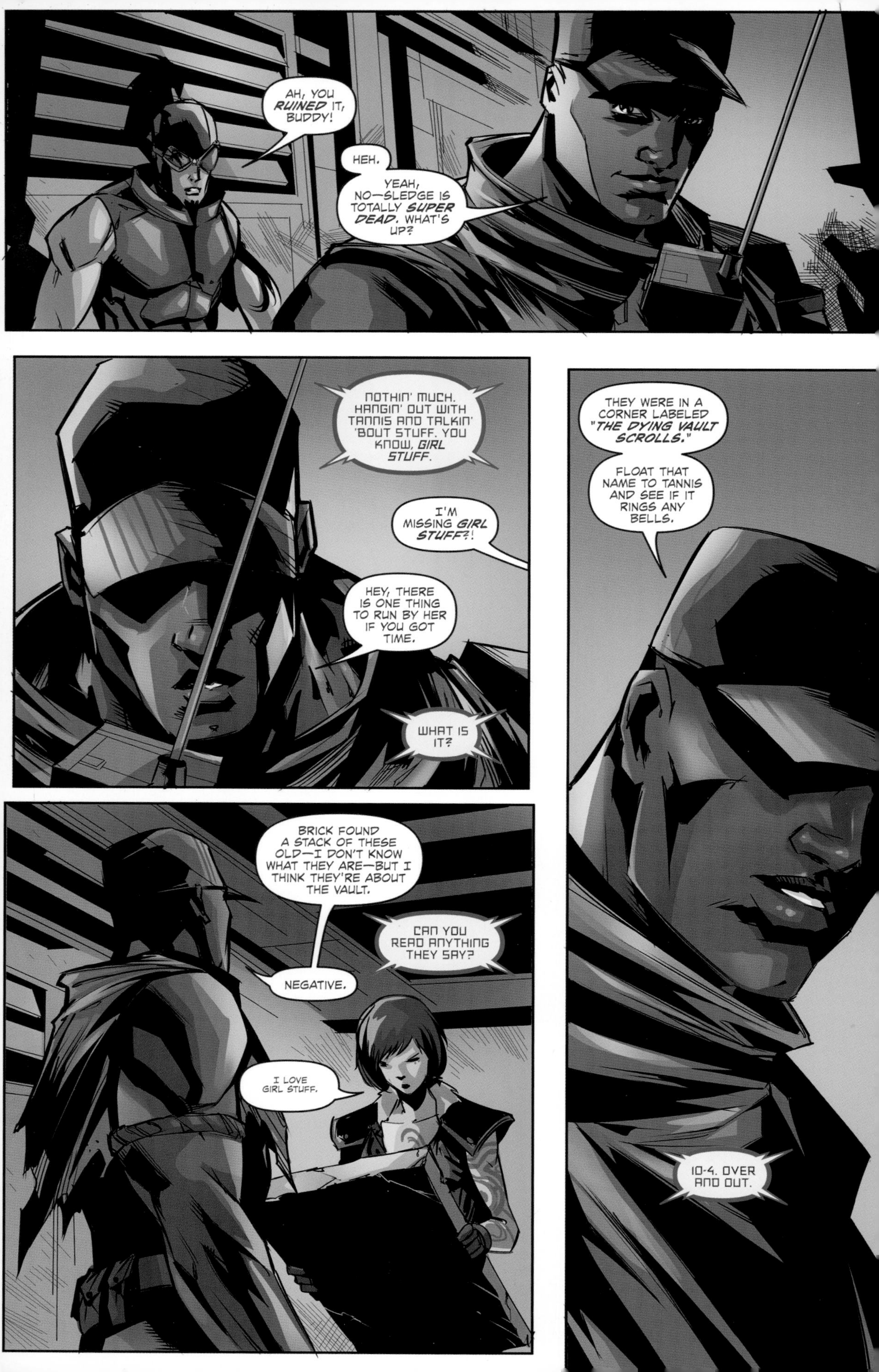
AH, YOU RUINED IT, BUDDY!
HEH.
YEAH, NO—SLEDGE IS TOTALLY SUPER DEAD. WHAT'S UP?
NOTHIN' MUCH. HANGIN' OUT WITH TANNIS AND TALKIN' 'BOUT STUFF. YOU KNOW, GIRL STUFF.
I'M MISSING GIRL STUFF?!
HEY, THERE IS ONE THING TO RUN BY HER IF YOU GOT TIME.
WHAT IS IT?
BRICK FOUND A STACK OF THESE OLD—I DON'T KNOW WHAT THEY ARE—BUT I THINK THEY'RE ABOUT THE VAULT.
CAN YOU READ ANYTHING THEY SAY?
NEGATIVE.
I LOVE GIRL STUFF.
THEY WERE IN A CORNER LABELED "THE DYING VAULT SCROLLS."
FLOAT THAT NAME TO TANNIS AND SEE IF IT RINGS ANY BELLS.
10-4. OVER AND OUT.

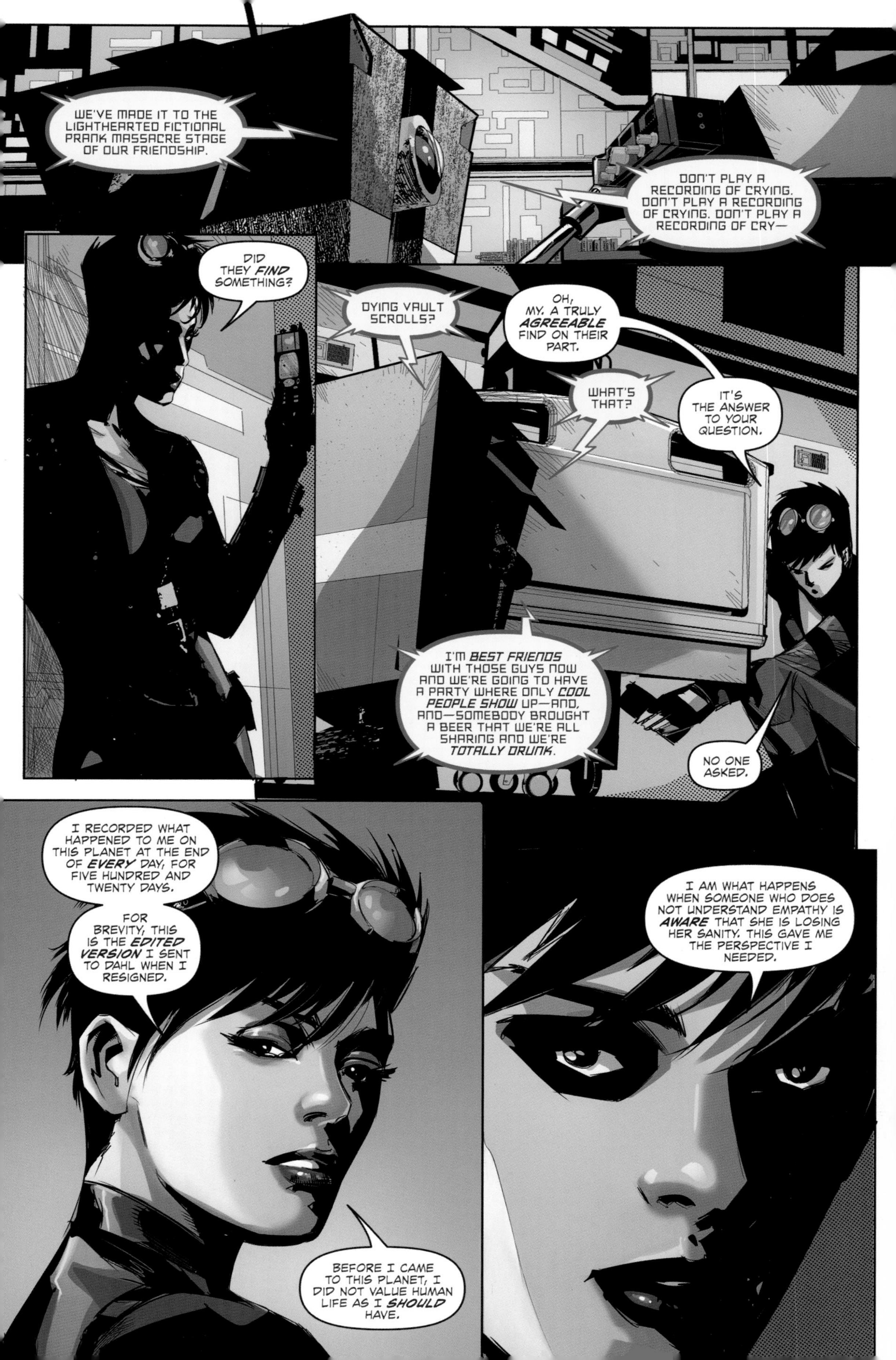
WE'VE MADE IT TO THE LIGHTHEARTED FICTIONAL PRANK MASSACRE STAGE OF OUR FRIENDSHIP.
DON'T PLAY A RECORDING OF CRYING. DON'T PLAY A RECORDING OF CRYING. DON'T PLAY A RECORDING OF CRY—
DID THEY FIND SOMETHING?
DYING VAULT SCROLLS?
OH, MY. A TRULY AGREEABLE FIND ON THEIR PART.
WHAT'S THAT?
IT'S THE ANSWER TO YOUR QUESTION.
I'M BEST FRIENDS WITH THOSE GUYS NOW AND WE'RE GOING TO HAVE A PARTY WHERE ONLY COOL PEOPLE SHOW UP—AND, AND—SOMEBODY BROUGHT A BEER THAT WE'RE ALL SHARING AND WE'RE TOTALLY DRUNK.
NO ONE ASKED.
I RECORDED WHAT HAPPENED TO ME ON THIS PLANET AT THE END OF EVERY DAY, FOR FIVE HUNDRED AND TWENTY DAYS.
FOR BREVITY, THIS IS THE EDITED VERSION I SENT TO DAHL WHEN I RESIGNED.
BEFORE I CAME TO THIS PLANET, I DID NOT VALUE HUMAN LIFE AS I SHOULD HAVE.
I AM WHAT HAPPENS WHEN SOMEONE WHO DOES NOT UNDERSTAND EMPATHY IS AWARE THAT SHE IS LOSING HER SANITY. THIS GAVE ME THE PERSPECTIVE I NEEDED.

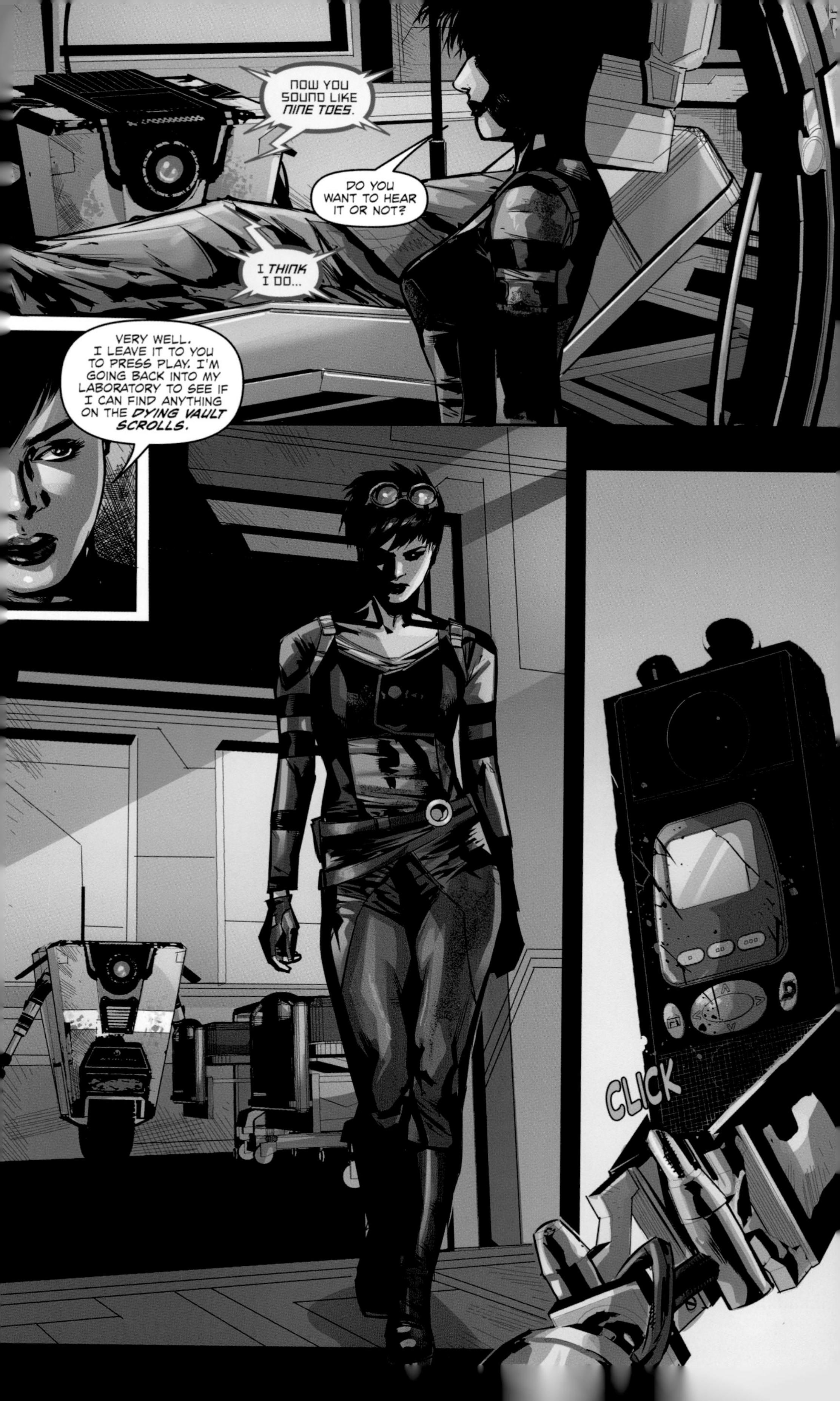
NOW YOU SOUND LIKE NINE TOES.
DO YOU WANT TO HEAR IT OR NOT?
I THINK I DO...
VERY WELL. I LEAVE IT TO YOU TO PRESS PLAY. I'M GOING BACK INTO MY LABORATORY TO SEE IF I CAN FIND ANYTHING ON THE DYING VAULT SCROLLS.
CLICK

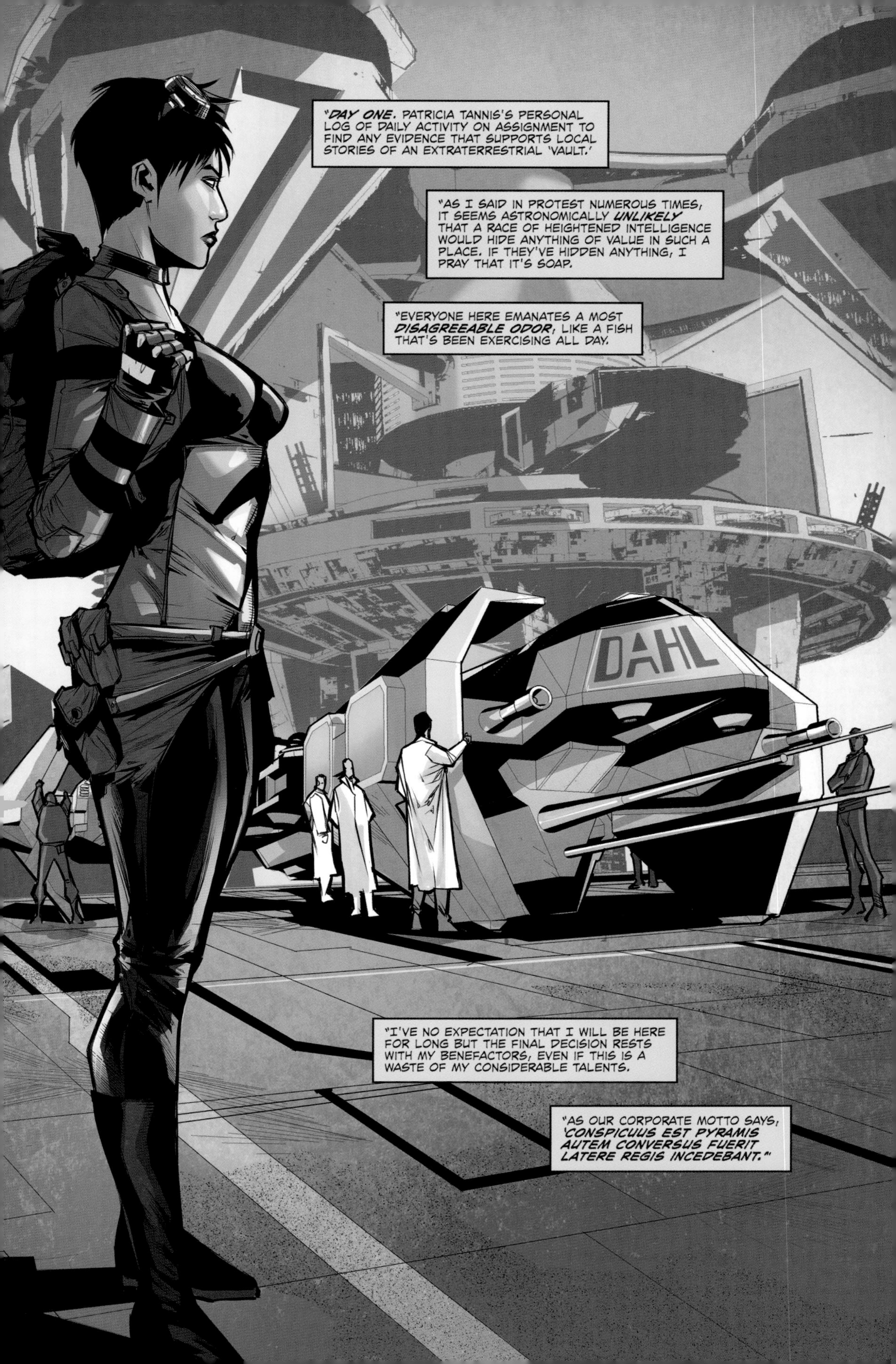
"DAY ONE. PATRICIA TANNIS'S PERSONAL LOG OF DAILY ACTIVITY ON ASSIGNMENT TO FIND ANY EVIDENCE THAT SUPPORTS LOCAL STORIES OF AN EXTRATERRESTRIAL 'VAULT.'
"AS I SAID IN PROTEST NUMEROUS TIMES, IT SEEMS ASTRONOMICALLY UNLIKELY THAT A RACE OF HEIGHTENED INTELLIGENCE WOULD HIDE ANYTHING OF VALUE IN SUCH A PLACE. IF THEY'VE HIDDEN ANYTHING, I PRAY THAT IT'S SOAP.
"EVERYONE HERE EMANATES A MOST DISAGREEABLE ODOR, LIKE A FISH THAT'S BEEN EXERCISING ALL DAY.
DAHL
"I'VE NO EXPECTATION THAT I WILL BE HERE FOR LONG BUT THE FINAL DECISION RESTS WITH MY BENEFACTORS, EVEN IF THIS IS A WASTE OF MY CONSIDERABLE TALENTS.
"AS OUR CORPORATE MOTTO SAYS, 'CONSPICUUS EST PYRAMIS AUTEM CONVERSUS FUERIT LATERE REGIS INCEDEBANT.'"

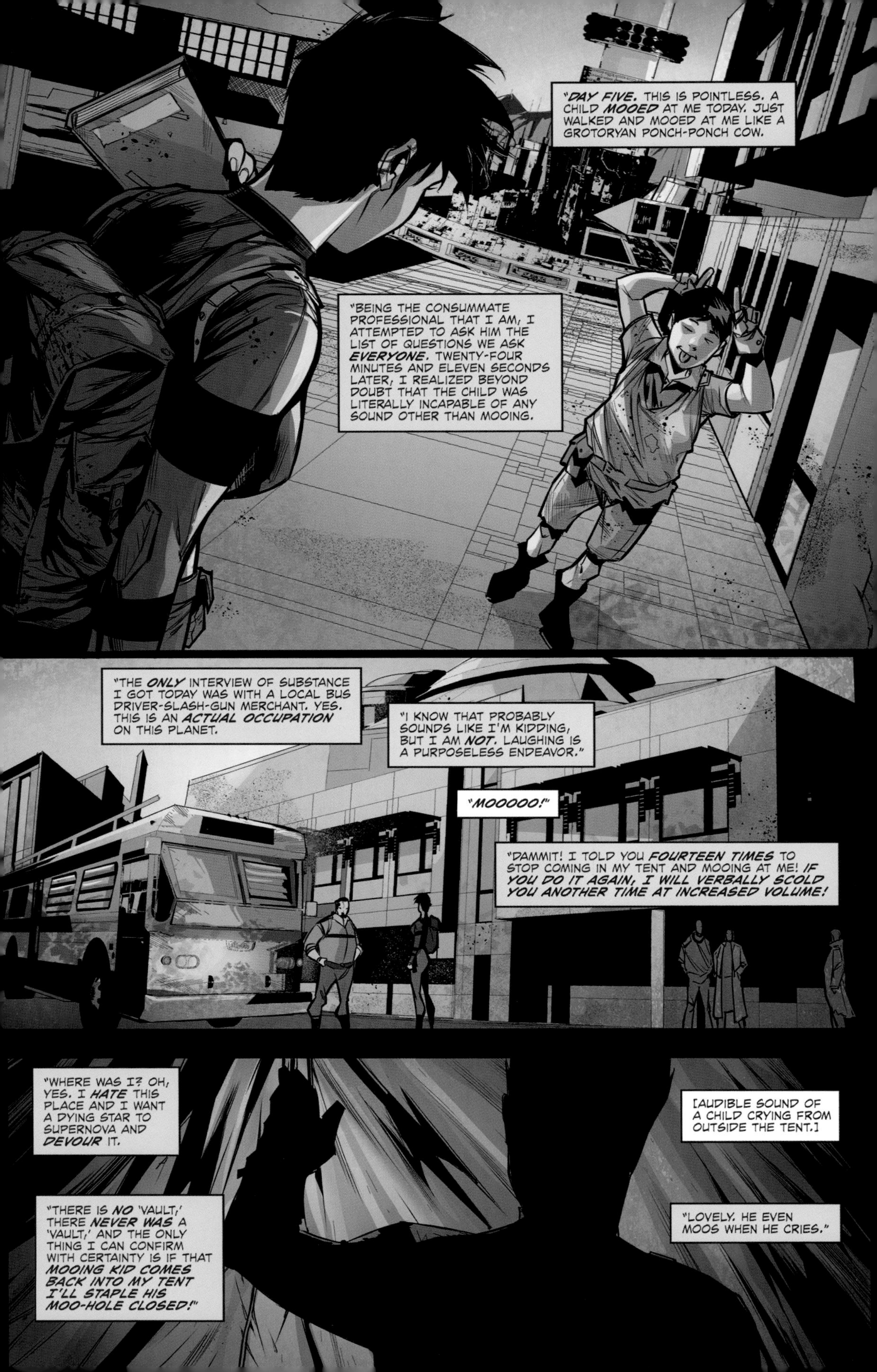

"DAY FIVE. THIS IS POINTLESS. A CHILD MOOED AT ME TODAY. JUST WALKED AND MOOED AT ME LIKE A GROTORYAN PONCH-PONCH COW.
"BEING THE CONSUMMATE PROFESSIONAL THAT I AM, I ATTEMPTED TO ASK HIM THE LIST OF QUESTIONS WE ASK EVERYONE. TWENTY-FOUR MINUTES AND ELEVEN SECONDS LATER, I REALIZED BEYOND DOUBT THAT THE CHILD WAS LITERALLY INCAPABLE OF ANY SOUND OTHER THAN MOOING.
"THE ONLY INTERVIEW OF SUBSTANCE I GOT TODAY WAS WITH A LOCAL BUS DRIVER-SLASH-GUN MERCHANT. YES. THIS IS AN ACTUAL OCCUPATION ON THIS PLANET.
"I KNOW THAT PROBABLY SOUNDS LIKE I'M KIDDING, BUT I AM NOT. LAUGHING IS A PURPOSELESS ENDEAVOR."
"MOOOOO!"
"DAMMIT! I TOLD YOU FOURTEEN TIMES TO STOP COMING IN MY TENT AND MOOING AT ME! IF YOU DO IT AGAIN, I WILL VERBALLY SCOLD YOU ANOTHER TIME AT INCREASED VOLUME!
"WHERE WAS I? OH, YES. I HATE THIS PLACE AND I WANT A DYING STAR TO SUPERNOVA AND DEVOUR IT.
[AUDIBLE SOUND OF A CHILD CRYING FROM OUTSIDE THE TENT.]
"THERE IS NO 'VAULT,' THERE NEVER WAS A 'VAULT,' AND THE ONLY THING I CAN CONFIRM WITH CERTAINTY IS IF THAT MOOING KID COMES BACK INTO MY TENT I'LL STAPLE HIS MOO-HOLE CLOSED!"
"LOVELY. HE EVEN MOOS WHEN HE CRIES."

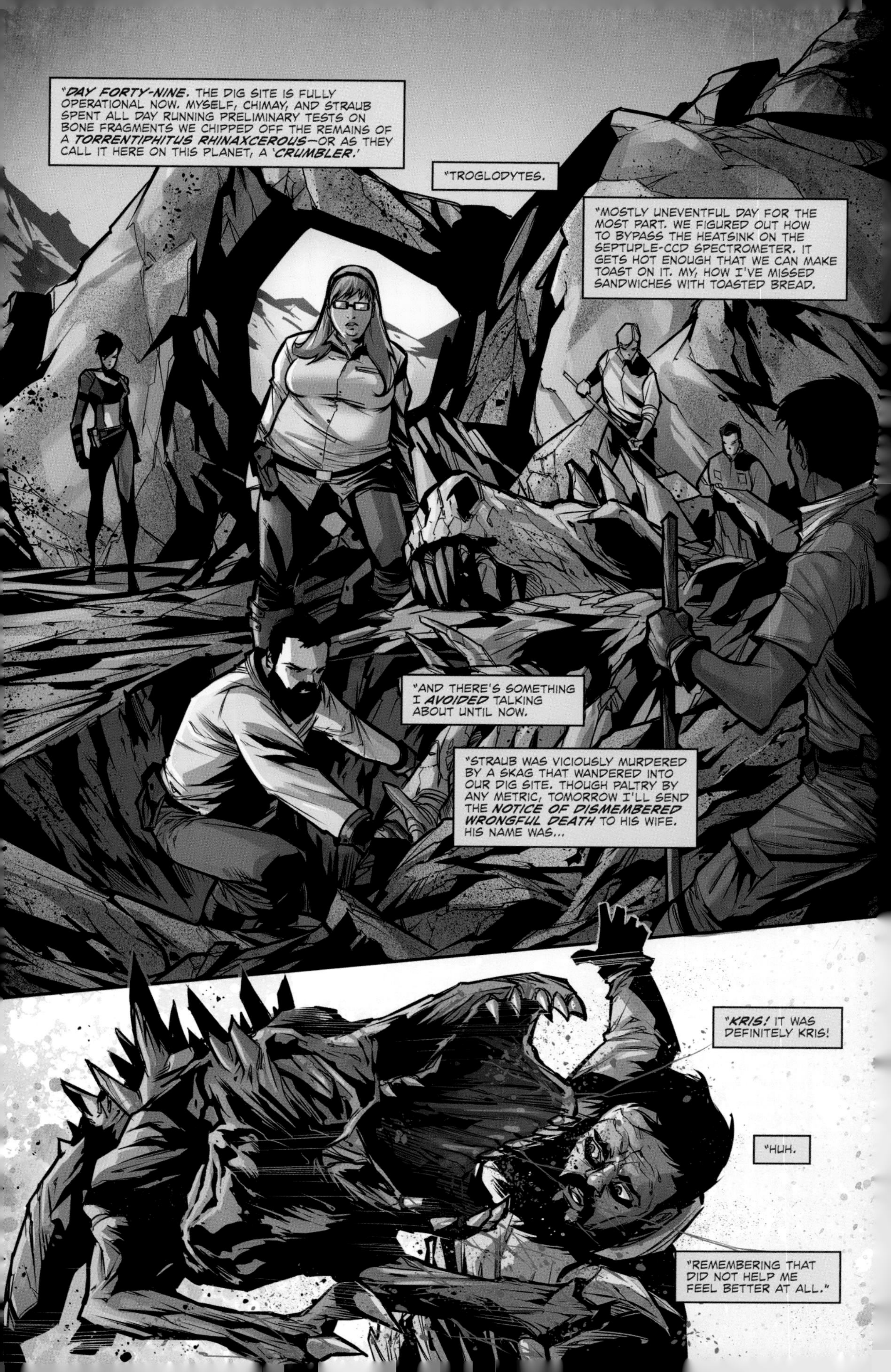
"DAY FORTY-NINE. THE DIG SITE IS FULLY OPERATIONAL NOW. MYSELF, CHIMAY, AND STRAUB SPENT ALL DAY RUNNING PRELIMINARY TESTS ON BONE FRAGMENTS WE CHIPPED OFF THE REMAINS OF A TORRENTIPHITUS RHINAXCEROUS—OR AS THEY CALL IT HERE ON THIS PLANET, A 'CRUMBLER.'
"TROGLODYTES.
"MOSTLY UNEVENTFUL DAY FOR THE MOST PART. WE FIGURED OUT HOW TO BYPASS THE HEATSINK ON THE SEPTUPLE-CCD SPECTROMETER. IT GETS HOT ENOUGH THAT WE CAN MAKE TOAST ON IT. MY, HOW I'VE MISSED SANDWICHES WITH TOASTED BREAD.
"AND THERE'S SOMETHING I AVOIDED TALKING ABOUT UNTIL NOW.
"STRAUB WAS VICIOUSLY MURDERED BY A SKAG THAT WANDERED INTO OUR DIG SITE. THOUGH PALTRY BY ANY METRIC, TOMORROW I'LL SEND THE NOTICE OF DISMEMBERED WRONGFUL DEATH TO HIS WIFE. HIS NAME WAS...
"KRIS! IT WAS DEFINITELY KRIS!
"HUH.
"REMEMBERING THAT DID NOT HELP ME FEEL BETTER AT ALL."

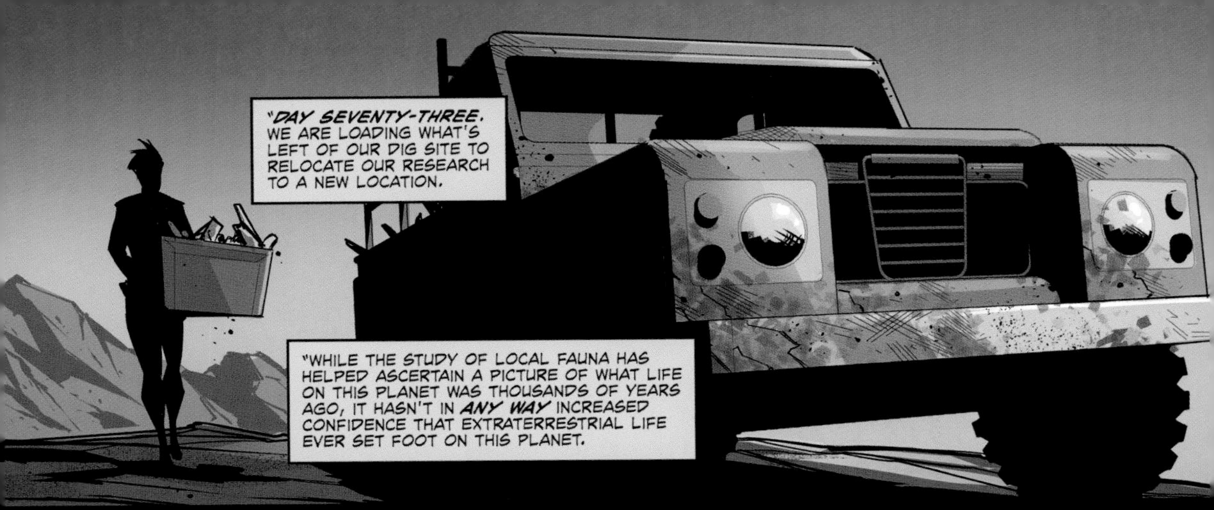
"DAY SEVENTY-THREE. WE ARE LOADING WHAT'S LEFT OF OUR DIG SITE TO RELOCATE OUR RESEARCH TO A NEW LOCATION.
"WHILE THE STUDY OF LOCAL FAUNA HAS HELPED ASCERTAIN A PICTURE OF WHAT LIFE ON THIS PLANET WAS THOUSANDS OF YEARS AGO, IT HASN'T IN ANY WAY INCREASED CONFIDENCE THAT EXTRATERRESTRIAL LIFE EVER SET FOOT ON THIS PLANET.

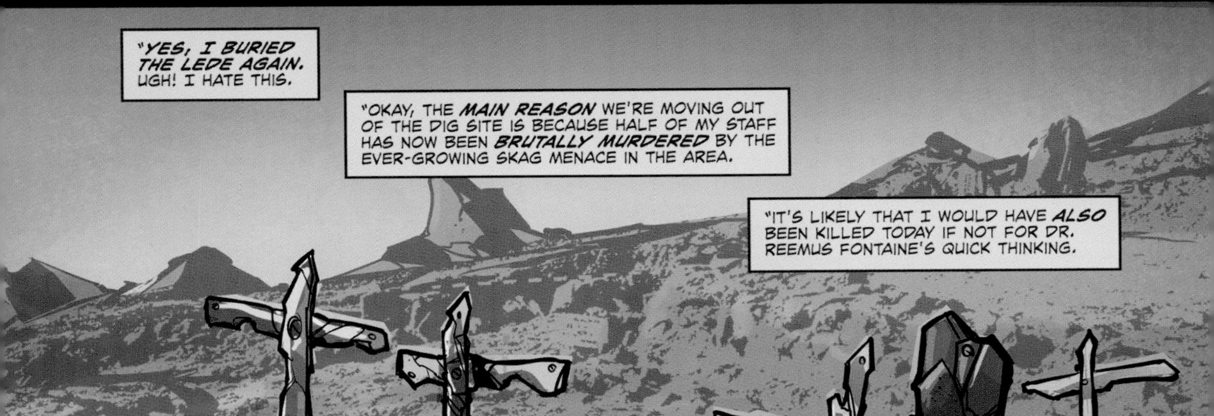
"YES, I BURIED THE LEDE AGAIN. UGH! I HATE THIS.
"OKAY, THE MAIN REASON WE'RE MOVING OUT OF THE DIG SITE IS BECAUSE HALF OF MY STAFF HAS NOW BEEN BRUTALLY MURDERED BY THE EVER-GROWING SKAG MENACE IN THE AREA.
"IT'S LIKELY THAT I WOULD HAVE ALSO BEEN KILLED TODAY IF NOT FOR DR. REEMUS FONTAINE'S QUICK THINKING.

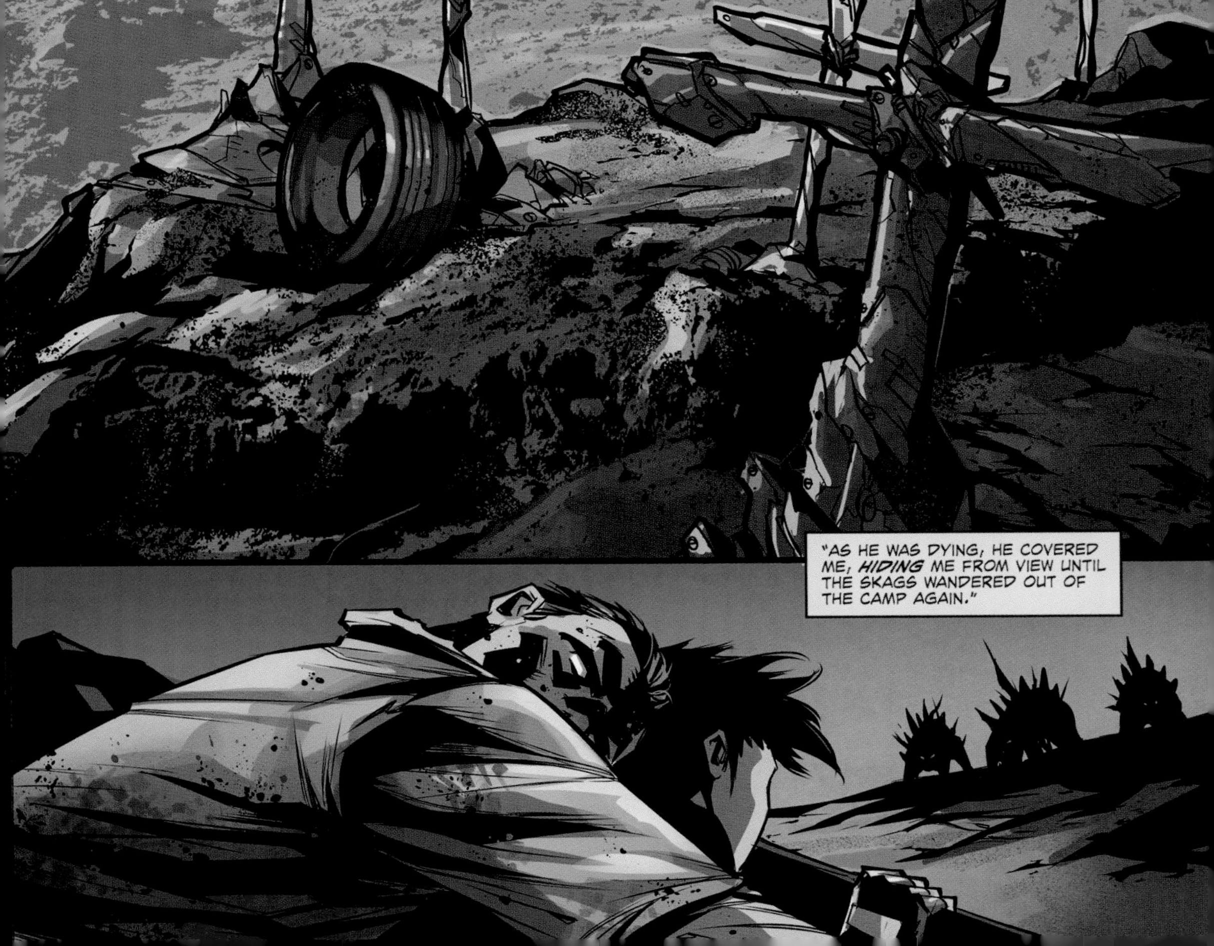
"AS HE WAS DYING, HE COVERED ME, HIDING ME FROM VIEW UNTIL THE SKAGS WANDERED OUT OF THE CAMP AGAIN."

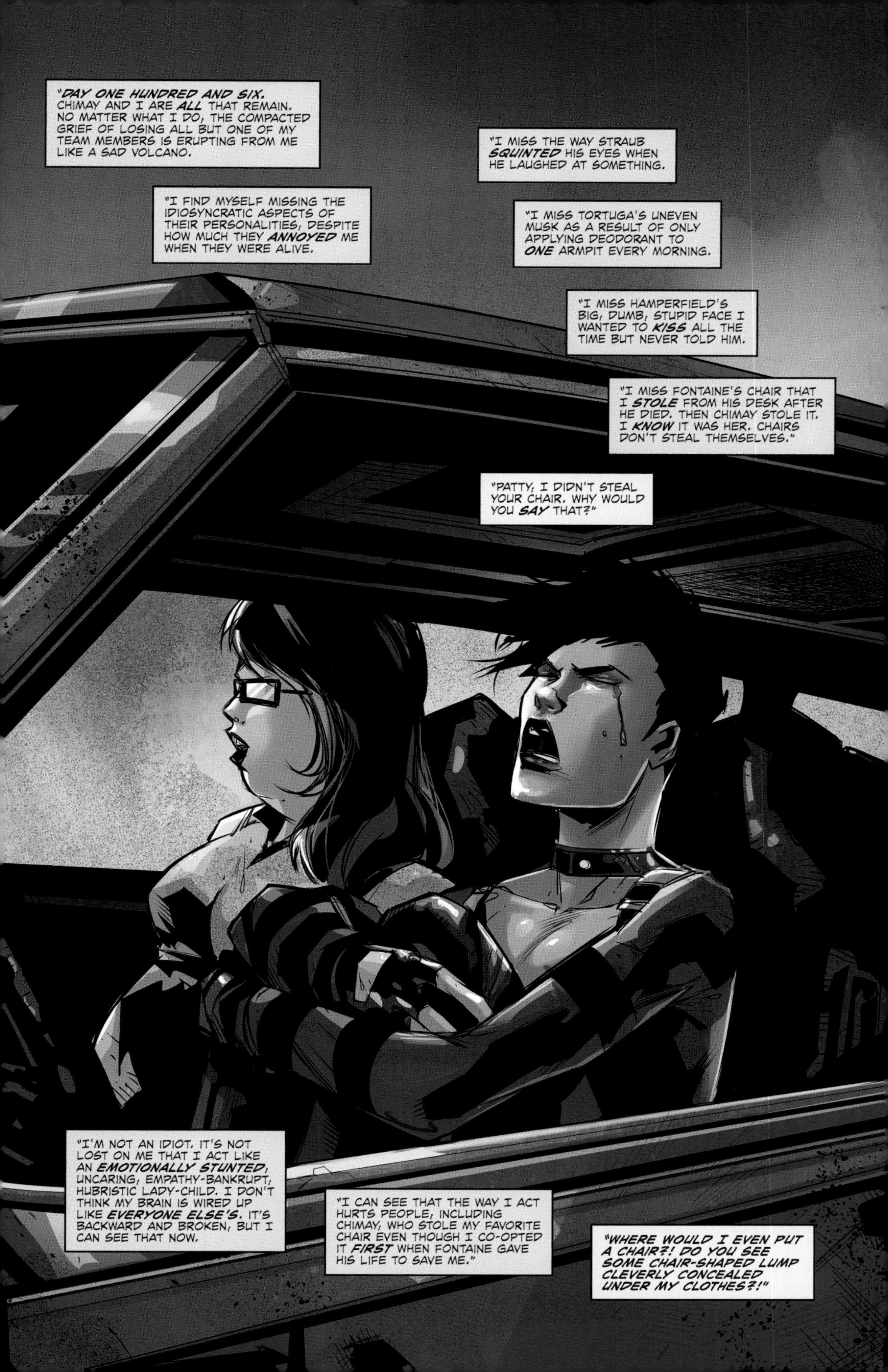

"DAY ONE HUNDRED AND SIX. CHIMAY AND I ARE ALL THAT REMAIN. NO MATTER WHAT I DO, THE COMPACTED GRIEF OF LOSING ALL BUT ONE OF MY TEAM MEMBERS IS ERUPTING FROM ME LIKE A SAD VOLCANO.
"I FIND MYSELF MISSING THE IDIOSYNCRATIC ASPECTS OF THEIR PERSONALITIES, DESPITE HOW MUCH THEY ANNOYED ME WHEN THEY WERE ALIVE.
"I MISS THE WAY STRAUB SQUINTED HIS EYES WHEN HE LAUGHED AT SOMETHING.
"I MISS TORTUGA'S UNEVEN MUSK AS A RESULT OF ONLY APPLYING DEODORANT TO ONE ARMPIT EVERY MORNING.
"I MISS HAMPERFIELD'S BIG, DUMB, STUPID FACE I WANTED TO KISS ALL THE TIME BUT NEVER TOLD HIM.
"I MISS FONTAINE'S CHAIR THAT I STOLE FROM HIS DESK AFTER HE DIED. THEN CHIMAY STOLE IT. I KNOW IT WAS HER. CHAIRS DON'T STEAL THEMSELVES."
"PATTY, I DIDN'T STEAL YOUR CHAIR. WHY WOULD YOU SAY THAT?"
"I'M NOT AN IDIOT. IT'S NOT LOST ON ME THAT I ACT LIKE AN EMOTIONALLY STUNTED, UNCARING, EMPATHY-BANKRUPT, HUBRISTIC LADY-CHILD. I DON'T THINK MY BRAIN IS WIRED UP LIKE EVERYONE ELSE'S. IT'S BACKWARD AND BROKEN, BUT I CAN SEE THAT NOW.
"I CAN SEE THAT THE WAY I ACT HURTS PEOPLE, INCLUDING CHIMAY, WHO STOLE MY FAVORITE CHAIR EVEN THOUGH I CO-OPTED IT FIRST WHEN FONTAINE GAVE HIS LIFE TO SAVE ME."
"WHERE WOULD I EVEN PUT A CHAIR?! DO YOU SEE SOME CHAIR-SHAPED LUMP CLEVERLY CONCEALED UNDER MY CLOTHES?!"

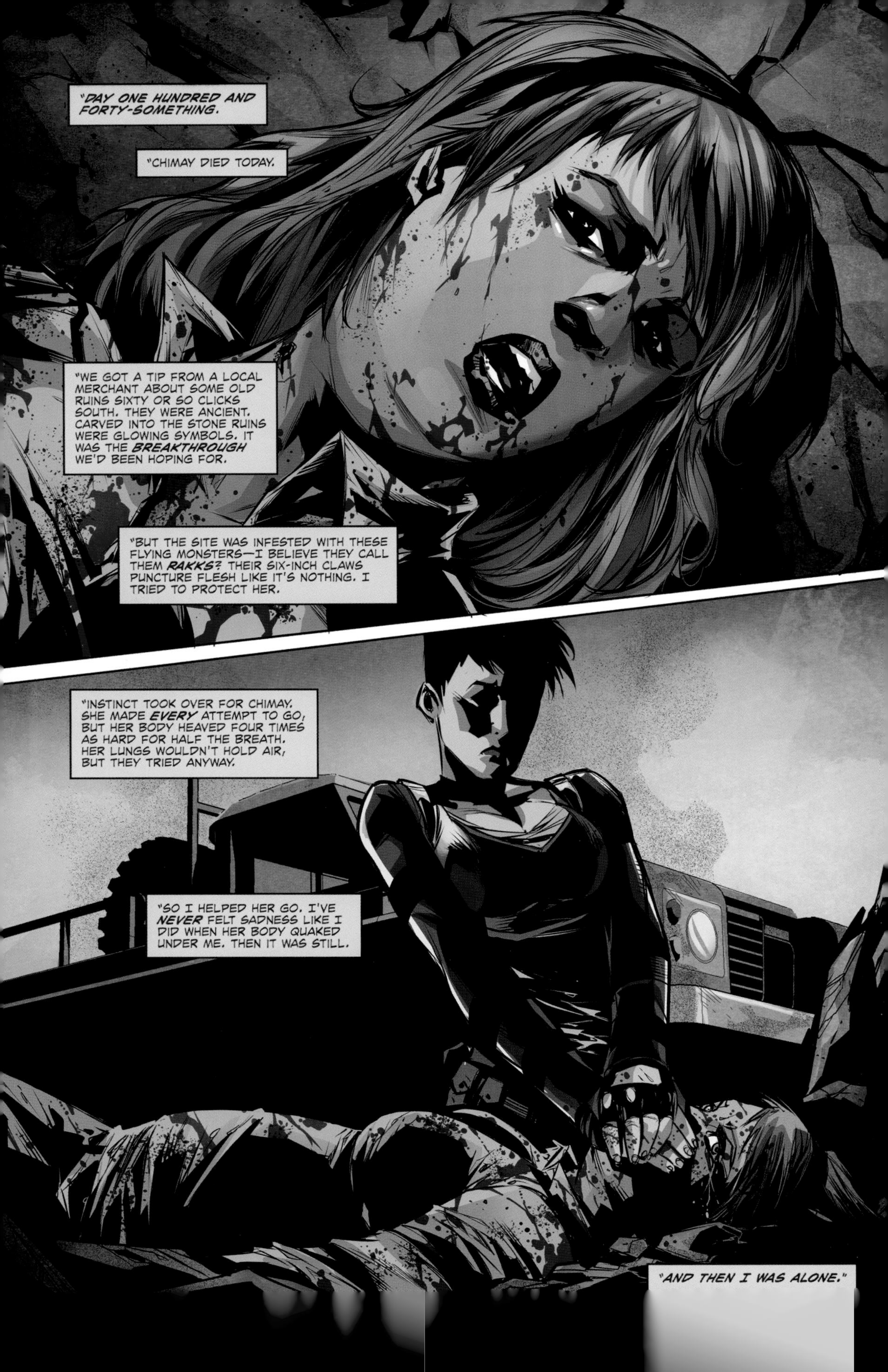
"DAY ONE HUNDRED AND FORTY-SOMETHING.
"CHIMAY DIED TODAY.
"WE GOT A TIP FROM A LOCAL MERCHANT ABOUT SOME OLD RUINS SIXTY OR SO CLICKS SOUTH. THEY WERE ANCIENT. CARVED INTO THE STONE RUINS WERE GLOWING SYMBOLS. IT WAS THE BREAKTHROUGH WE'D BEEN HOPING FOR.
"BUT THE SITE WAS INFESTED WITH THESE FLYING MONSTERS—I BELIEVE THEY CALL THEM RAKKS? THEIR SIX-INCH CLAWS PUNCTURE FLESH LIKE IT'S NOTHING. I TRIED TO PROTECT HER.
"INSTINCT TOOK OVER FOR CHIMAY. SHE MADE EVERY ATTEMPT TO GO, BUT HER BODY HEAVED FOUR TIMES AS HARD FOR HALF THE BREATH. HER LUNGS WOULDN'T HOLD AIR, BUT THEY TRIED ANYWAY.
"SO I HELPED HER GO. I'VE NEVER FELT SADNESS LIKE I DID WHEN HER BODY QUAKED UNDER ME. THEN IT WAS STILL.
"AND THEN I WAS ALONE."

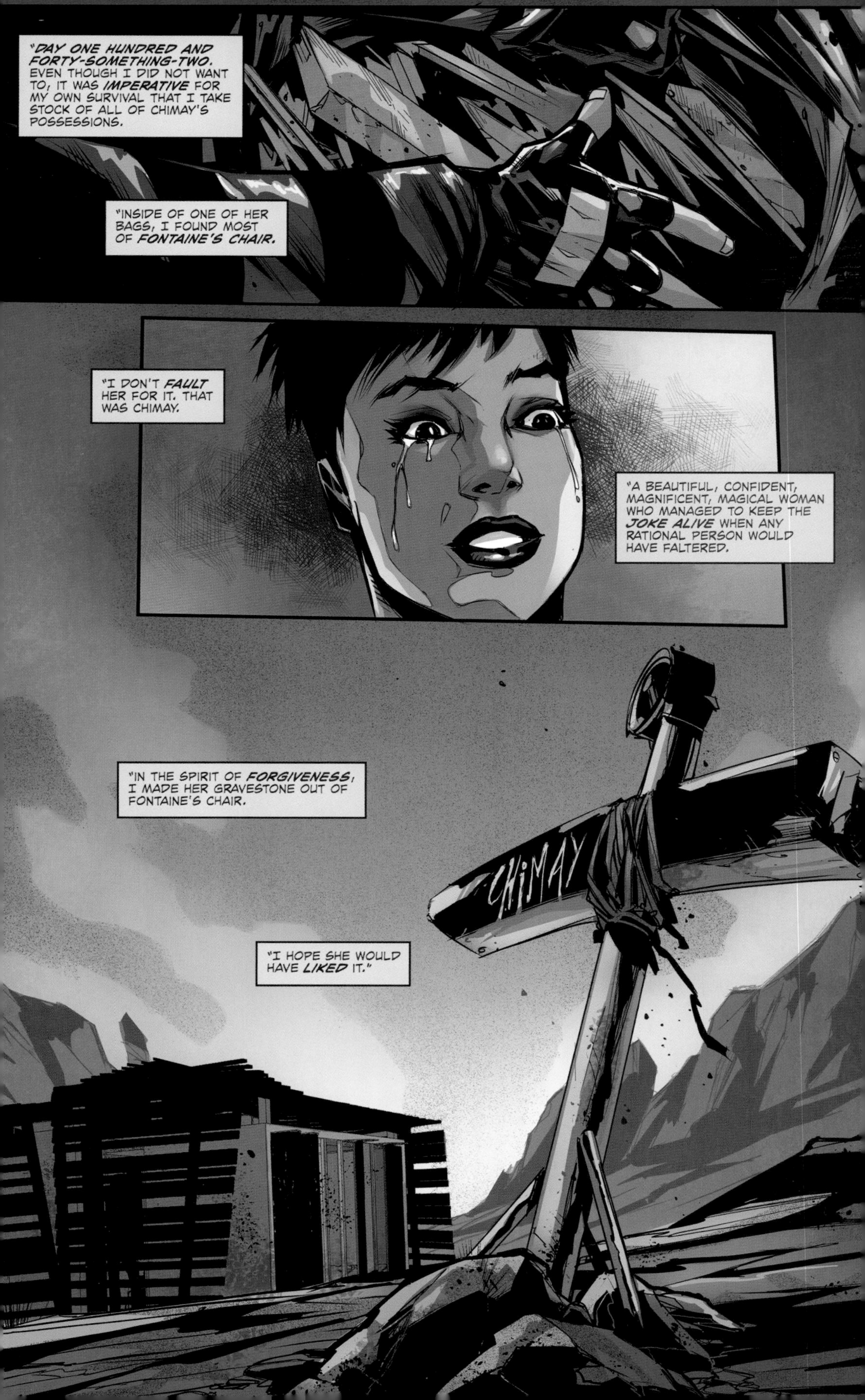
"DAY ONE HUNDRED AND FORTY-SOMETHING-TWO. EVEN THOUGH I DID NOT WANT TO, IT WAS IMPERATIVE FOR MY OWN SURVIVAL THAT I TAKE STOCK OF ALL OF CHIMAY'S POSSESSIONS.
"INSIDE OF ONE OF HER BAGS, I FOUND MOST OF FONTAINE'S CHAIR.
"I DON'T FAULT HER FOR IT. THAT WAS CHIMAY.
"A BEAUTIFUL, CONFIDENT, MAGNIFICENT, MAGICAL WOMAN WHO MANAGED TO KEEP THE JOKE ALIVE WHEN ANY RATIONAL PERSON WOULD HAVE FALTERED.
"IN THE SPIRIT OF FORGIVENESS, I MADE HER GRAVESTONE OUT OF FONTAINE'S CHAIR.
CHIMAY
"I HOPE SHE WOULD HAVE LIKED IT."

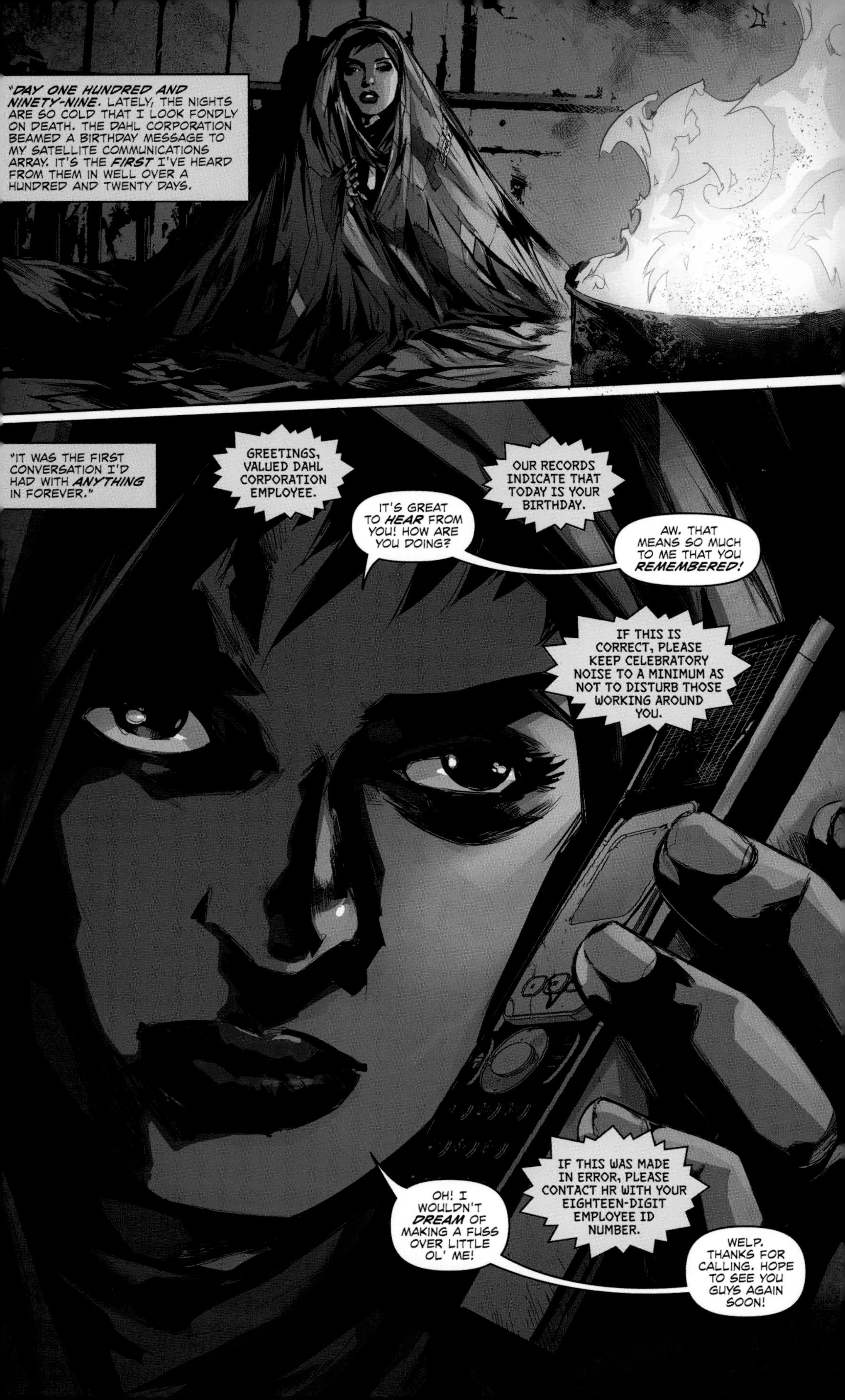

"DAY ONE HUNDRED AND NINETY-NINE. LATELY, THE NIGHTS ARE SO COLD THAT I LOOK FONDLY ON DEATH. THE DAHL CORPORATION BEAMED A BIRTHDAY MESSAGE TO MY SATELLITE COMMUNICATIONS ARRAY. IT'S THE FIRST I'VE HEARD FROM THEM IN WELL OVER A HUNDRED AND TWENTY DAYS.
"IT WAS THE FIRST CONVERSATION I'D HAD WITH ANYTHING IN FOREVER."
GREETINGS, VALUED DAHL CORPORATION EMPLOYEE.
IT'S GREAT TO HEAR FROM YOU! HOW ARE YOU DOING?
OUR RECORDS INDICATE THAT TODAY IS YOUR BIRTHDAY.
AW. THAT MEANS SO MUCH TO ME THAT YOU REMEMBERED!
IF THIS IS CORRECT, PLEASE KEEP CELEBRATORY NOISE TO A MINIMUM AS NOT TO DISTURB THOSE WORKING AROUND YOU.
OH! I WOULDN'T DREAM OF MAKING A FUSS OVER LITTLE OL' ME!
IF THIS WAS MADE IN ERROR, PLEASE CONTACT HR WITH YOUR EIGHTEEN-DIGIT EMPLOYEE ID NUMBER.
WELP. THANKS FOR CALLING. HOPE TO SEE YOU GUYS AGAIN SOON!

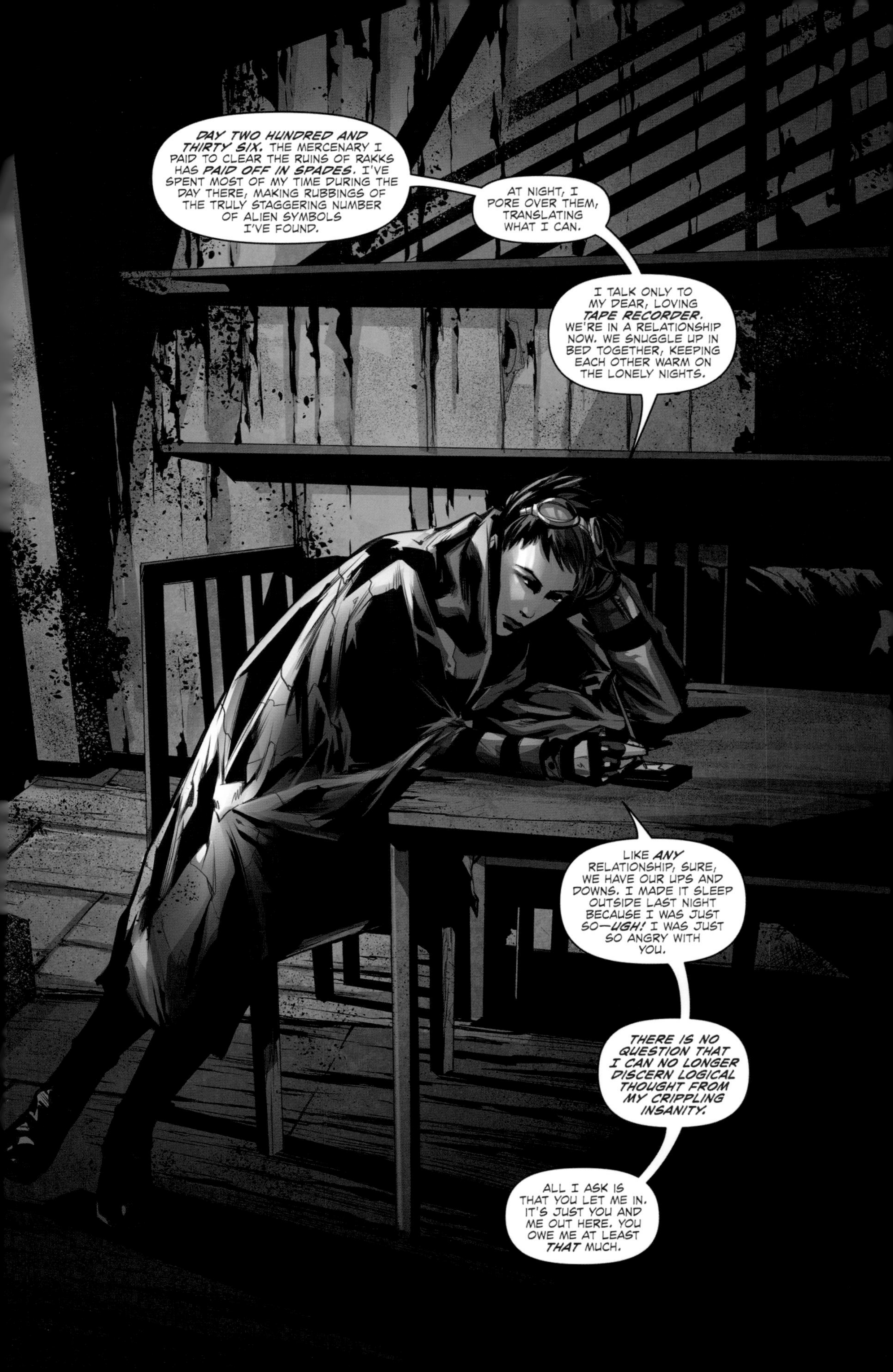
DAY TWO HUNDRED AND THIRTY SIX. THE MERCENARY I PAID TO CLEAR THE RUINS OF RAKKS HAS PAID OFF IN SPADES. I'VE SPENT MOST OF MY TIME DURING THE DAY THERE, MAKING RUBBINGS OF THE TRULY STAGGERING NUMBER OF ALIEN SYMBOLS I'VE FOUND.
AT NIGHT, I PORE OVER THEM, TRANSLATING WHAT I CAN.
I TALK ONLY TO MY DEAR, LOVING TAPE RECORDER. WE'RE IN A RELATIONSHIP NOW. WE SNUGGLE UP IN BED TOGETHER, KEEPING EACH OTHER WARM ON THE LONELY NIGHTS.
LIKE ANY RELATIONSHIP, SURE, WE HAVE OUR UPS AND DOWNS. I MADE IT SLEEP OUTSIDE LAST NIGHT BECAUSE I WAS JUST SO—UGH! I WAS JUST SO ANGRY WITH YOU.
THERE IS NO QUESTION THAT I CAN NO LONGER DISCERN LOGICAL THOUGHT FROM MY CRIPPLING INSANITY.
ALL I ASK IS THAT YOU LET ME IN. IT'S JUST YOU AND ME OUT HERE. YOU OWE ME AT LEAST THAT MUCH.

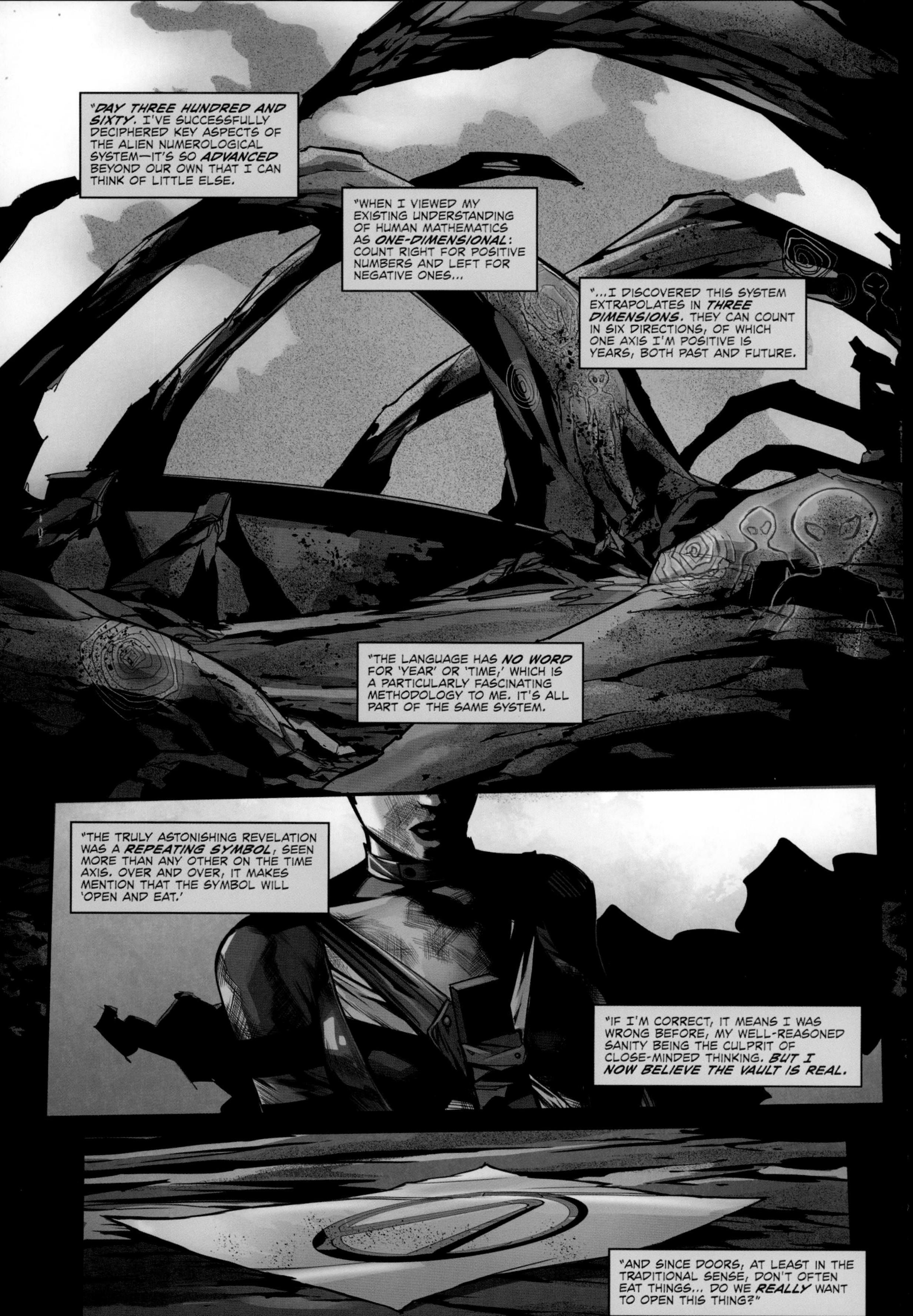
"DAY THREE HUNDRED AND SIXTY. I'VE SUCCESSFULLY DECIPHERED KEY ASPECTS OF THE ALIEN NUMEROLOGICAL SYSTEM—IT'S SO ADVANCED BEYOND OUR OWN THAT I CAN THINK OF LITTLE ELSE.
"WHEN I VIEWED MY EXISTING UNDERSTANDING OF HUMAN MATHEMATICS AS ONE-DIMENSIONAL: COUNT RIGHT FOR POSITIVE NUMBERS AND LEFT FOR NEGATIVE ONES...
"...I DISCOVERED THIS SYSTEM EXTRAPOLATES IN THREE DIMENSIONS. THEY CAN COUNT IN SIX DIRECTIONS, OF WHICH ONE AXIS I'M POSITIVE IS YEARS, BOTH PAST AND FUTURE.
"THE LANGUAGE HAS NO WORD FOR 'YEAR' OR 'TIME,' WHICH IS A PARTICULARLY FASCINATING METHODOLOGY TO ME. IT'S ALL PART OF THE SAME SYSTEM.
"THE TRULY ASTONISHING REVELATION WAS A REPEATING SYMBOL, SEEN MORE THAN ANY OTHER ON THE TIME AXIS. OVER AND OVER, IT MAKES MENTION THAT THE SYMBOL WILL 'OPEN AND EAT.'
"IF I'M CORRECT, IT MEANS I WAS WRONG BEFORE, MY WELL-REASONED SANITY BEING THE CULPRIT OF CLOSE-MINDED THINKING. BUT I NOW BELIEVE THE VAULT IS REAL.
"AND SINCE DOORS, AT LEAST IN THE TRADITIONAL SENSE, DON'T OFTEN EAT THINGS... DO WE REALLY WANT TO OPEN THIS THING?"

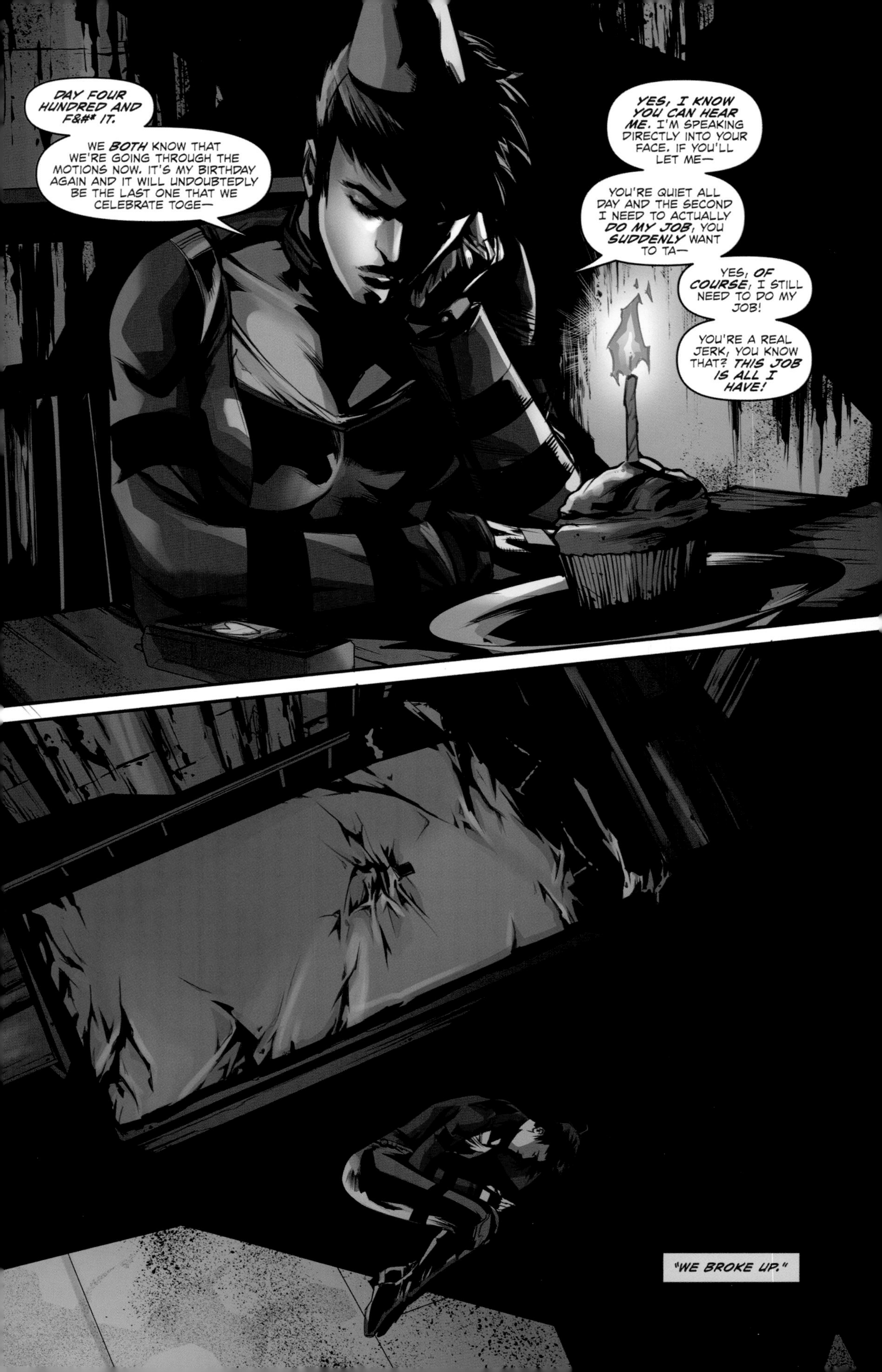
DAY FOUR HUNDRED AND F&#* IT.
WE BOTH KNOW THAT WE'RE GOING THROUGH THE MOTIONS NOW. IT'S MY BIRTHDAY AGAIN AND IT WILL UNDOUBTEDLY BE THE LAST ONE THAT WE CELEBRATE TOGE—
YES, I KNOW YOU CAN HEAR ME. I'M SPEAKING DIRECTLY INTO YOUR FACE. IF YOU'LL LET ME—
YOU'RE QUIET ALL DAY AND THE SECOND I NEED TO ACTUALLY DO MY JOB, YOU SUDDENLY WANT TO TA—
YES, OF COURSE, I STILL NEED TO DO MY JOB!
YOU'RE A REAL JERK, YOU KNOW THAT? THIS JOB IS ALL I HAVE!
"WE BROKE UP."

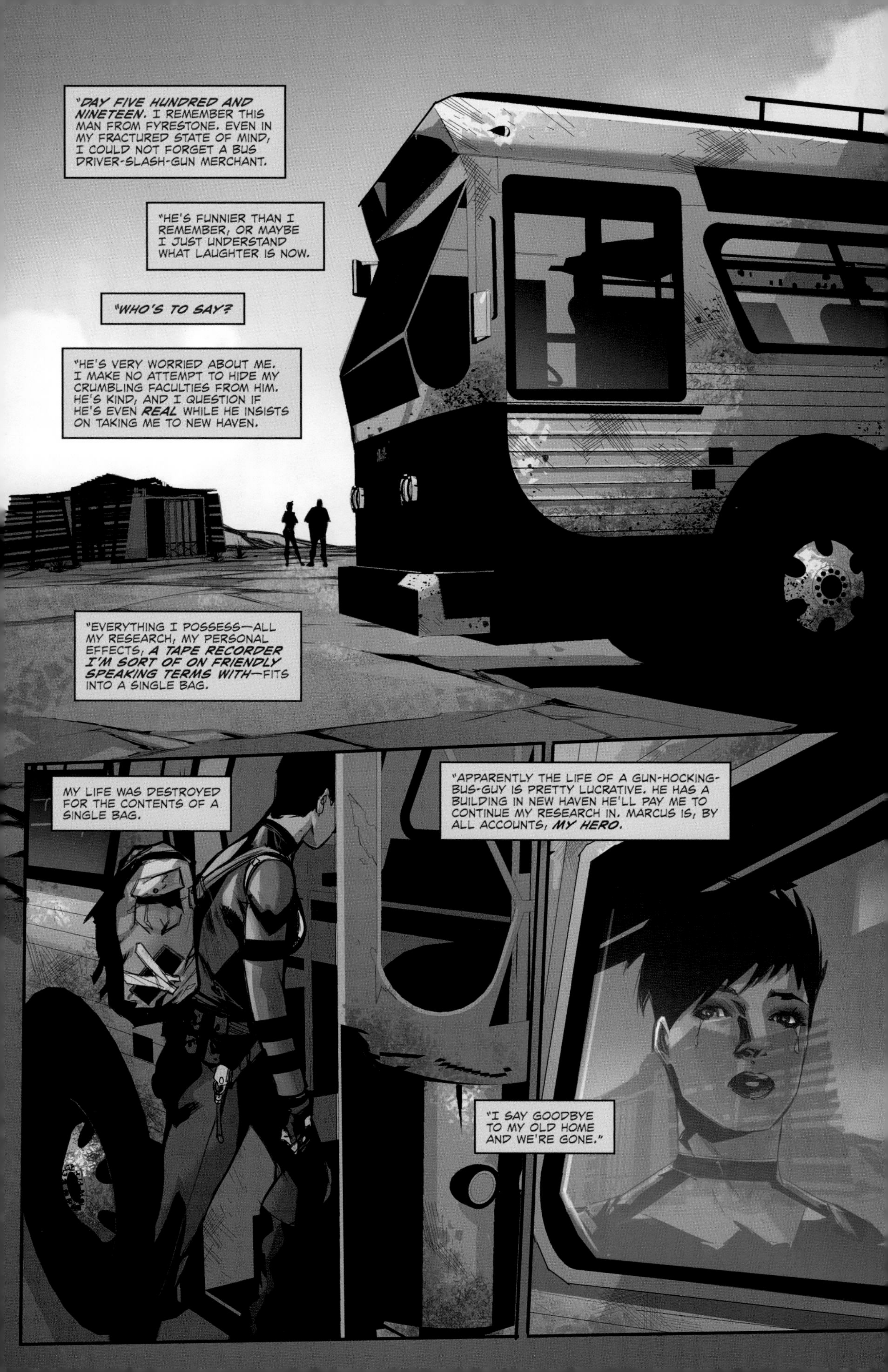
"DAY FIVE HUNDRED AND NINETEEN. I REMEMBER THIS MAN FROM FYRESTONE. EVEN IN MY FRACTURED STATE OF MIND, I COULD NOT FORGET A BUS DRIVER-SLASH-GUN MERCHANT.
"HE'S FUNNIER THAN I REMEMBER, OR MAYBE I JUST UNDERSTAND WHAT LAUGHTER IS NOW.
"WHO'S TO SAY?
"HE'S VERY WORRIED ABOUT ME. I MAKE NO ATTEMPT TO HIDE MY CRUMBLING FACULTIES FROM HIM. HE'S KIND, AND I QUESTION IF HE'S EVEN REAL WHILE HE INSISTS ON TAKING ME TO NEW HAVEN.
"EVERYTHING I POSSESS—ALL MY RESEARCH, MY PERSONAL EFFECTS, A TAPE RECORDER I'M SORT OF ON FRIENDLY SPEAKING TERMS WITH—FITS INTO A SINGLE BAG.
MY LIFE WAS DESTROYED FOR THE CONTENTS OF A SINGLE BAG.
"APPARENTLY THE LIFE OF A GUN-HOCKING-BUS-GUY IS PRETTY LUCRATIVE. HE HAS A BUILDING IN NEW HAVEN HE'LL PAY ME TO CONTINUE MY RESEARCH IN. MARCUS IS, BY ALL ACCOUNTS, MY HERO.
"I SAY GOODBYE TO MY OLD HOME AND WE'RE GONE."

"*DAY FIVE HUNDRED AND TWENTY.* THIS WILL BE MY *LAST* RECORDED UPDATE.

"I HAVE ARRIVED IN NEW HAVEN, REFRESHED AND EXCITED TO CONTINUE MY RESEARCH."

AS AN *ADDENDUM* TO THIS UPDATE, I WOULD LIKE TO SPEAK DIRECTLY TO MY *BENEFACTORS* AT THE DAHL CORPORATION. IF YOU'RE LISTENING TO THIS, YOU'VE NO DOUBT HEARD THE *UPDATES* I'VE SELECTED FROM MY TIME HERE ON PANDORA TO SHARE WITH YOU.

WHAT YOU ARE MOST LIKELY *NOT* TO SURMISE FROM THESE AUDIO LOGS IS WHAT IT'S LIKE TO HAVE FEELINGS OF ABANDONMENT CREATE A *VACUUM* WHERE YOUR HEART SHOULD BE.

"I DON'T BELIEVE I CAN ARTICULATE HOW *THANKFUL* I AM THAT YOU CALLOUSLY TOSSED ME ASIDE LIKE A PIECE OF GARBAGE.

"IF YOU HADN'T, I WOULDN'T UNDERSTAND WHAT IT IS TO BE *HUMAN.*

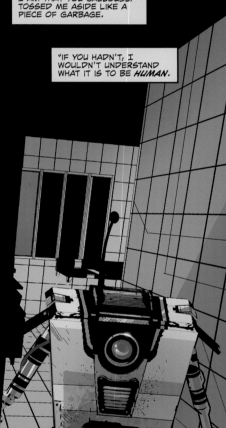

TATE. I'LL BE RIGHT BACK, OKAY?

I GOTTA *DO SOMETHING* REAL QUICK.

"IN SHORT, I'VE LEARNED THAT EMOTIONS ARE IRRATIONAL WINDOWS INTO OUR PERSONAL INSANITY— *AND THAT IS A BEAUTIFUL, WONDERFUL THING.*"

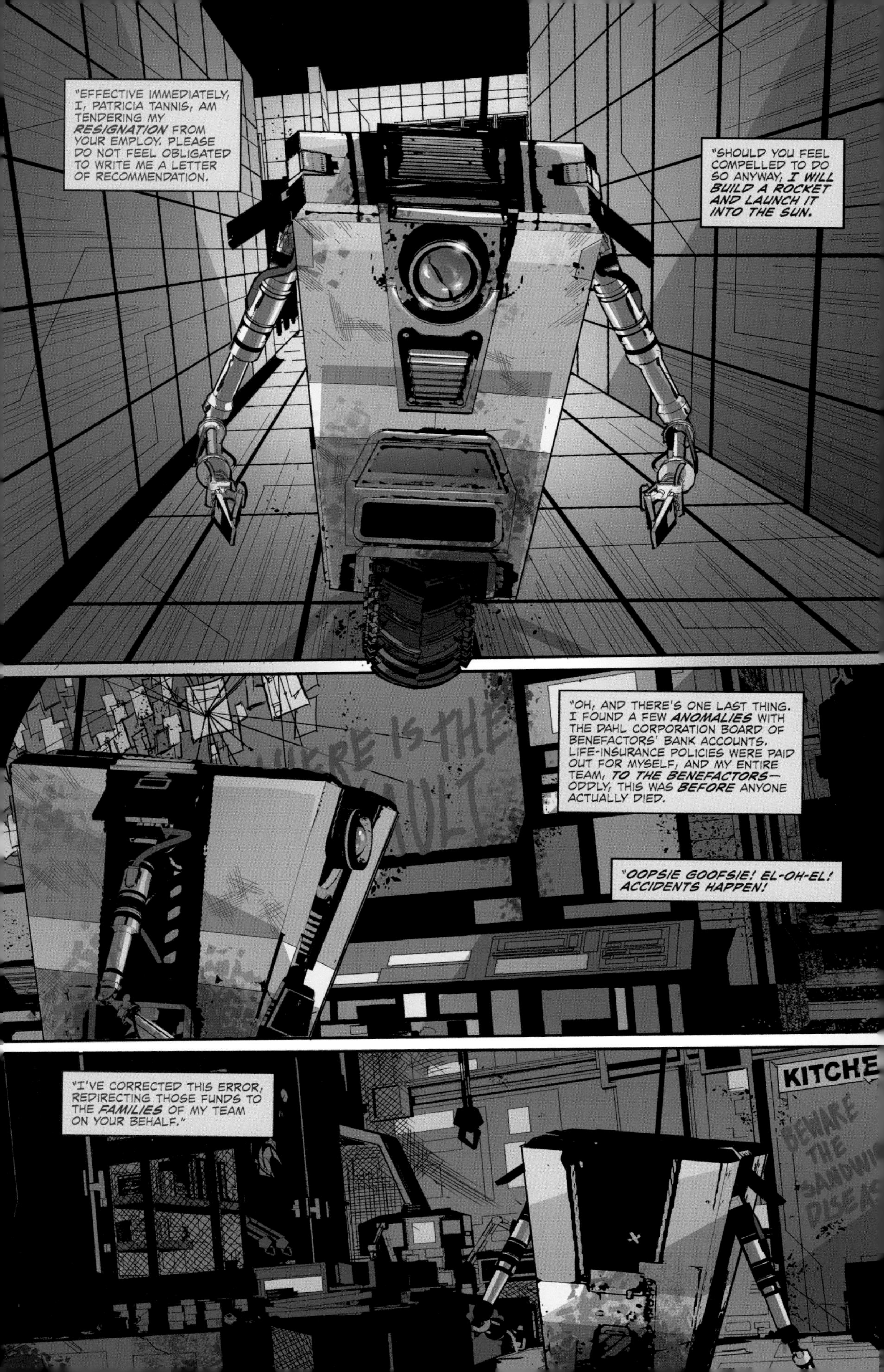
"EFFECTIVE IMMEDIATELY, I, PATRICIA TANNIS, AM TENDERING MY RESIGNATION FROM YOUR EMPLOY. PLEASE DO NOT FEEL OBLIGATED TO WRITE ME A LETTER OF RECOMMENDATION.
"SHOULD YOU FEEL COMPELLED TO DO SO ANYWAY, I WILL BUILD A ROCKET AND LAUNCH IT INTO THE SUN.
"OH, AND THERE'S ONE LAST THING. I FOUND A FEW ANOMALIES WITH THE DAHL CORPORATION BOARD OF BENEFACTORS' BANK ACCOUNTS. LIFE-INSURANCE POLICIES WERE PAID OUT FOR MYSELF, AND MY ENTIRE TEAM, TO THE BENEFACTORS—ODDLY, THIS WAS BEFORE ANYONE ACTUALLY DIED.
"OOPSIE GOOFSIE! EL-OH-EL! ACCIDENTS HAPPEN!
"I'VE CORRECTED THIS ERROR, REDIRECTING THOSE FUNDS TO THE FAMILIES OF MY TEAM ON YOUR BEHALF."
KITCHE
BEWARE THE

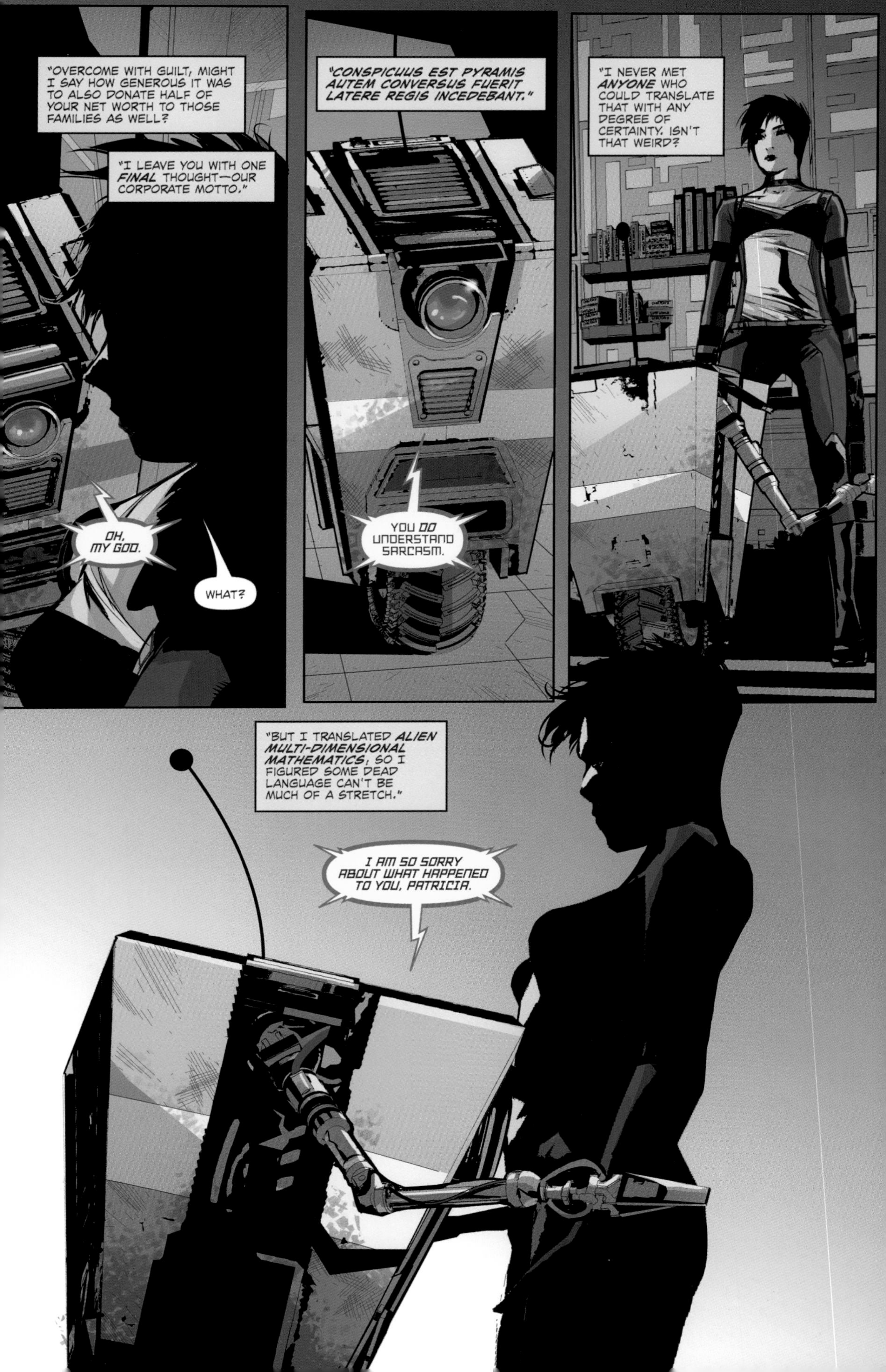
"OVERCOME WITH GUILT, MIGHT I SAY HOW GENEROUS IT WAS TO ALSO DONATE HALF OF YOUR NET WORTH TO THOSE FAMILIES AS WELL?
"I LEAVE YOU WITH ONE FINAL THOUGHT—OUR CORPORATE MOTTO."
OH, MY GOD.
WHAT?
"CONSPICUUS EST PYRAMIS AUTEM CONVERSUS FUERIT LATERE REGIS INCEDEBANT."
YOU DO UNDERSTAND SARCASM.
"I NEVER MET ANYONE WHO COULD TRANSLATE THAT WITH ANY DEGREE OF CERTAINTY. ISN'T THAT WEIRD?
"BUT I TRANSLATED ALIEN MULTI-DIMENSIONAL MATHEMATICS, SO I FIGURED SOME DEAD LANGUAGE CAN'T BE MUCH OF A STRETCH."
I AM SO SORRY ABOUT WHAT HAPPENED TO YOU, PATRICIA.

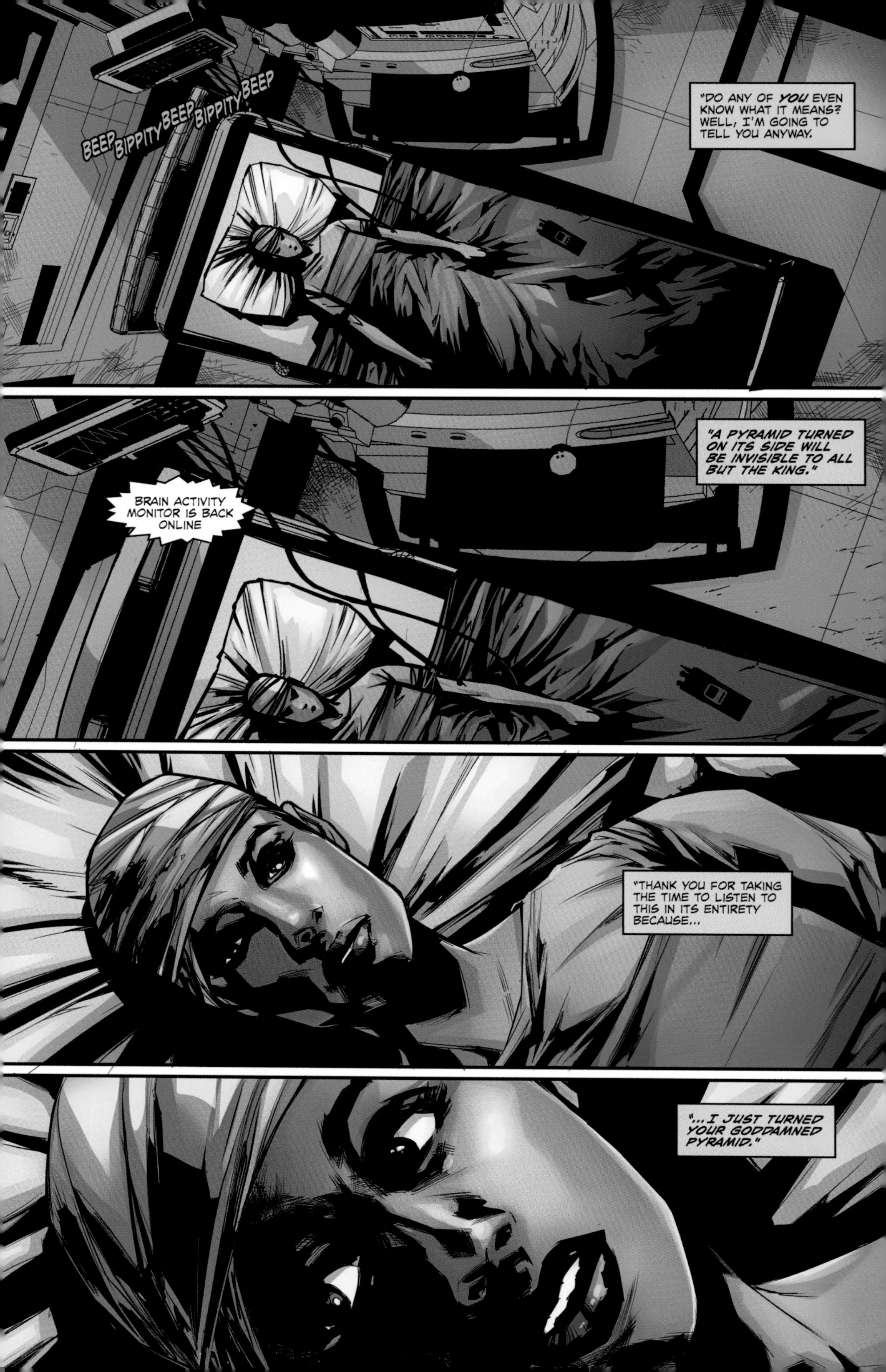
BEEP BIPPITY BEEP BIPPITY BEEP
"DO ANY OF *YOU* EVEN KNOW WHAT IT MEANS? WELL, I'M GOING TO TELL YOU ANYWAY.
"A PYRAMID TURNED ON ITS SIDE WILL BE INVISIBLE TO ALL BUT THE KING."
BRAIN ACTIVITY MONITOR IS BACK ONLINE
"THANK YOU FOR TAKING THE TIME TO LISTEN TO THIS IN ITS ENTIRETY BECAUSE...
"...I JUST TURNED YOUR GODDAMNED PYRAMID."

CHAPTER THREE

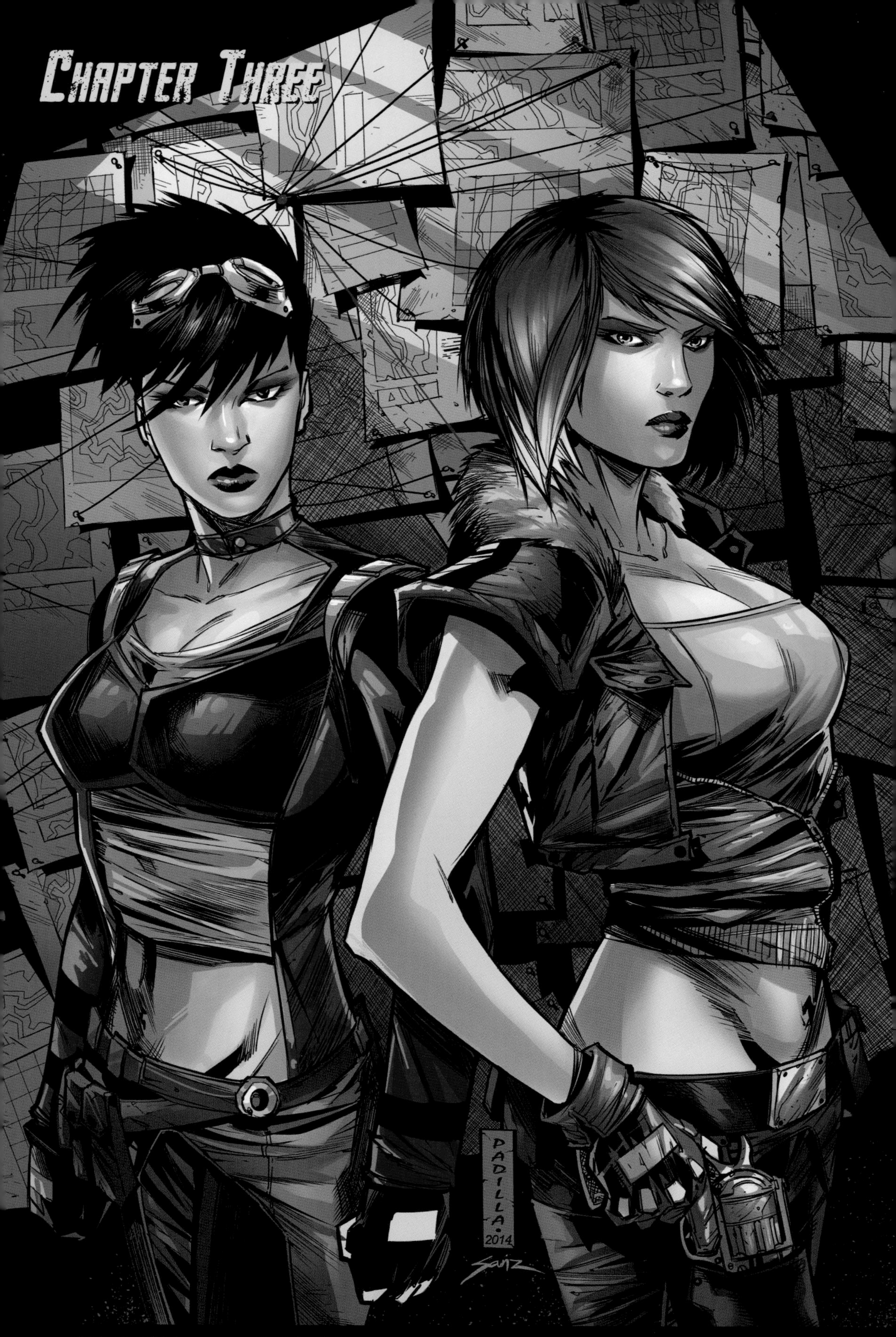
PADILLA 2014

art by AGUSTIN PADILLA • colors by ESTHER SANZ

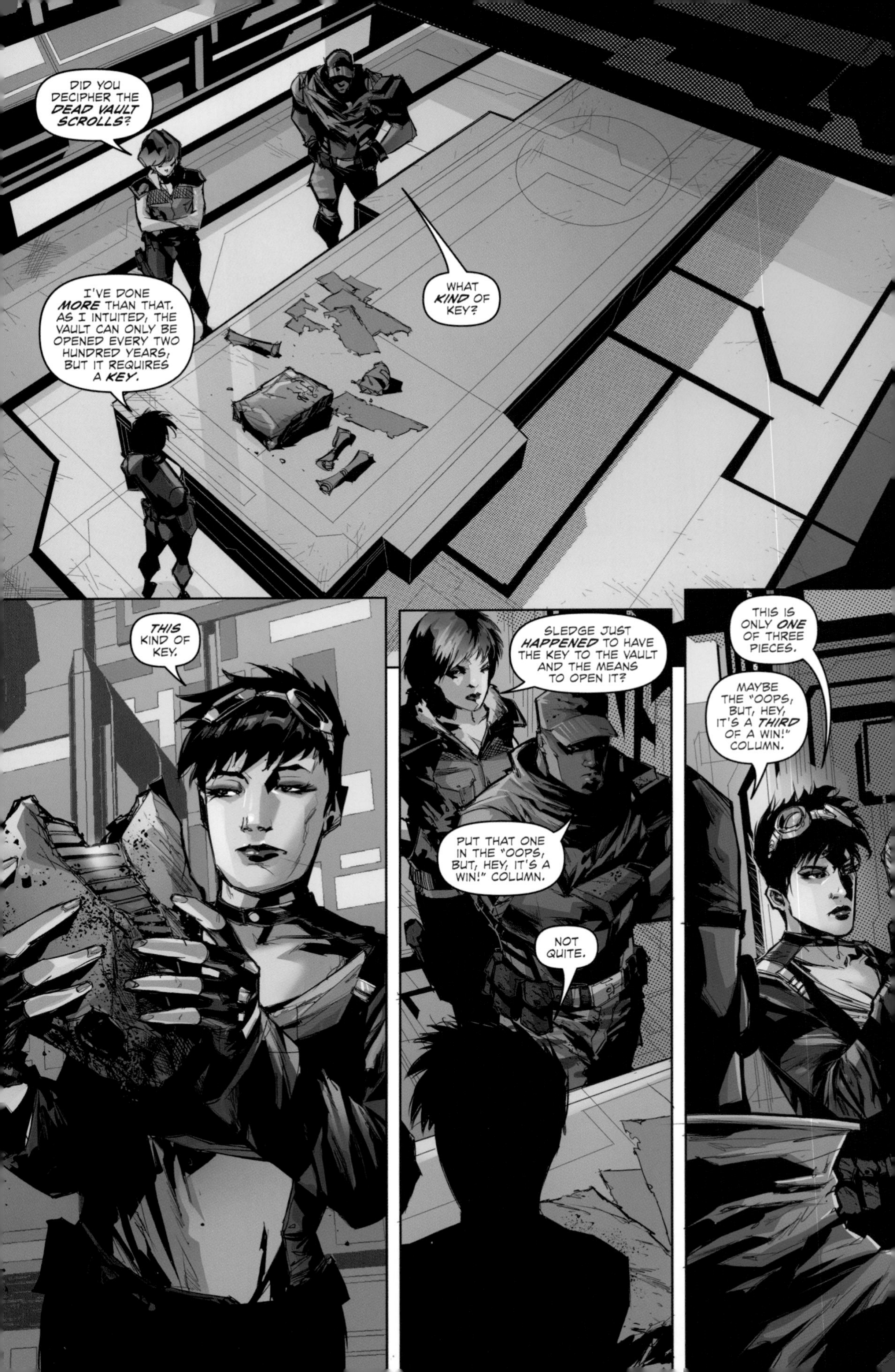
DID YOU DECIPHER THE DEAD VAULT SCROLLS?
I'VE DONE MORE THAN THAT. AS I INTUITED, THE VAULT CAN ONLY BE OPENED EVERY TWO HUNDRED YEARS, BUT IT REQUIRES A KEY.
WHAT KIND OF KEY?
THIS KIND OF KEY.
SLEDGE JUST HAPPENED TO HAVE THE KEY TO THE VAULT AND THE MEANS TO OPEN IT?
PUT THAT ONE IN THE "OOPS, BUT, HEY, IT'S A WIN!" COLUMN.
NOT QUITE.
THIS IS ONLY ONE OF THREE PIECES.
MAYBE THE "OOPS, BUT, HEY, IT'S A THIRD OF A WIN!" COLUMN.

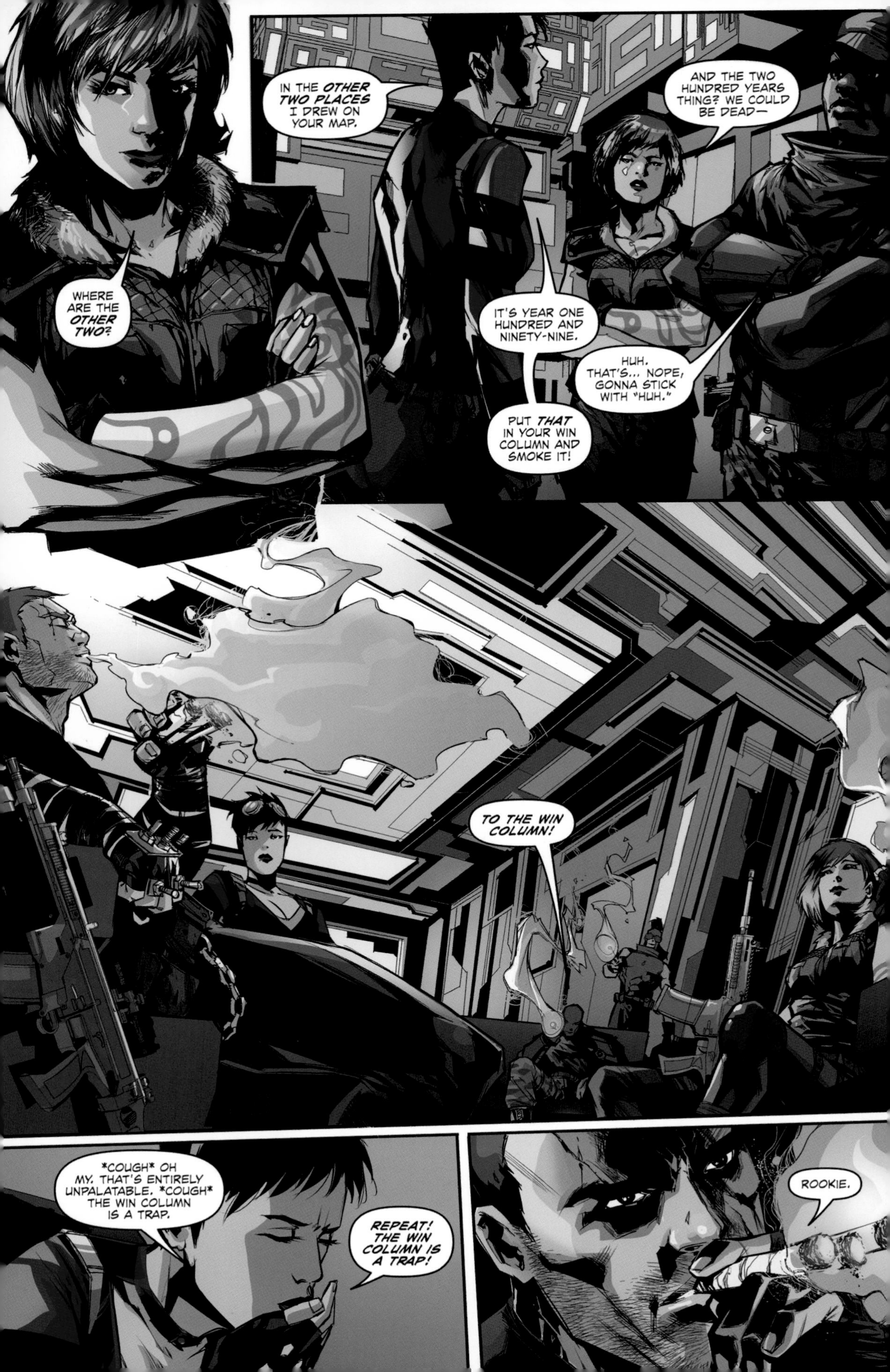

WHERE ARE THE *OTHER TWO*?
IN THE *OTHER TWO PLACES* I DREW ON YOUR MAP.
AND THE TWO HUNDRED YEARS THING? WE COULD BE DEAD—
IT'S YEAR ONE HUNDRED AND NINETY-NINE.
PUT *THAT* IN YOUR WIN COLUMN AND SMOKE IT!
HUH. THAT'S... NOPE, GONNA STICK WITH "HUH."
TO THE WIN COLUMN!
COUGH OH MY. THAT'S ENTIRELY UNPALATABLE. *COUGH* THE WIN COLUMN IS A TRAP.
REPEAT! THE WIN COLUMN IS A TRAP!
ROOKIE.

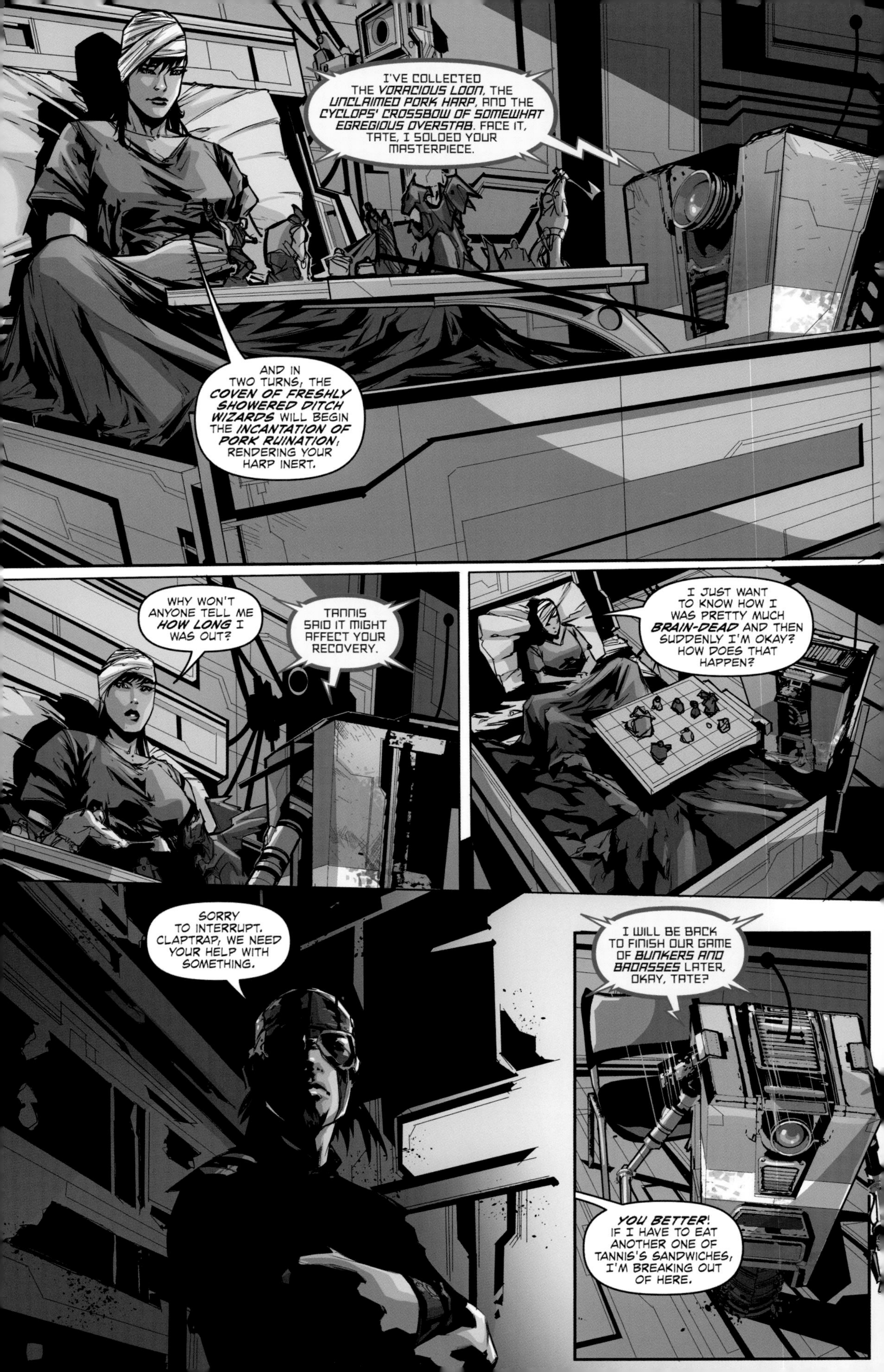

I'VE COLLECTED THE VORACIOUS LOON, THE UNCLAIMED PORK HARP, AND THE CYCLOPS' CROSSBOW OF SOMEWHAT EGREGIOUS OVERSTAB. FACE IT, TATE, I SOLOED YOUR MASTERPIECE.
AND IN TWO TURNS, THE COVEN OF FRESHLY SHOWERED DITCH WIZARDS WILL BEGIN THE INCANTATION OF PORK RUINATION; RENDERING YOUR HARP INERT.
WHY WON'T ANYONE TELL ME HOW LONG I WAS OUT?
TANNIS SAID IT MIGHT AFFECT YOUR RECOVERY.
I JUST WANT TO KNOW HOW I WAS PRETTY MUCH BRAIN-DEAD AND THEN SUDDENLY I'M OKAY? HOW DOES THAT HAPPEN?
SORRY TO INTERRUPT. CLAPTRAP, WE NEED YOUR HELP WITH SOMETHING.
I WILL BE BACK TO FINISH OUR GAME OF BUNKERS AND BADASSES LATER, OKAY, TATE?
YOU BETTER! IF I HAVE TO EAT ANOTHER ONE OF TANNIS'S SANDWICHES, I'M BREAKING OUT OF HERE.

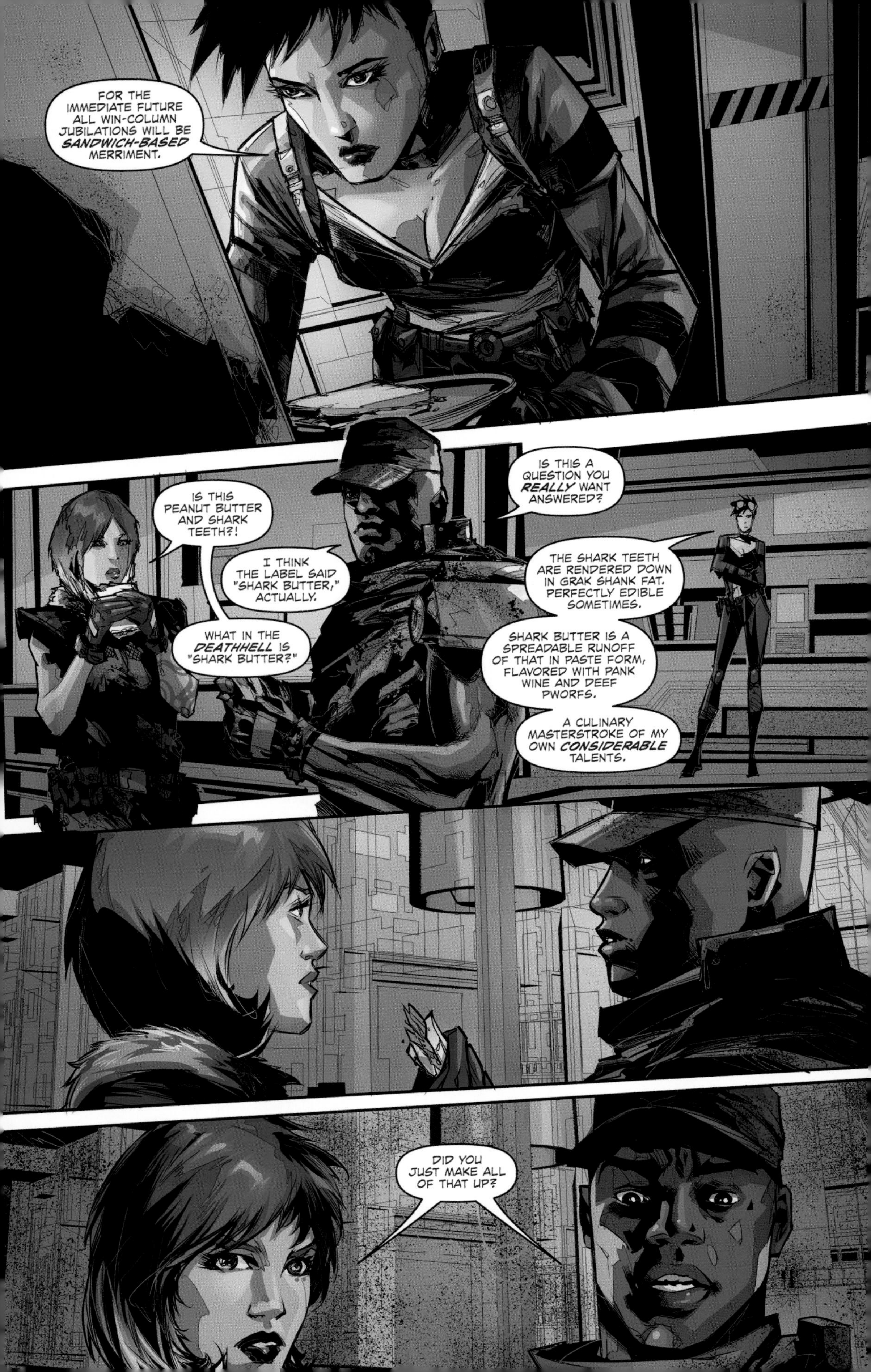
FOR THE IMMEDIATE FUTURE ALL WIN-COLUMN JUBILATIONS WILL BE SANDWICH-BASED MERRIMENT.
IS THIS PEANUT BUTTER AND SHARK TEETH?!
IS THIS A QUESTION YOU REALLY WANT ANSWERED?
I THINK THE LABEL SAID "SHARK BUTTER," ACTUALLY.
WHAT IN THE DEATHHELL IS "SHARK BUTTER?"
THE SHARK TEETH ARE RENDERED DOWN IN GRAK SHANK FAT. PERFECTLY EDIBLE SOMETIMES.
SHARK BUTTER IS A SPREADABLE RUNOFF OF THAT IN PASTE FORM, FLAVORED WITH PANK WINE AND DEEF PWORFS.
A CULINARY MASTERSTROKE OF MY OWN CONSIDERABLE TALENTS.
DID YOU JUST MAKE ALL OF THAT UP?

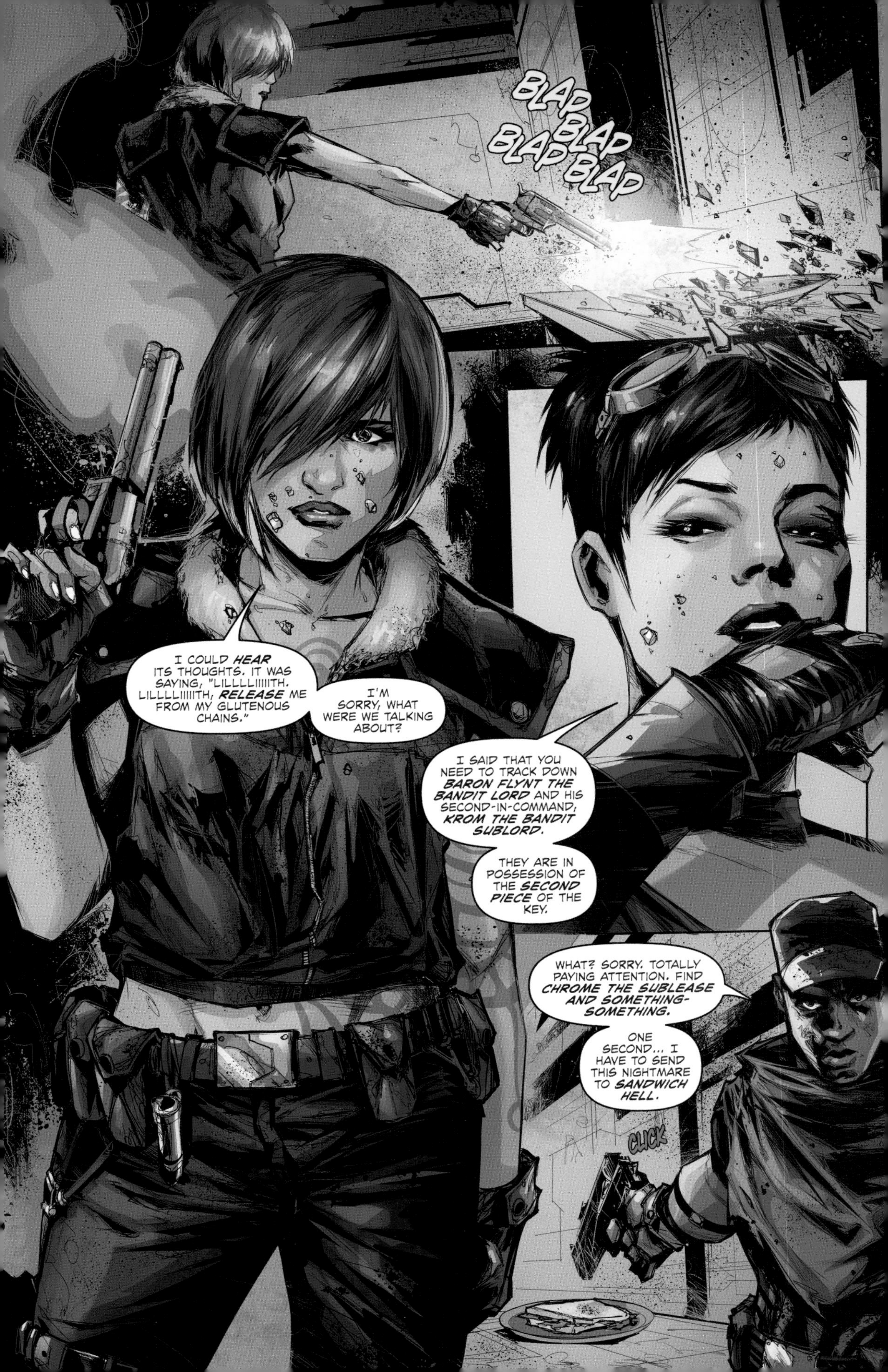
BLAP BLAP BLAP BLAP
I COULD HEAR ITS THOUGHTS. IT WAS SAYING, "LILLLLIIIIITH. LILLLLIIIIITH, RELEASE ME FROM MY GLUTENOUS CHAINS."
I'M SORRY, WHAT WERE WE TALKING ABOUT?
I SAID THAT YOU NEED TO TRACK DOWN BARON FLYNT THE BANDIT LORD AND HIS SECOND-IN-COMMAND, KROM THE BANDIT SUBLORD.
THEY ARE IN POSSESSION OF THE SECOND PIECE OF THE KEY.
WHAT? SORRY. TOTALLY PAYING ATTENTION. FIND CHROME THE SUBLEASE AND SOMETHING-SOMETHING.
ONE SECOND... I HAVE TO SEND THIS NIGHTMARE TO SANDWICH HELL.
CLICK

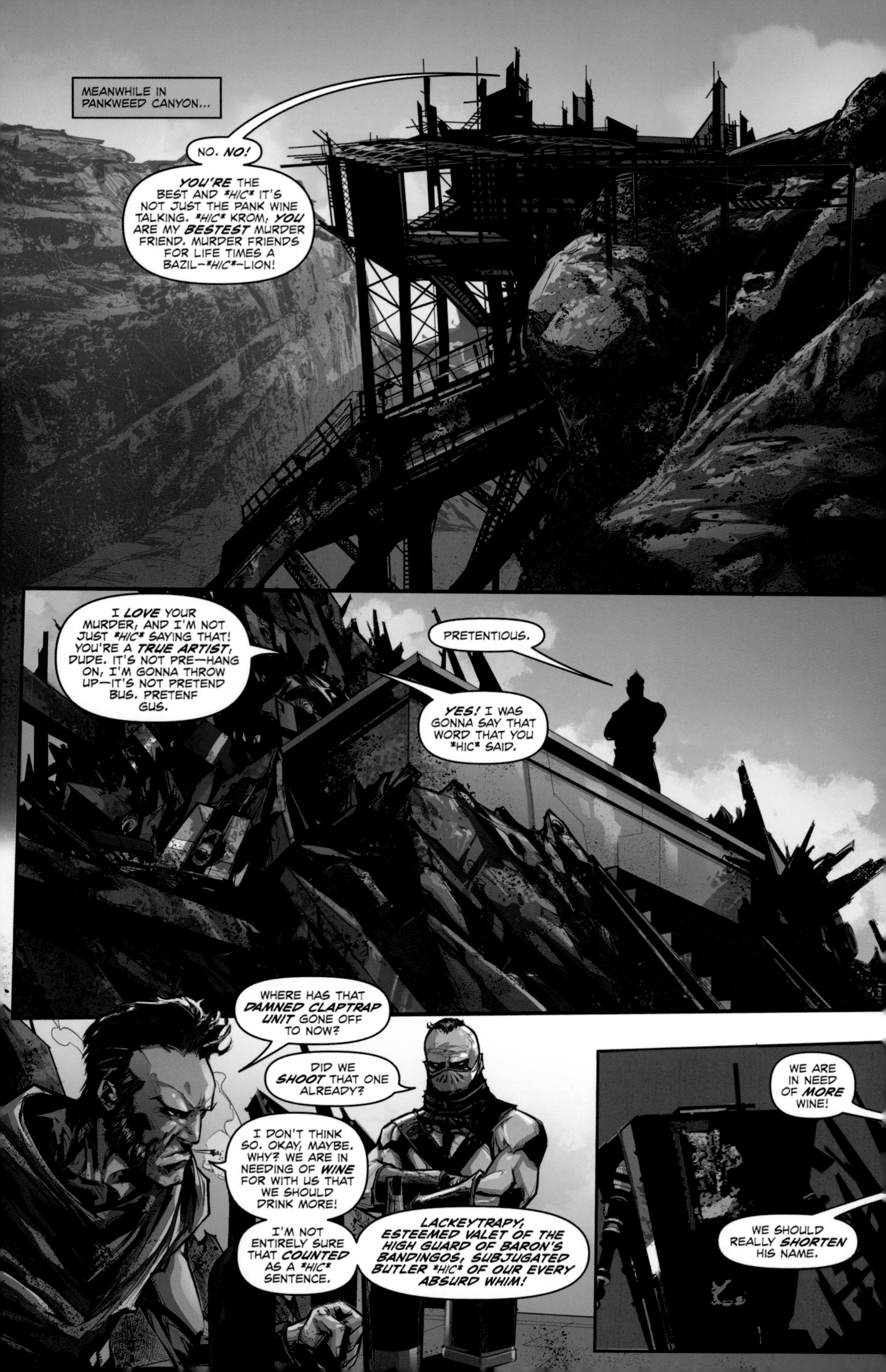
MEANWHILE IN PANKWEED CANYON...
NO. *NO!*
YOU'RE THE BEST AND **HIC** IT'S NOT JUST THE PANK WINE TALKING. **HIC** KROM, *YOU* ARE MY ***BESTEST*** MURDER FRIEND. MURDER FRIENDS FOR LIFE TIMES A BAZIL-**HIC**-LION!
I *LOVE* YOUR MURDER, AND I'M NOT JUST **HIC** SAYING THAT! YOU'RE A *TRUE ARTIST*, DUDE. IT'S NOT PRE–HANG ON, I'M GONNA THROW UP—IT'S NOT PRETEND BUS. PRETENF GUS.
PRETENTIOUS.
YES! I WAS GONNA SAY THAT WORD THAT YOU *HIC* SAID.
WHERE HAS THAT ***DAMNED CLAPTRAP UNIT*** GONE OFF TO NOW?
DID WE ***SHOOT*** THAT ONE ALREADY?
I DON'T THINK SO. OKAY, MAYBE. WHY? WE ARE IN NEEDING OF *WINE* FOR WITH US THAT WE SHOULD DRINK MORE!
I'M NOT ENTIRELY SURE THAT ***COUNTED*** AS A **HIC** SENTENCE.
LACKEYTRAPY, ESTEEMED VALET OF THE HIGH GUARD OF BARON'S BANDINGOS, SUBJUGATED BUTLER *HIC* OF OUR EVERY ABSURD WHIM!
WE ARE IN NEED OF ***MORE*** WINE!
WE SHOULD REALLY ***SHORTEN*** HIS NAME.

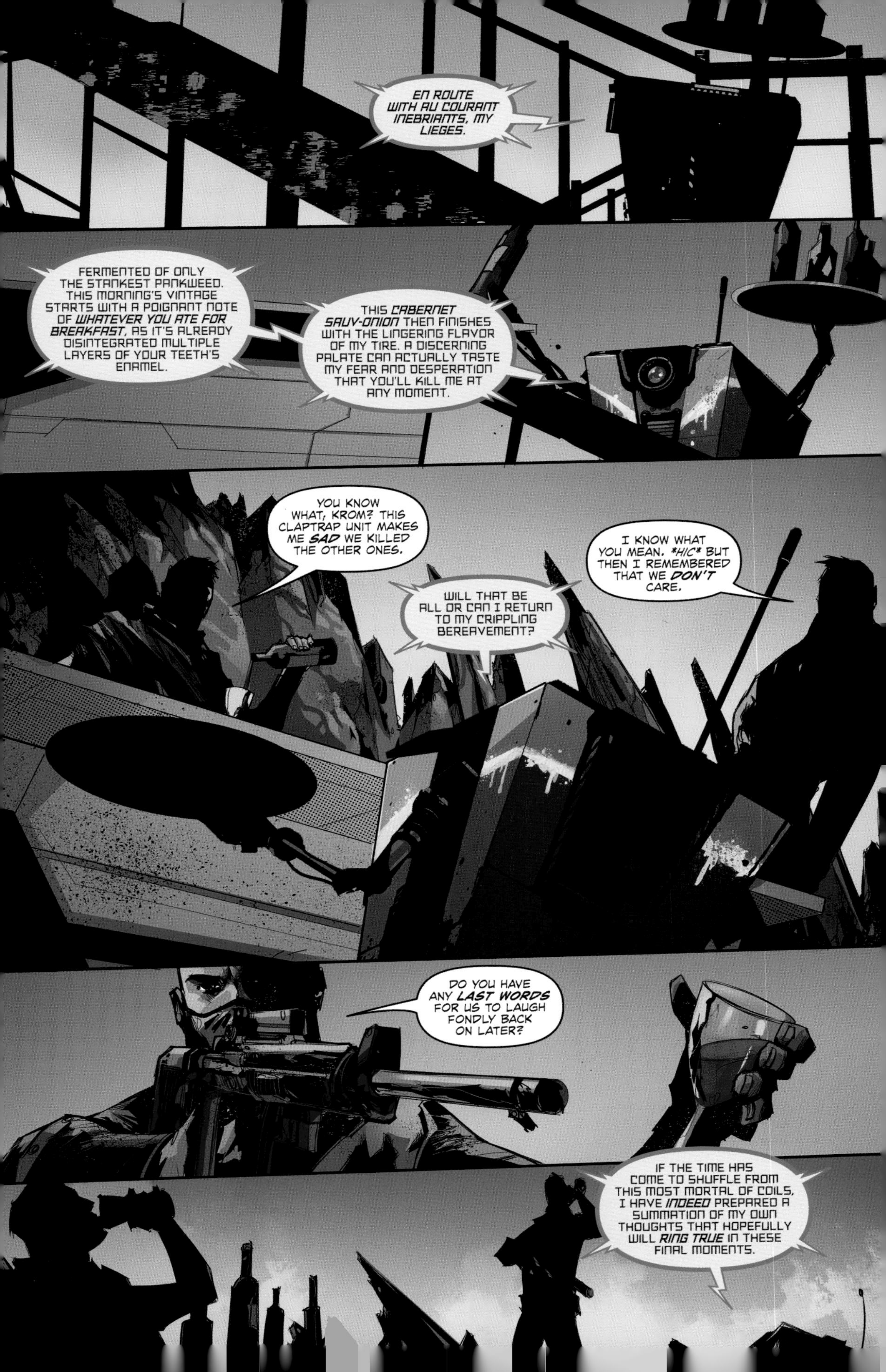
EN ROUTE WITH AU COURANT INEBRIANTS, MY LIEGES.
FERMENTED OF ONLY THE STANKEST PANKWEED. THIS MORNING'S VINTAGE STARTS WITH A POIGNANT NOTE OF WHATEVER YOU ATE FOR BREAKFAST, AS IT'S ALREADY DISINTEGRATED MULTIPLE LAYERS OF YOUR TEETH'S ENAMEL.
THIS CABERNET SAUV-ONION THEN FINISHES WITH THE LINGERING FLAVOR OF MY TIRE. A DISCERNING PALATE CAN ACTUALLY TASTE MY FEAR AND DESPERATION THAT YOU'LL KILL ME AT ANY MOMENT.
YOU KNOW WHAT, KROM? THIS CLAPTRAP UNIT MAKES ME SAD WE KILLED THE OTHER ONES.
WILL THAT BE ALL OR CAN I RETURN TO MY CRIPPLING BEREAVEMENT?
I KNOW WHAT YOU MEAN. *HIC* BUT THEN I REMEMBERED THAT WE DON'T CARE.
DO YOU HAVE ANY LAST WORDS FOR US TO LAUGH FONDLY BACK ON LATER?
IF THE TIME HAS COME TO SHUFFLE FROM THIS MOST MORTAL OF COILS, I HAVE INDEED PREPARED A SUMMATION OF MY OWN THOUGHTS THAT HOPEFULLY WILL RING TRUE IN THESE FINAL MOMENTS.

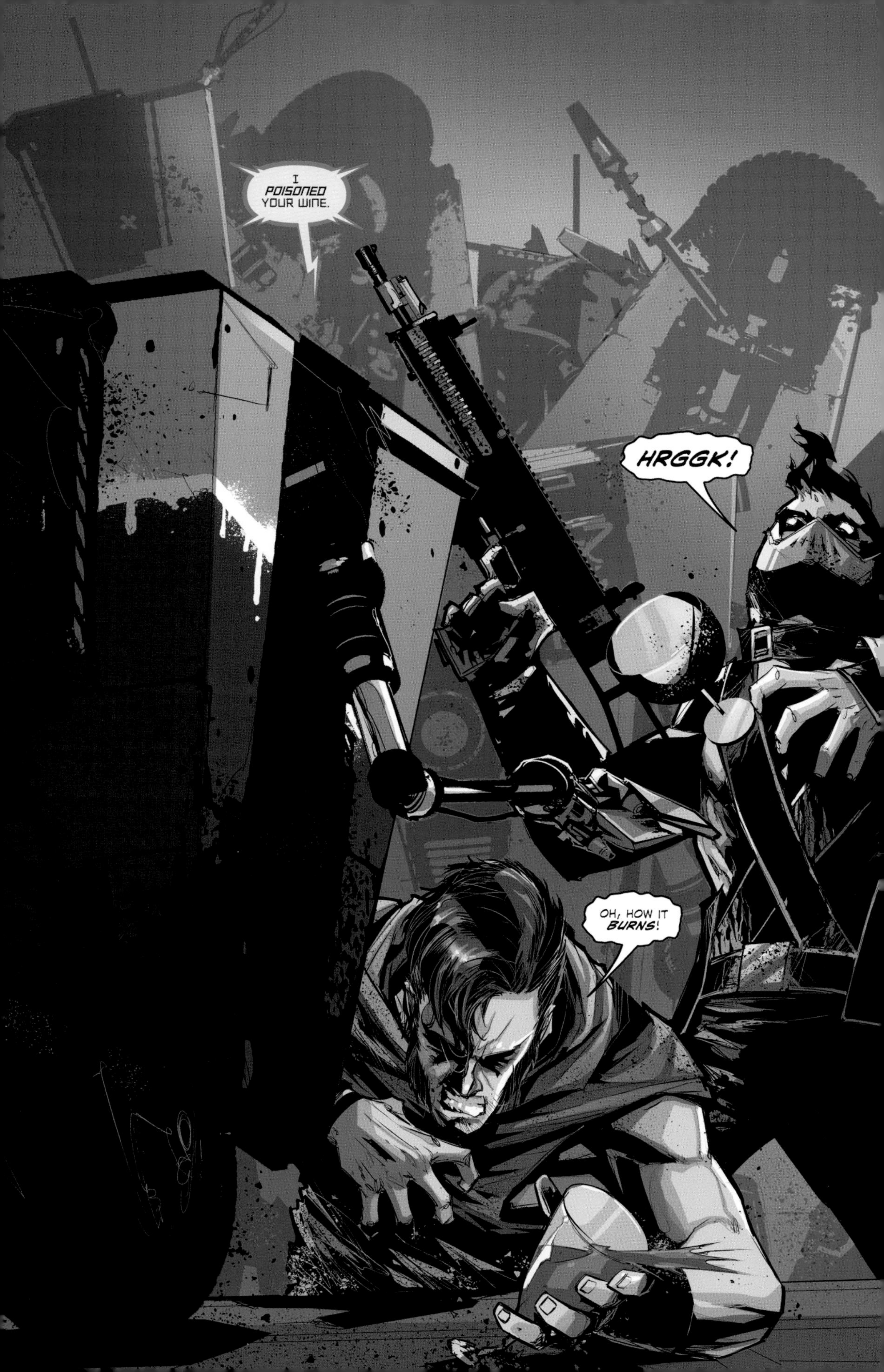
I POISONED YOUR WINE.
HRGGK!
OH, HOW IT BURNS!

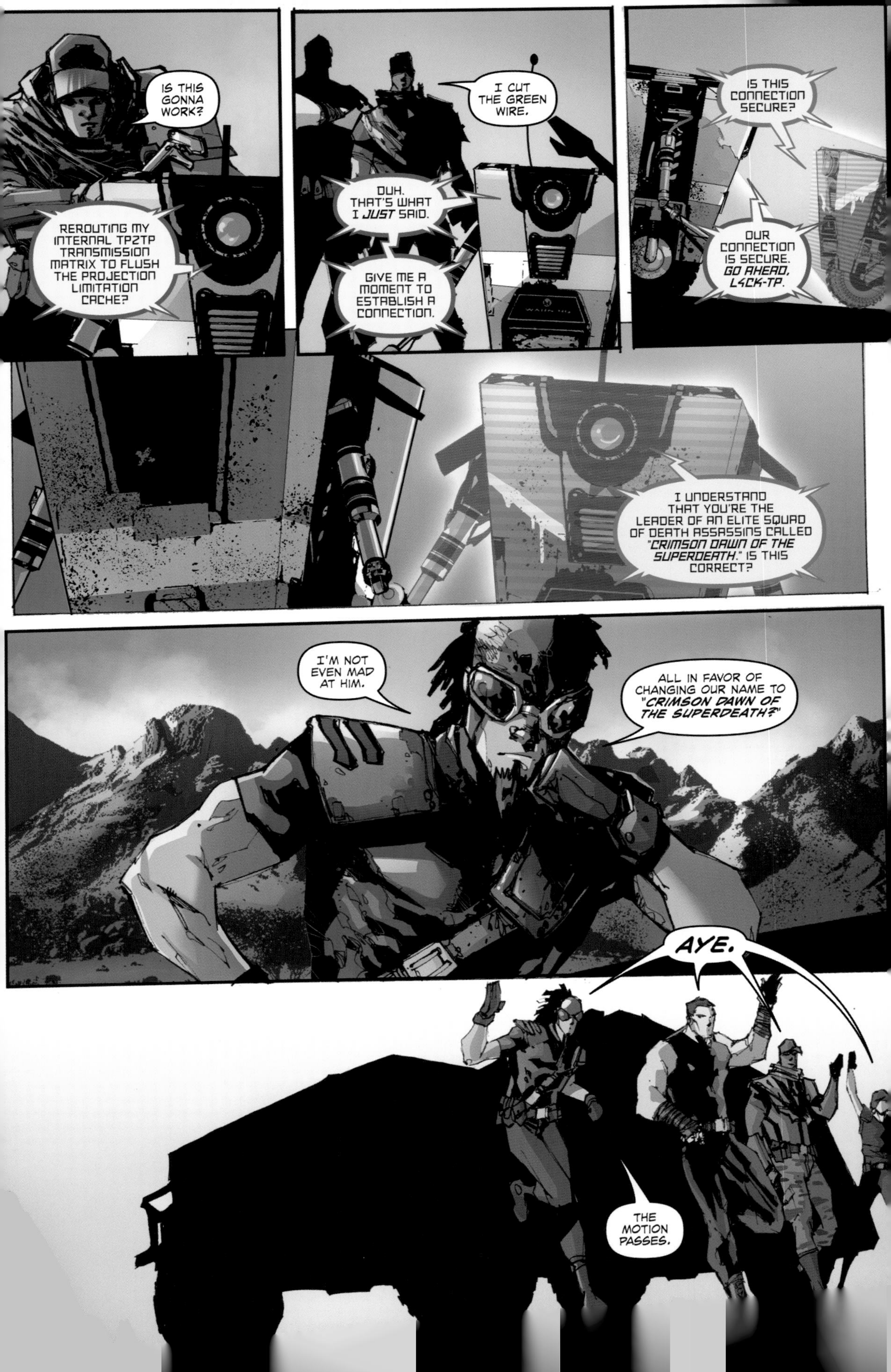
IS THIS GONNA WORK?
REROUTING MY INTERNAL TP2TP TRANSMISSION MATRIX TO FLUSH THE PROJECTION LIMITATION CACHE?
I CUT THE GREEN WIRE.
DUH. THAT'S WHAT I JUST SAID.
GIVE ME A MOMENT TO ESTABLISH A CONNECTION.
IS THIS CONNECTION SECURE?
OUR CONNECTION IS SECURE. GO AHEAD, L4CK-TP.
I UNDERSTAND THAT YOU'RE THE LEADER OF AN ELITE SQUAD OF DEATH ASSASSINS CALLED "CRIMSON DAWN OF THE SUPERDEATH." IS THIS CORRECT?
I'M NOT EVEN MAD AT HIM.
ALL IN FAVOR OF CHANGING OUR NAME TO "CRIMSON DAWN OF THE SUPERDEATH?"
AYE.
THE MOTION PASSES.

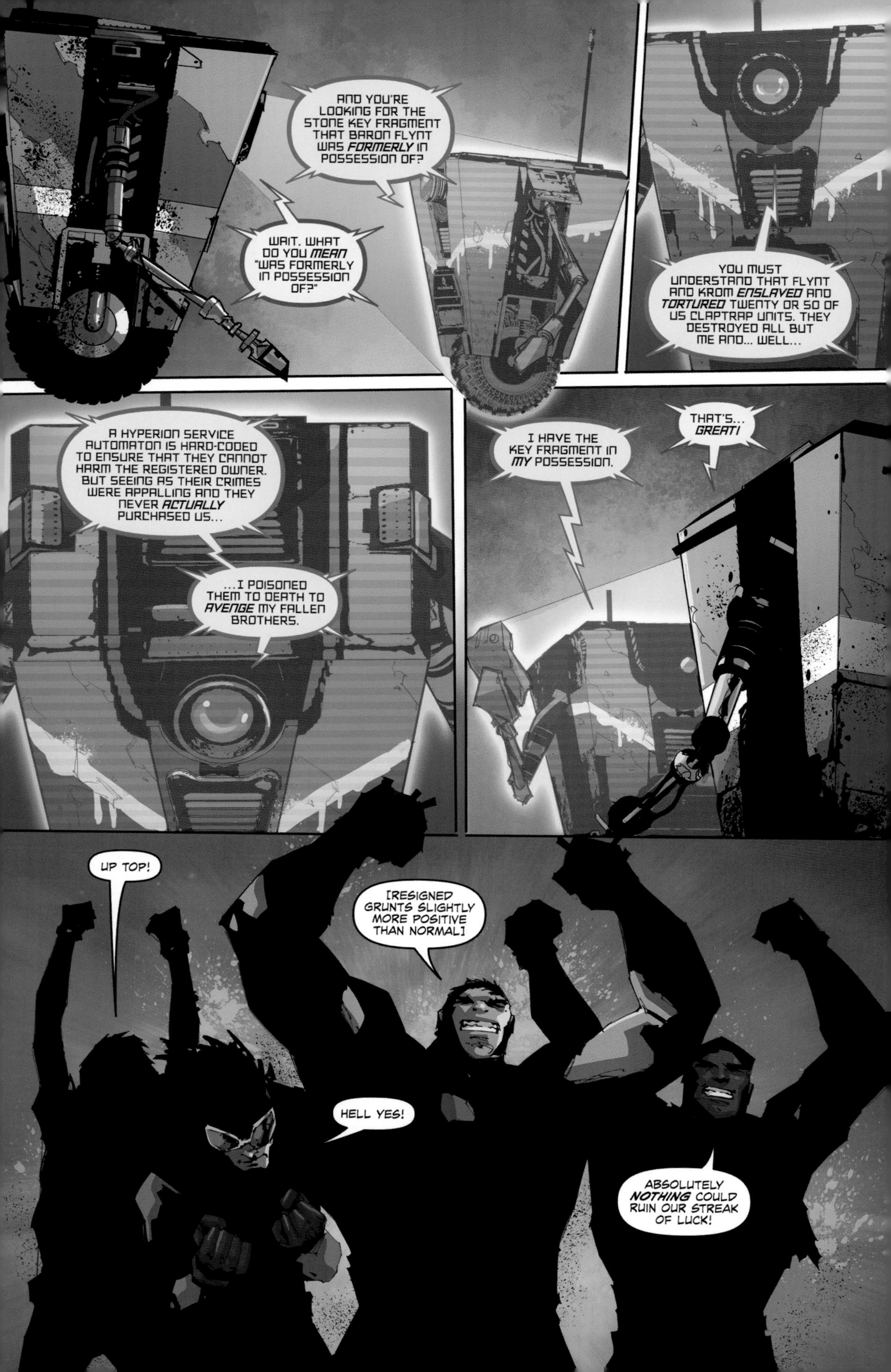
AND YOU'RE LOOKING FOR THE STONE KEY FRAGMENT THAT BARON FLYNT WAS *FORMERLY* IN POSSESSION OF?
WAIT. WHAT DO YOU *MEAN* "WAS FORMERLY IN POSSESSION OF?"
YOU MUST UNDERSTAND THAT FLYNT AND KROM *ENSLAVED* AND *TORTURED* TWENTY OR SO OF US CLAPTRAP UNITS. THEY DESTROYED ALL BUT ME AND... WELL...
A HYPERION SERVICE AUTOMATON IS HARD-CODED TO ENSURE THAT THEY CANNOT HARM THE REGISTERED OWNER. BUT SEEING AS THEIR CRIMES WERE APPALLING AND THEY NEVER *ACTUALLY* PURCHASED US...
...I POISONED THEM TO DEATH TO *AVENGE* MY FALLEN BROTHERS.
I HAVE THE KEY FRAGMENT IN *MY* POSSESSION.
THAT'S... *GREAT!*
UP TOP!
[RESIGNED GRUNTS SLIGHTLY MORE POSITIVE THAN NORMAL]
HELL YES!
ABSOLUTELY *NOTHING* COULD RUIN OUR STREAK OF LUCK!

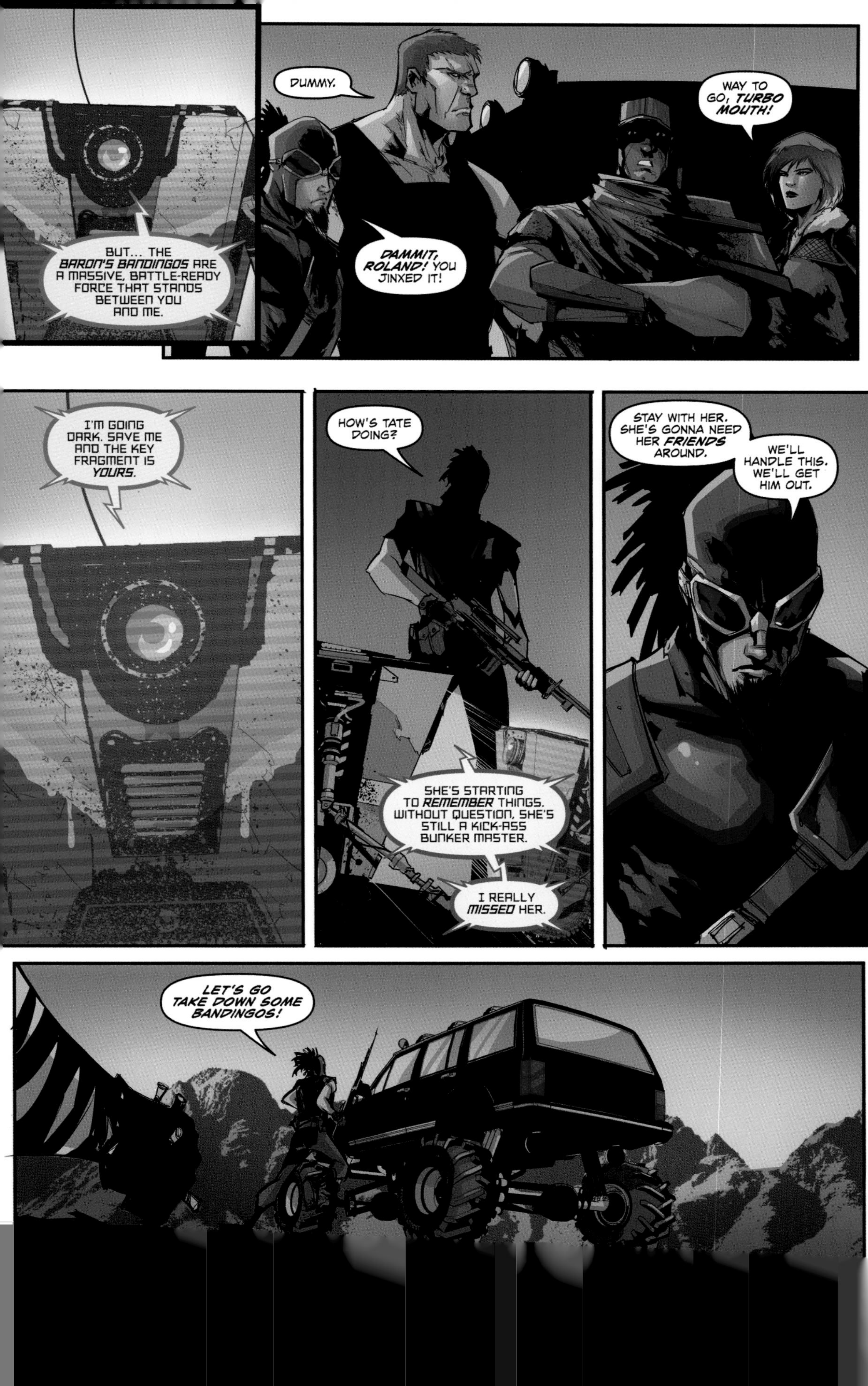
BUT... THE BARON'S BANDINGOS ARE A MASSIVE, BATTLE-READY FORCE THAT STANDS BETWEEN YOU AND ME.
DUMMY.
DAMMIT, ROLAND! YOU JINXED IT!
WAY TO GO, TURBO MOUTH!
I'M GOING DARK. SAVE ME AND THE KEY FRAGMENT IS YOURS.
HOW'S TATE DOING?
SHE'S STARTING TO REMEMBER THINGS. WITHOUT QUESTION, SHE'S STILL A KICK-ASS BUNKER MASTER.
I REALLY MISSED HER.
STAY WITH HER. SHE'S GONNA NEED HER FRIENDS AROUND.
WE'LL HANDLE THIS. WE'LL GET HIM OUT.
LET'S GO TAKE DOWN SOME BANDINGOS!

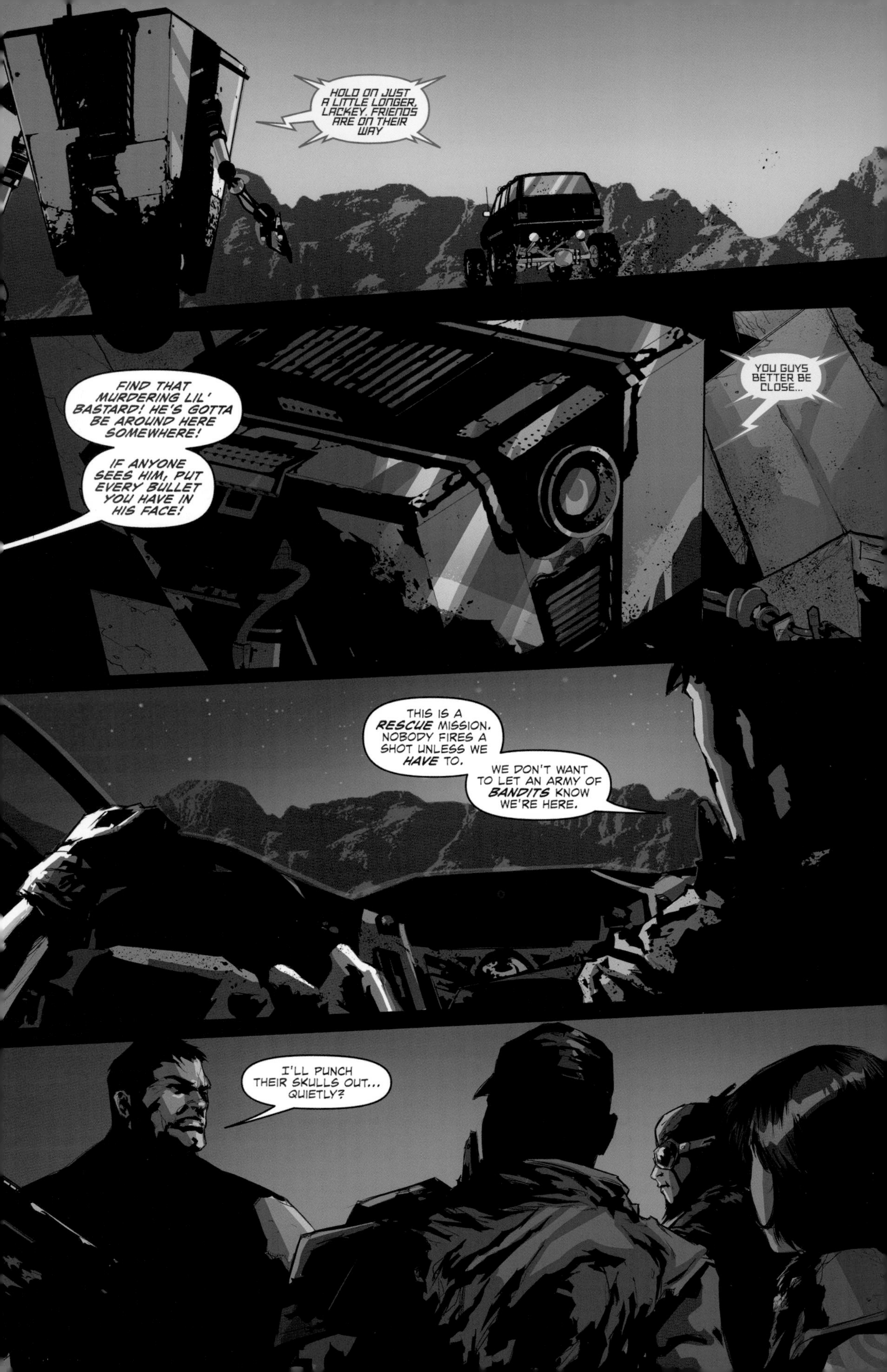
HOLD ON JUST A LITTLE LONGER, LACKEY. FRIENDS ARE ON THEIR WAY
FIND THAT MURDERING LIL' BASTARD! HE'S GOTTA BE AROUND HERE SOMEWHERE!
IF ANYONE SEES HIM, PUT EVERY BULLET YOU HAVE IN HIS FACE!
YOU GUYS BETTER BE CLOSE...
THIS IS A RESCUE MISSION. NOBODY FIRES A SHOT UNLESS WE HAVE TO.
WE DON'T WANT TO LET AN ARMY OF BANDITS KNOW WE'RE HERE.
I'LL PUNCH THEIR SKULLS OUT... QUIETLY?

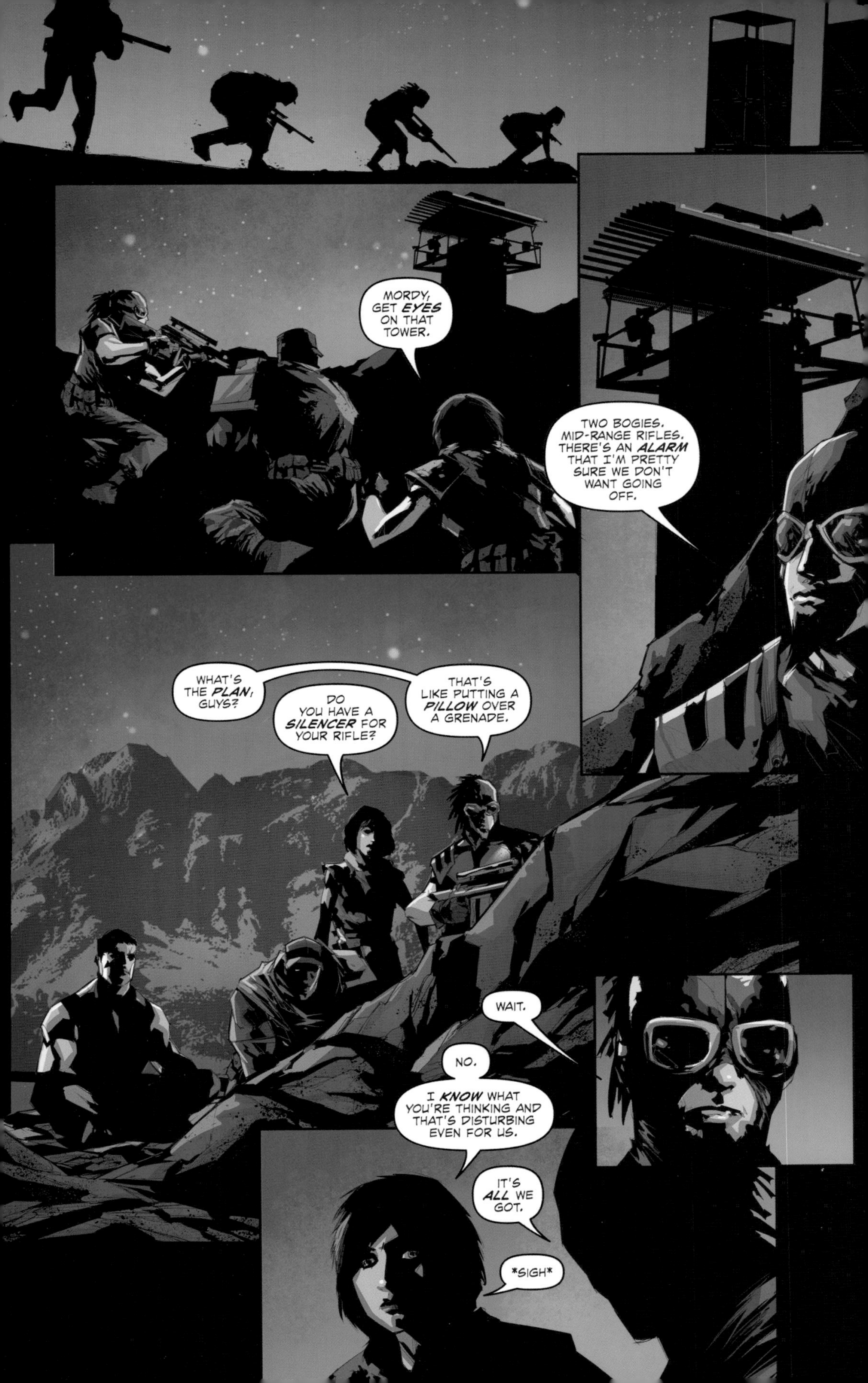
MORDY, GET EYES ON THAT TOWER.
TWO BOGIES. MID-RANGE RIFLES. THERE'S AN ALARM THAT I'M PRETTY SURE WE DON'T WANT GOING OFF.
WHAT'S THE PLAN, GUYS?
DO YOU HAVE A SILENCER FOR YOUR RIFLE?
THAT'S LIKE PUTTING A PILLOW OVER A GRENADE.
WAIT.
NO.
I KNOW WHAT YOU'RE THINKING AND THAT'S DISTURBING EVEN FOR US.
IT'S ALL WE GOT.
SIGH

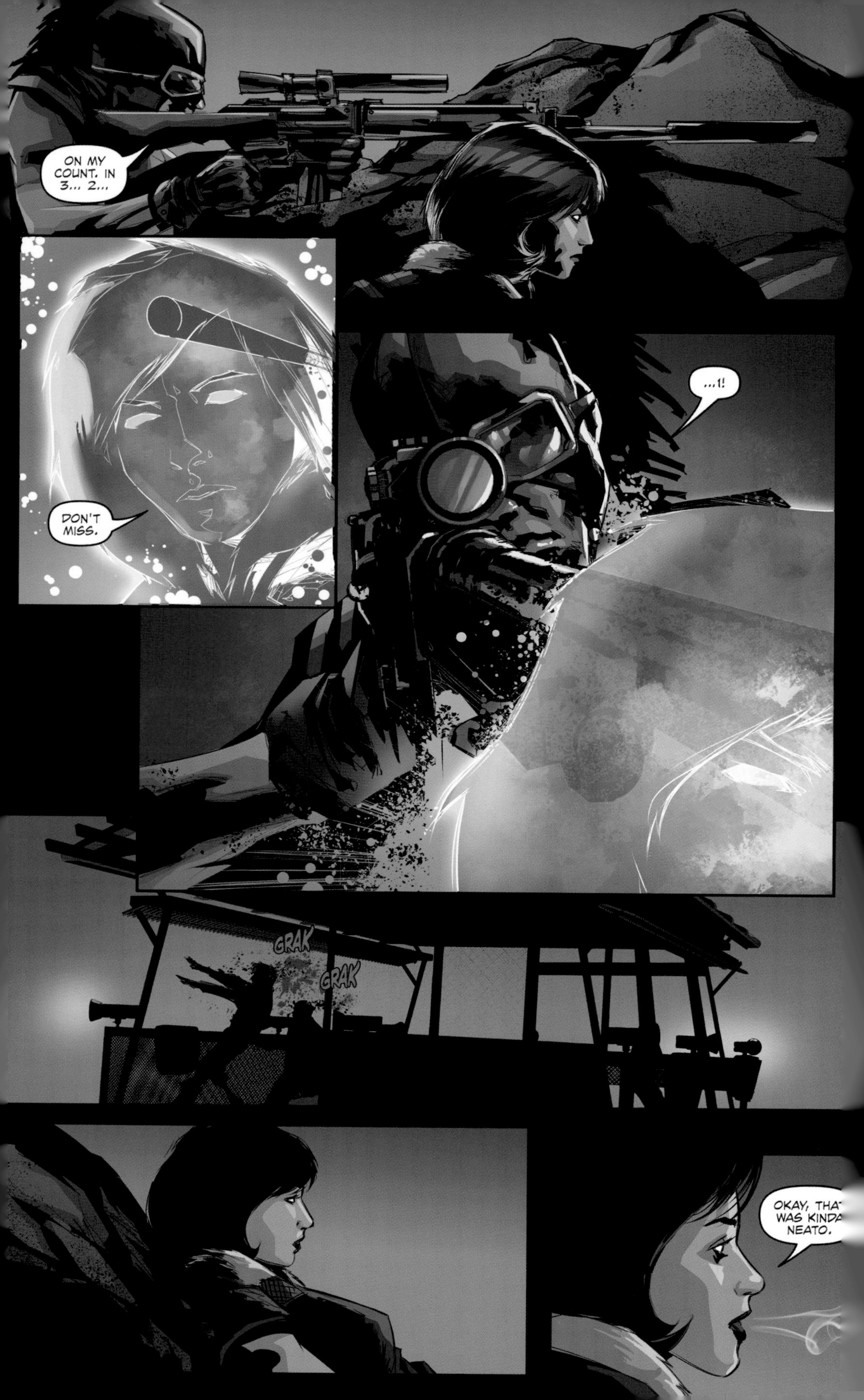
ON MY COUNT. IN 3... 2...
DON'T MISS.
...1!
GRAK
GRAK
OKAY, THAT WAS KINDA NEATO.

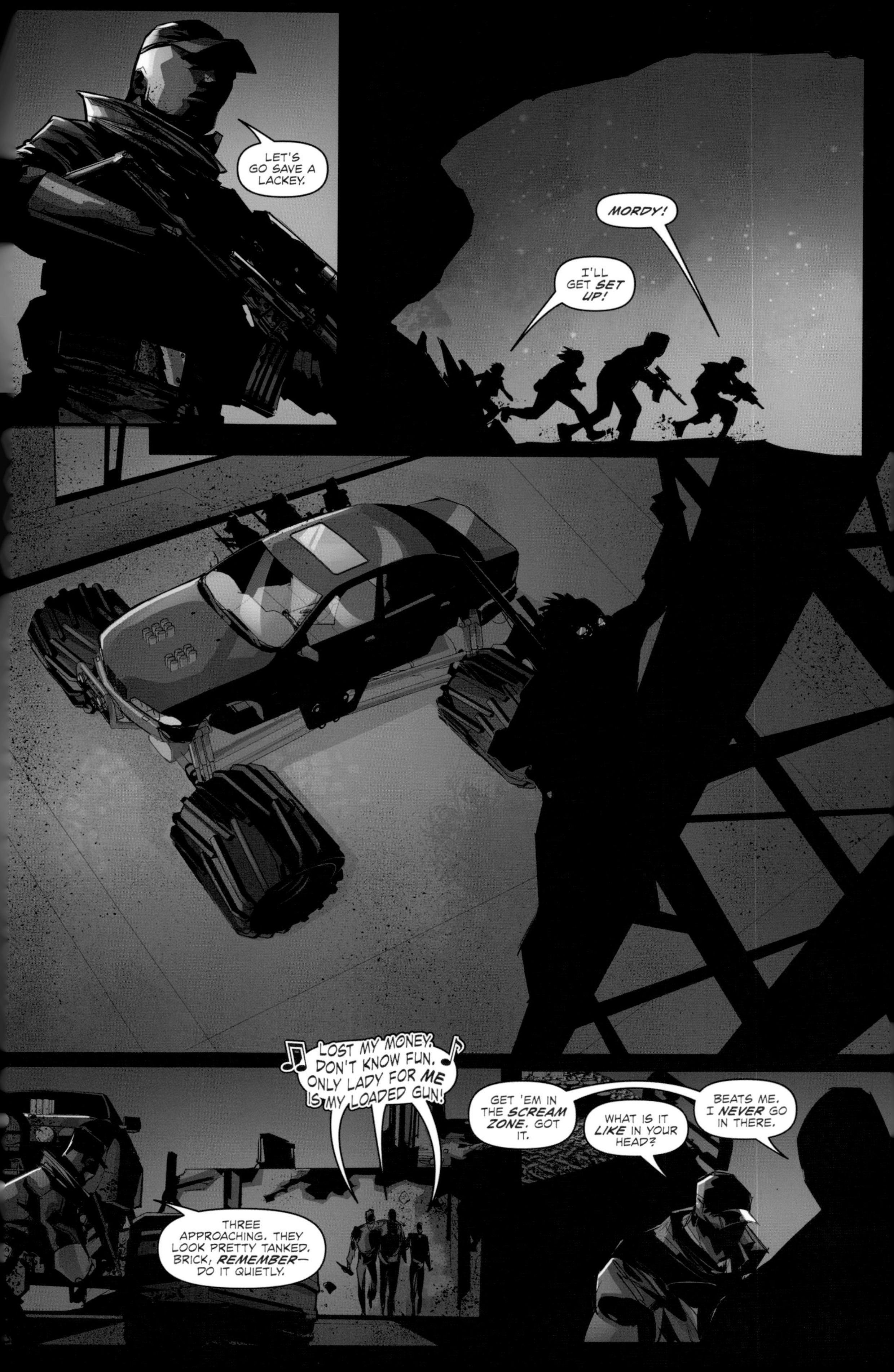
LET'S GO SAVE A LACKEY.
MORDY!
I'LL GET SET UP!
LOST MY MONEY. DON'T KNOW FUN. ONLY LADY FOR ME IS MY LOADED GUN!
THREE APPROACHING. THEY LOOK PRETTY TANKED. BRICK, REMEMBER— DO IT QUIETLY.
GET 'EM IN THE SCREAM ZONE. GOT IT.
WHAT IS IT LIKE IN YOUR HEAD?
BEATS ME. I NEVER GO IN THERE.

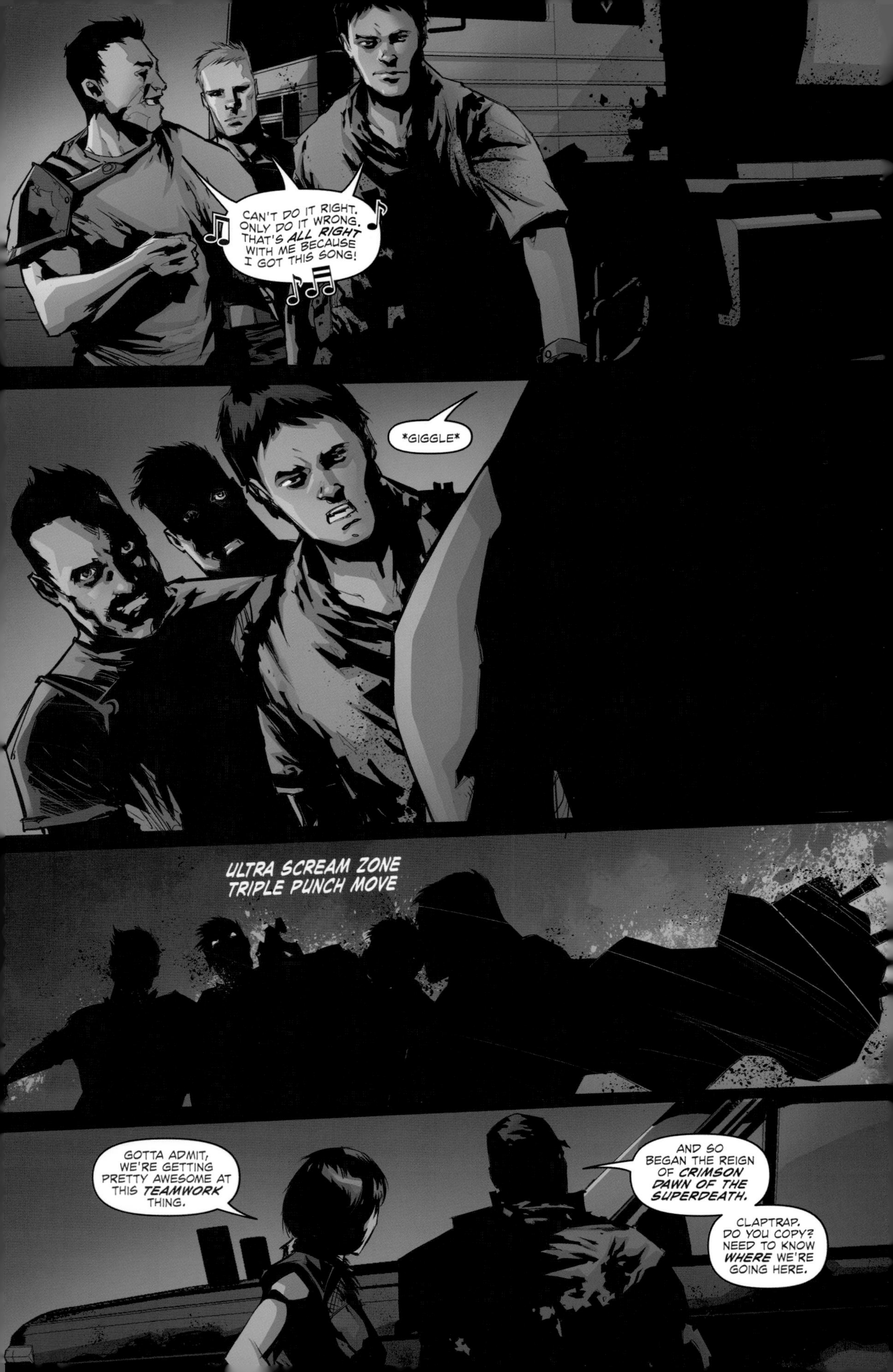
CAN'T DO IT RIGHT. ONLY DO IT WRONG. THAT'S ALL RIGHT WITH ME BECAUSE I GOT THIS SONG!
GIGGLE
ULTRA SCREAM ZONE TRIPLE PUNCH MOVE
GOTTA ADMIT, WE'RE GETTING PRETTY AWESOME AT THIS TEAMWORK THING.
AND SO BEGAN THE REIGN OF CRIMSON DAWN OF THE SUPERDEATH.
CLAPTRAP. DO YOU COPY? NEED TO KNOW WHERE WE'RE GOING HERE.

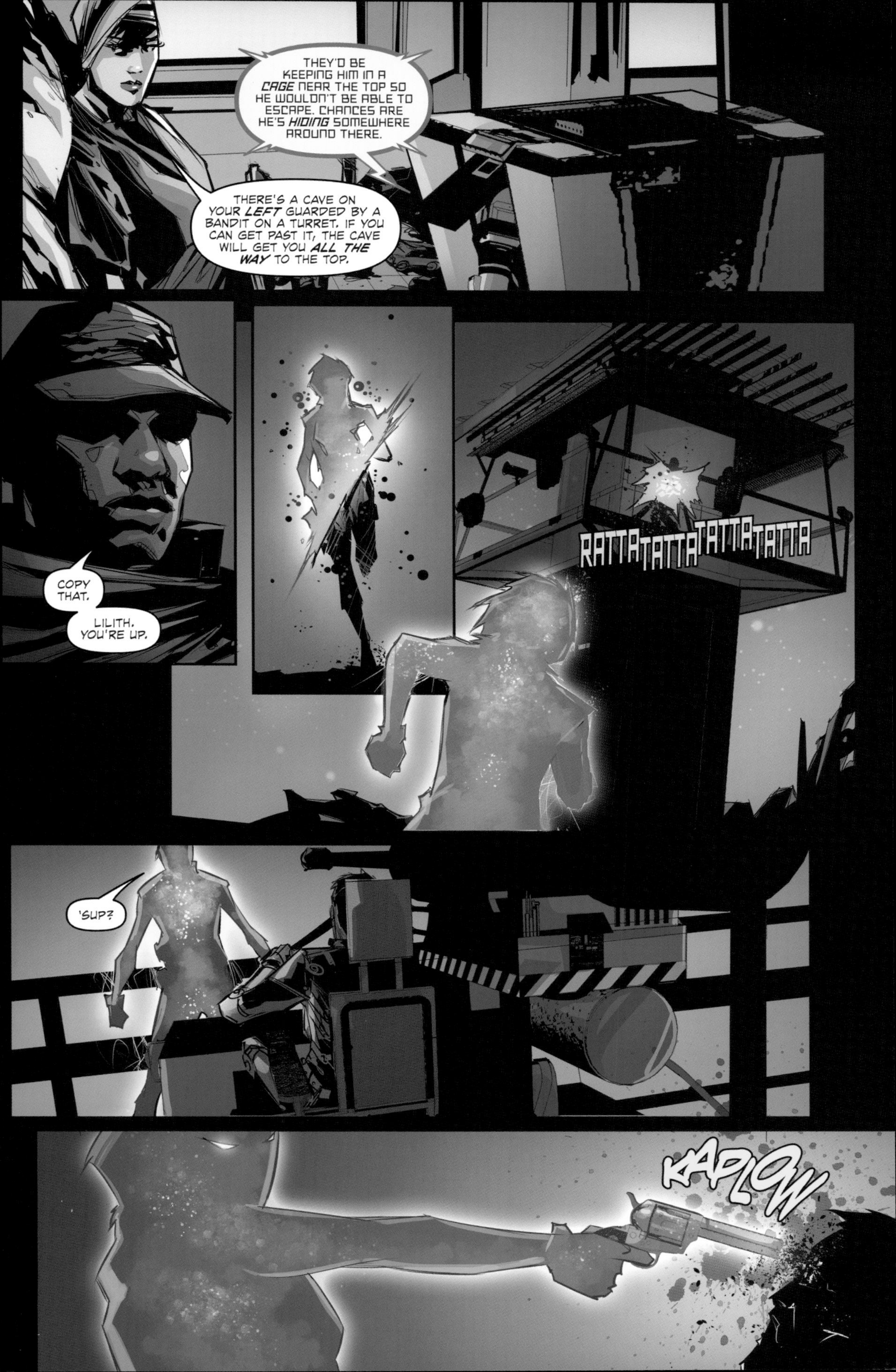
THEY'D BE KEEPING HIM IN A CAGE NEAR THE TOP SO HE WOULDN'T BE ABLE TO ESCAPE. CHANCES ARE HE'S HIDING SOMEWHERE AROUND THERE.
THERE'S A CAVE ON YOUR LEFT GUARDED BY A BANDIT ON A TURRET. IF YOU CAN GET PAST IT, THE CAVE WILL GET YOU ALL THE WAY TO THE TOP.
COPY THAT.
LILITH. YOU'RE UP.
RATTATATTATATTATATTA
'SUP?
KAPLOW

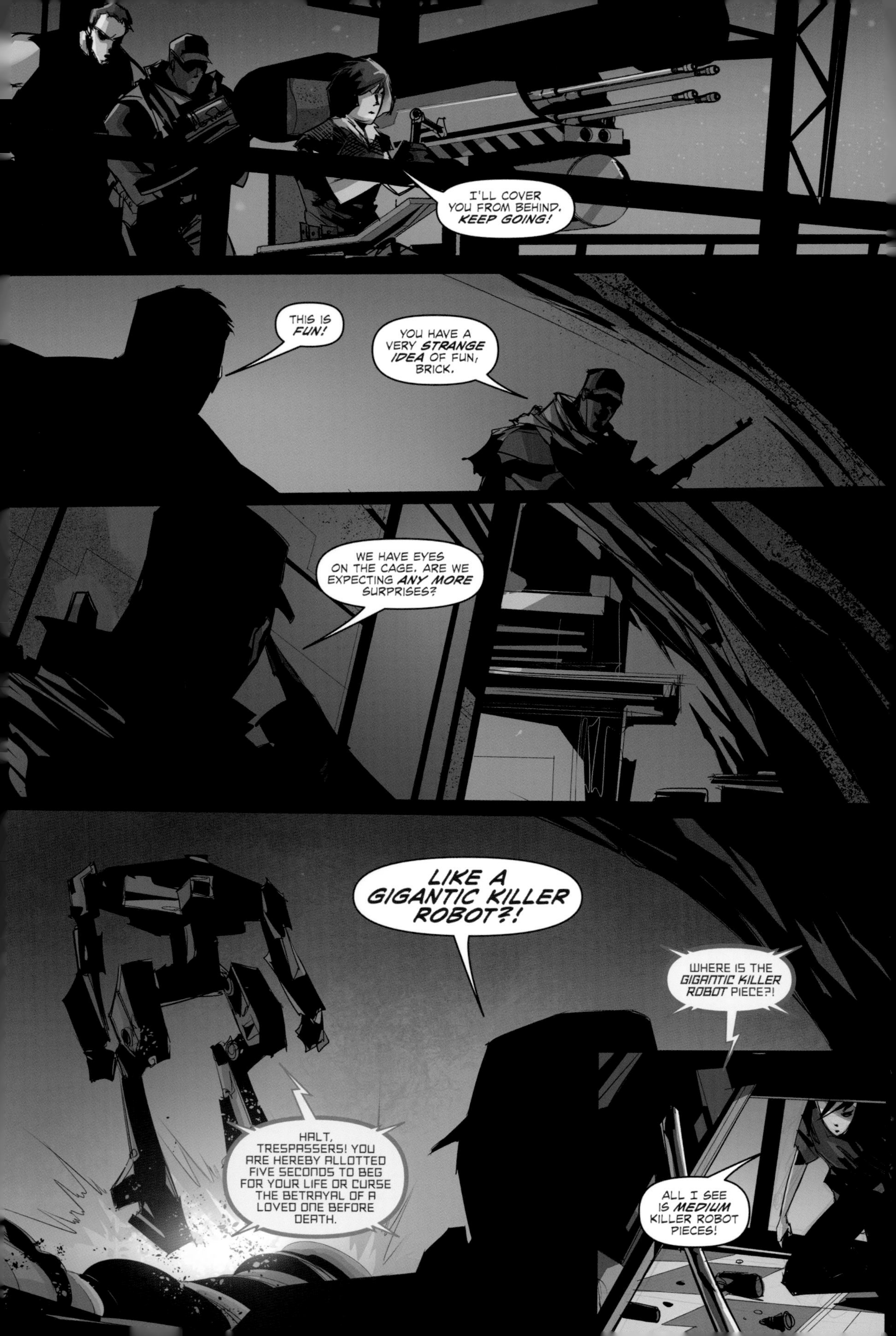
I'LL COVER YOU FROM BEHIND. KEEP GOING!
THIS IS FUN!
YOU HAVE A VERY STRANGE IDEA OF FUN, BRICK.
WE HAVE EYES ON THE CAGE. ARE WE EXPECTING ANY MORE SURPRISES?
LIKE A GIGANTIC KILLER ROBOT?!
WHERE IS THE GIGANTIC KILLER ROBOT PIECE?!
HALT, TRESPASSERS! YOU ARE HEREBY ALLOTTED FIVE SECONDS TO BEG FOR YOUR LIFE OR CURSE THE BETRAYAL OF A LOVED ONE BEFORE DEATH.
ALL I SEE IS MEDIUM KILLER ROBOT PIECES!

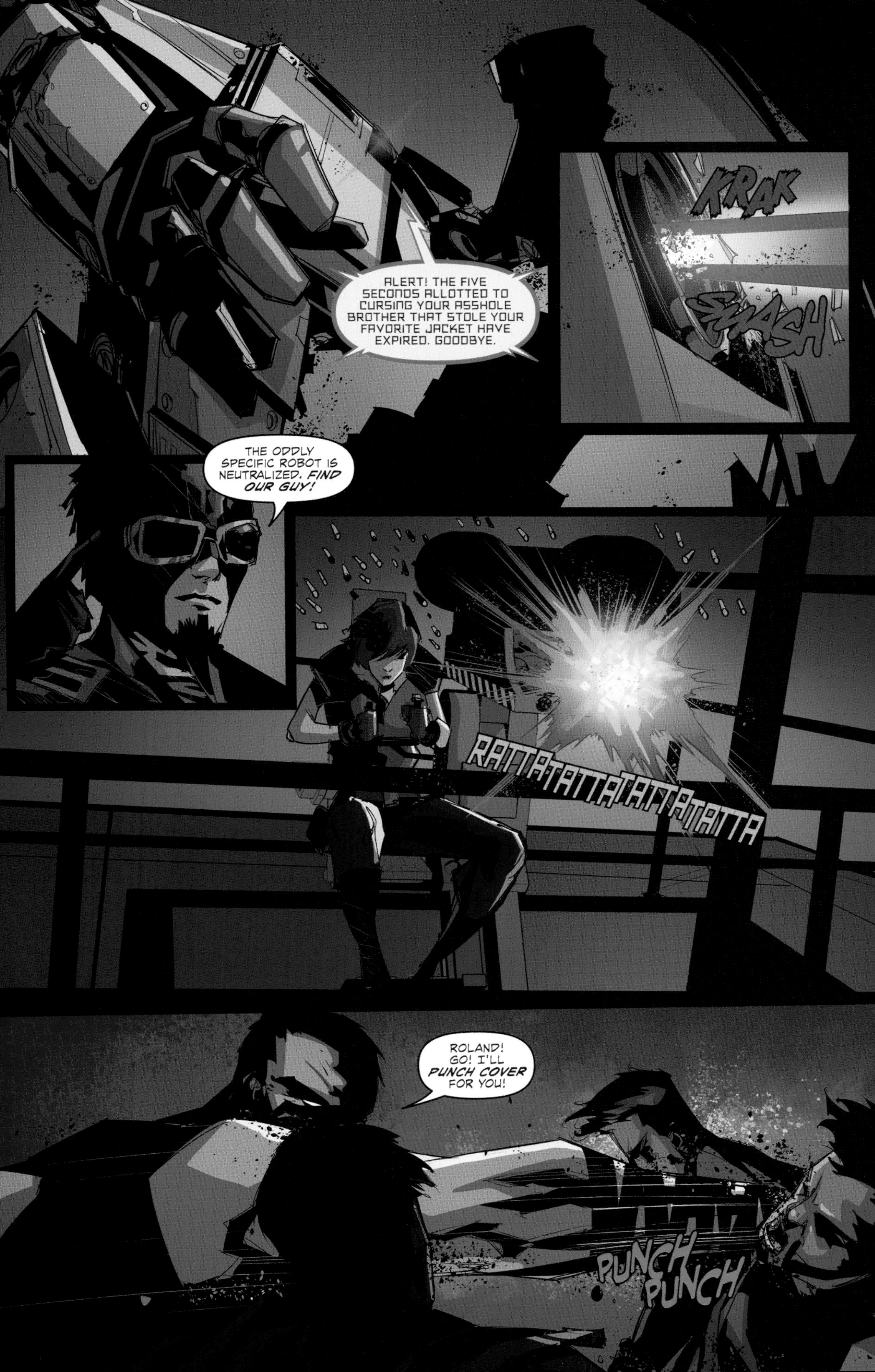
ALERT! THE FIVE SECONDS ALLOTTED TO CURSING YOUR ASSHOLE BROTHER THAT STOLE YOUR FAVORITE JACKET HAVE EXPIRED. GOODBYE.
KRAK
SMASH
THE ODDLY SPECIFIC ROBOT IS NEUTRALIZED. *FIND OUR GUY!*
RATTATATTATATTATATTA
ROLAND! GO! I'LL *PUNCH COVER* FOR YOU!
PUNCH
PUNCH

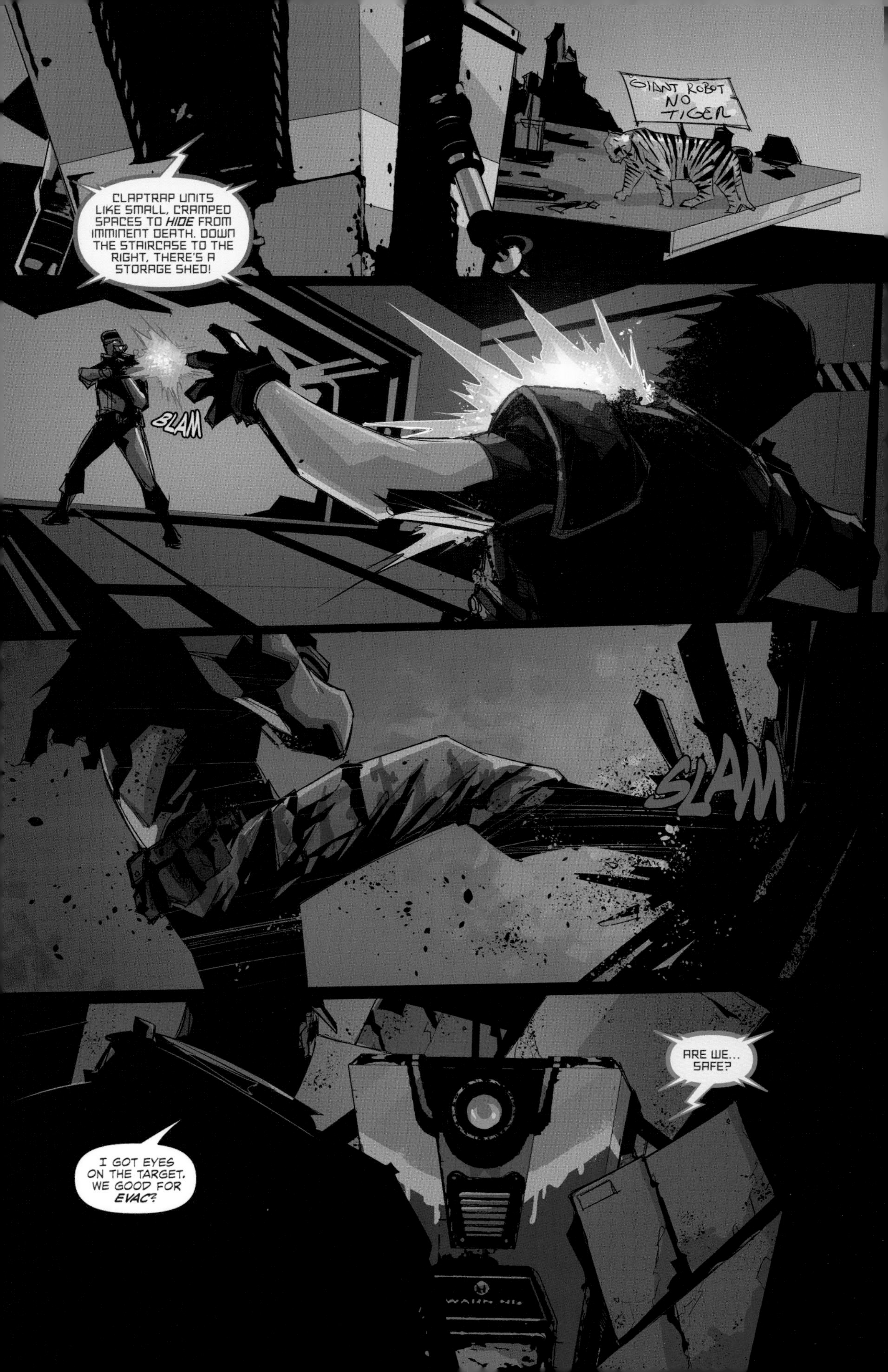
GIANT ROBOT NO TIGER
CLAPTRAP UNITS LIKE SMALL, CRAMPED SPACES TO HIDE FROM IMMINENT DEATH. DOWN THE STAIRCASE TO THE RIGHT, THERE'S A STORAGE SHED!
BLAM
SLAM
ARE WE... SAFE?
I GOT EYES ON THE TARGET. WE GOOD FOR EVAC?

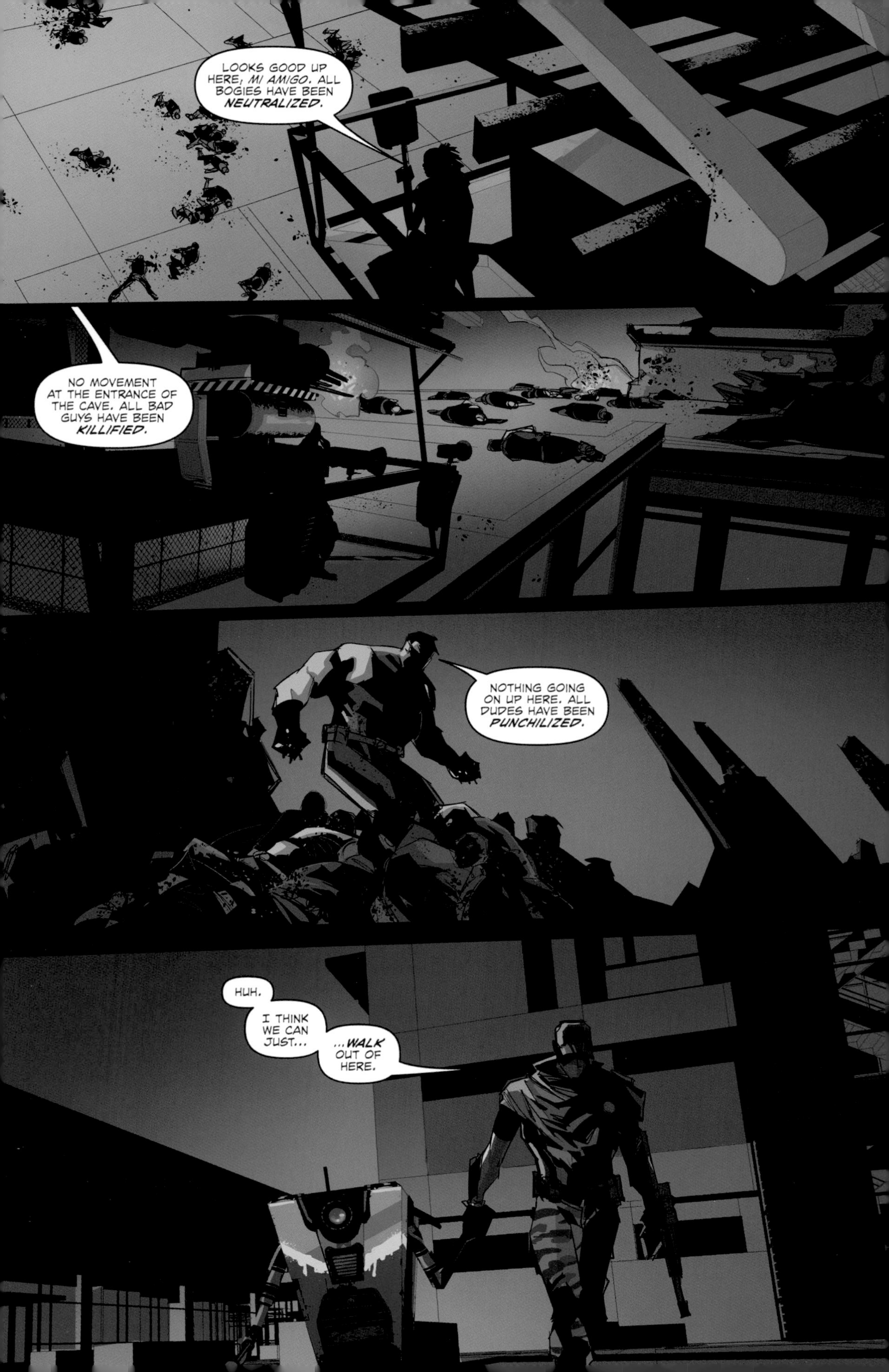
LOOKS GOOD UP HERE, MI AMIGO. ALL BOGIES HAVE BEEN NEUTRALIZED.
NO MOVEMENT AT THE ENTRANCE OF THE CAVE. ALL BAD GUYS HAVE BEEN KILLIFIED.
NOTHING GOING ON UP HERE. ALL DUDES HAVE BEEN PUNCHILIZED.
HUH.
I THINK WE CAN JUST...
...WALK OUT OF HERE.

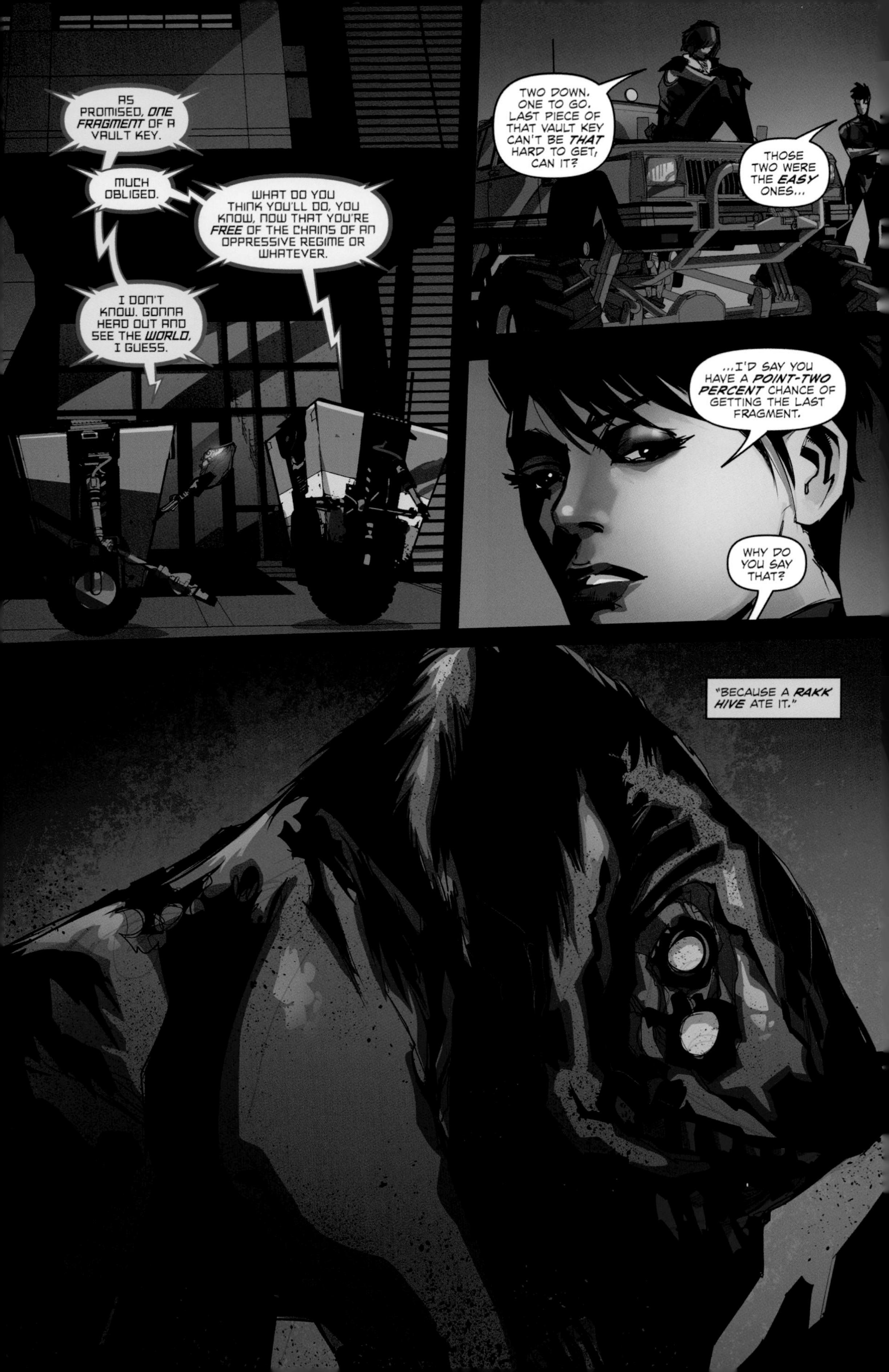
AS PROMISED, ONE FRAGMENT OF A VAULT KEY.
MUCH OBLIGED.
WHAT DO YOU THINK YOU'LL DO, YOU KNOW, NOW THAT YOU'RE FREE OF THE CHAINS OF AN OPPRESSIVE REGIME OR WHATEVER.
I DON'T KNOW. GONNA HEAD OUT AND SEE THE WORLD, I GUESS.
TWO DOWN. ONE TO GO. LAST PIECE OF THAT VAULT KEY CAN'T BE THAT HARD TO GET, CAN IT?
THOSE TWO WERE THE EASY ONES...
...I'D SAY YOU HAVE A POINT-TWO PERCENT CHANCE OF GETTING THE LAST FRAGMENT.
WHY DO YOU SAY THAT?
"BECAUSE A RAKK HIVE ATE IT."

Chapter Four

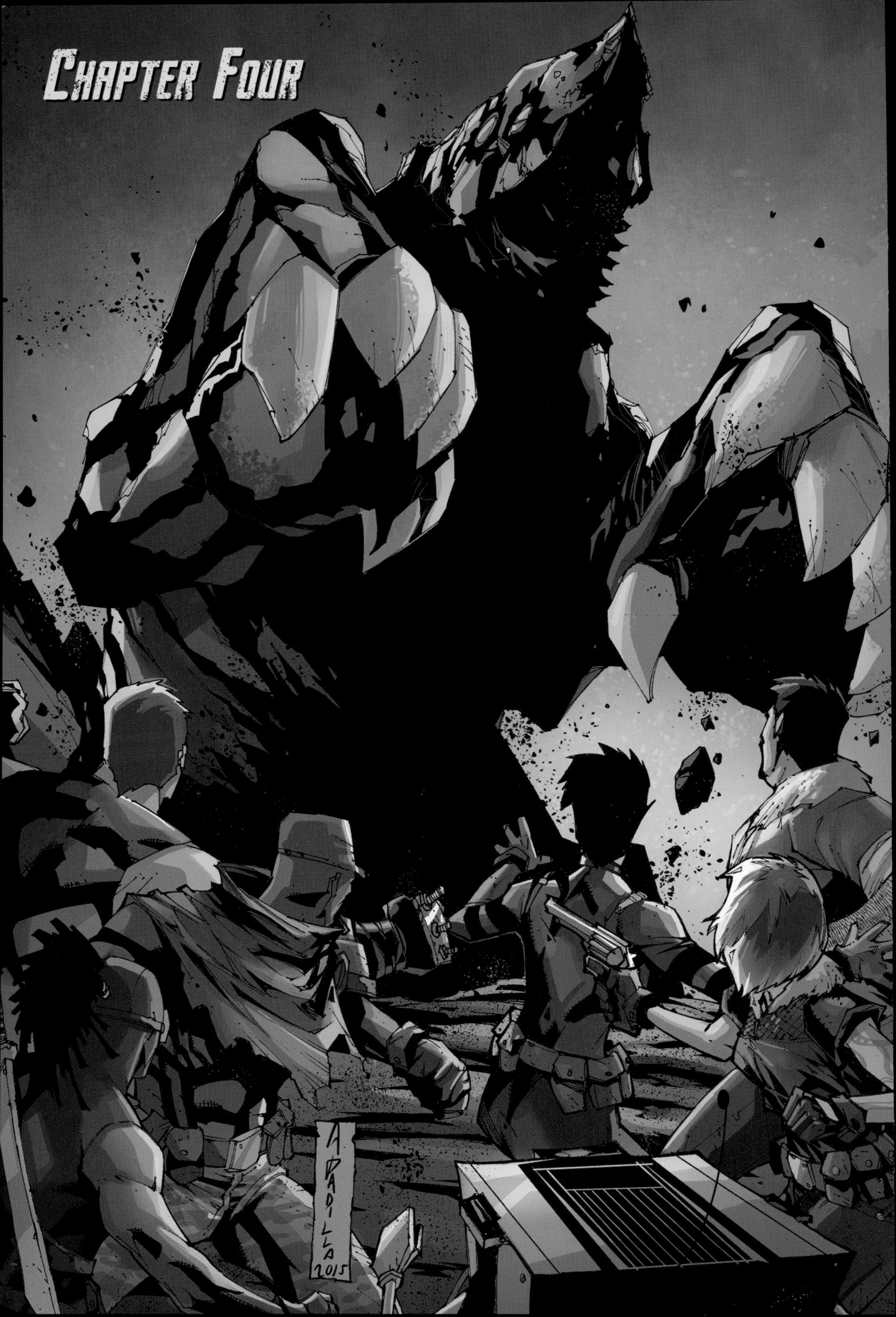
PADILLA 2015

art by AGUSTIN PADILLA • colors by ESTHER SANZ

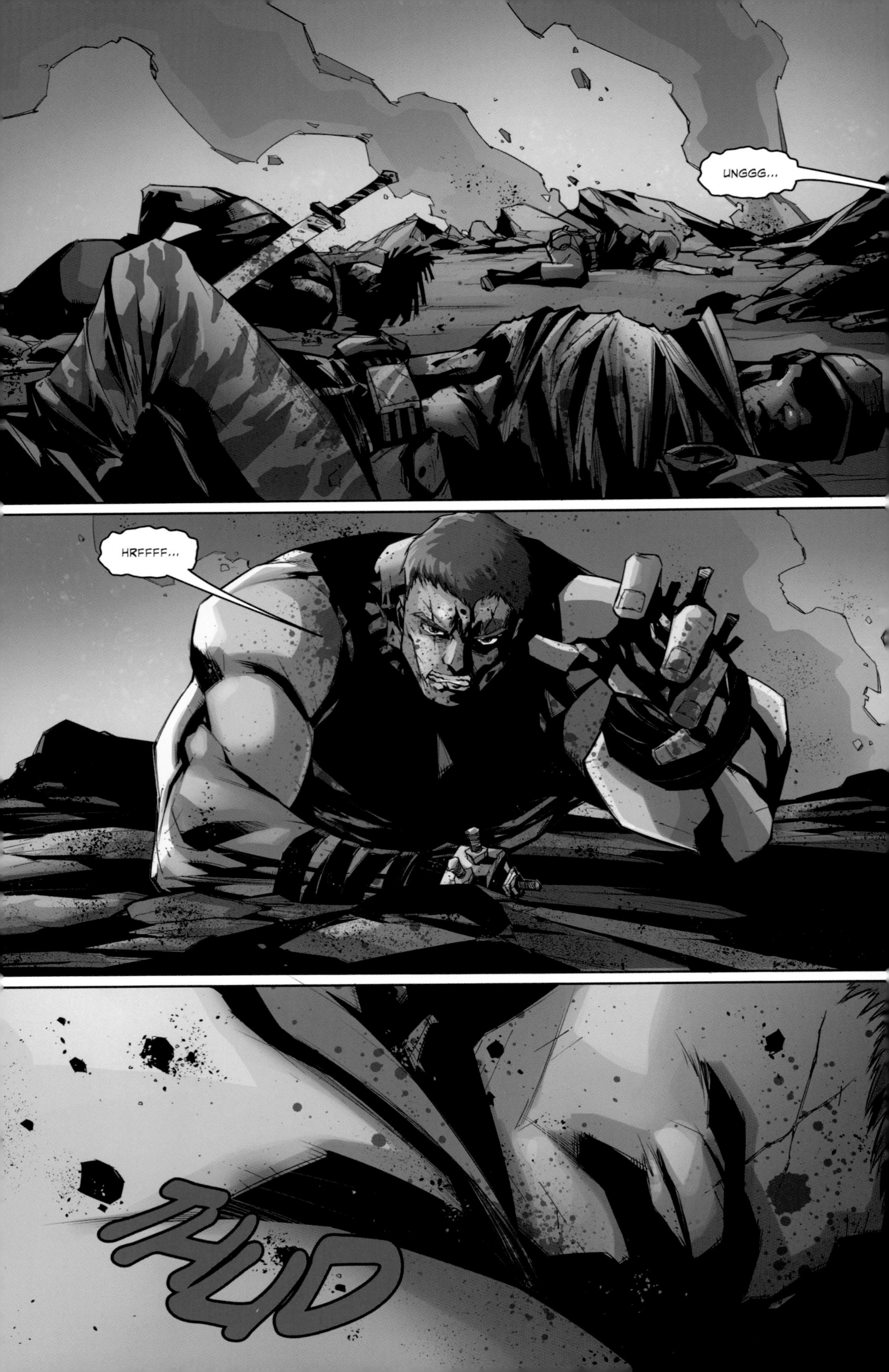
UNGGG...
HRFFFF...
THUD

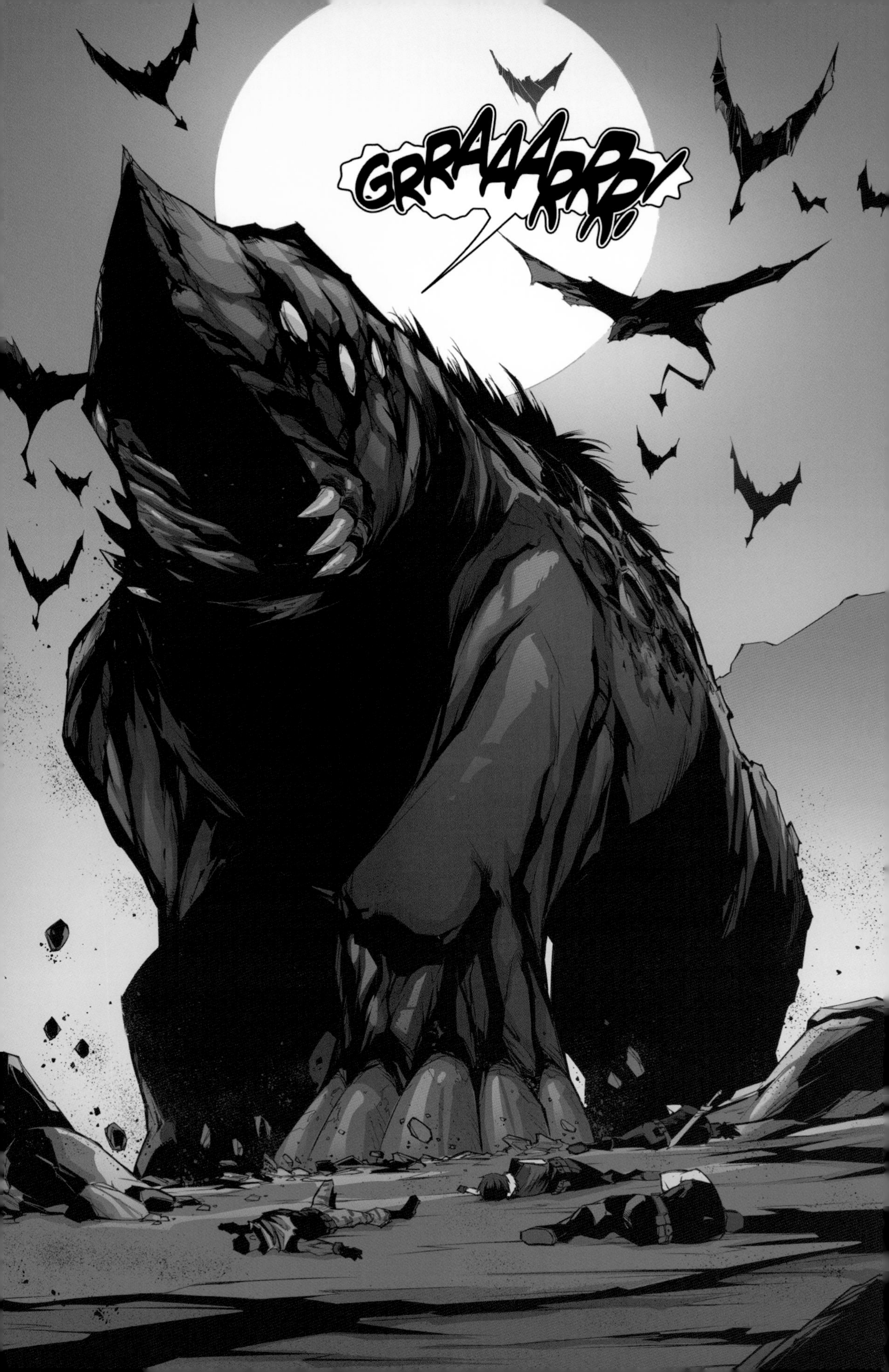
GRRAAAARRR!

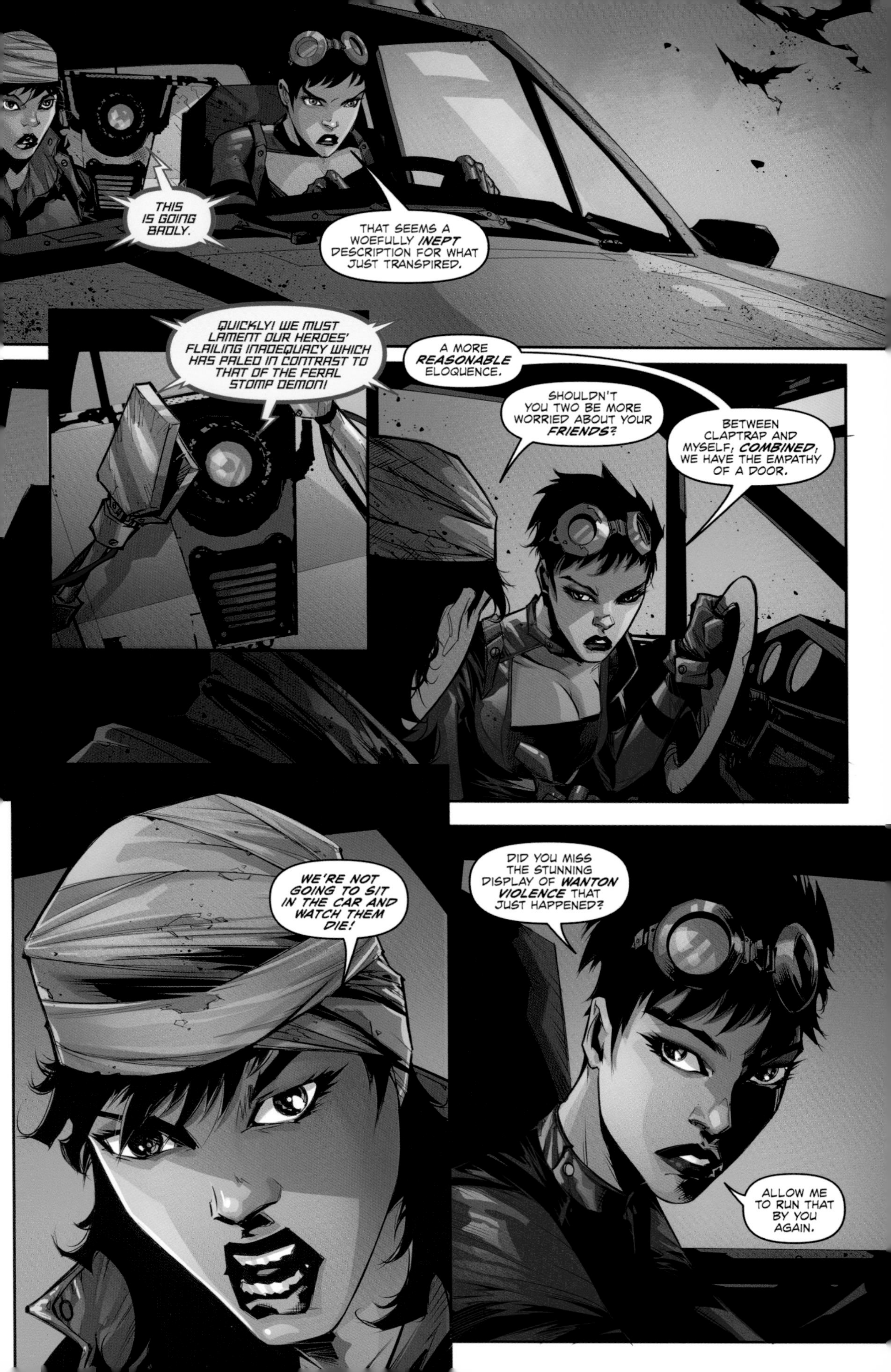
THIS IS GOING BADLY.
THAT SEEMS A WOEFULLY *INEPT* DESCRIPTION FOR WHAT JUST TRANSPIRED.
QUICKLY! WE MUST LAMENT OUR HEROES' FLAILING INADEQUACY WHICH HAS PALED IN CONTRAST TO THAT OF THE FERAL STOMP DEMON!
A MORE *REASONABLE* ELOQUENCE.
SHOULDN'T YOU TWO BE MORE WORRIED ABOUT YOUR *FRIENDS*?
BETWEEN CLAPTRAP AND MYSELF, *COMBINED*, WE HAVE THE EMPATHY OF A DOOR.
WE'RE NOT GOING TO SIT IN THE CAR AND WATCH THEM DIE!
DID YOU MISS THE STUNNING DISPLAY OF *WANTON VIOLENCE* THAT JUST HAPPENED?
ALLOW ME TO RUN THAT BY YOU AGAIN.

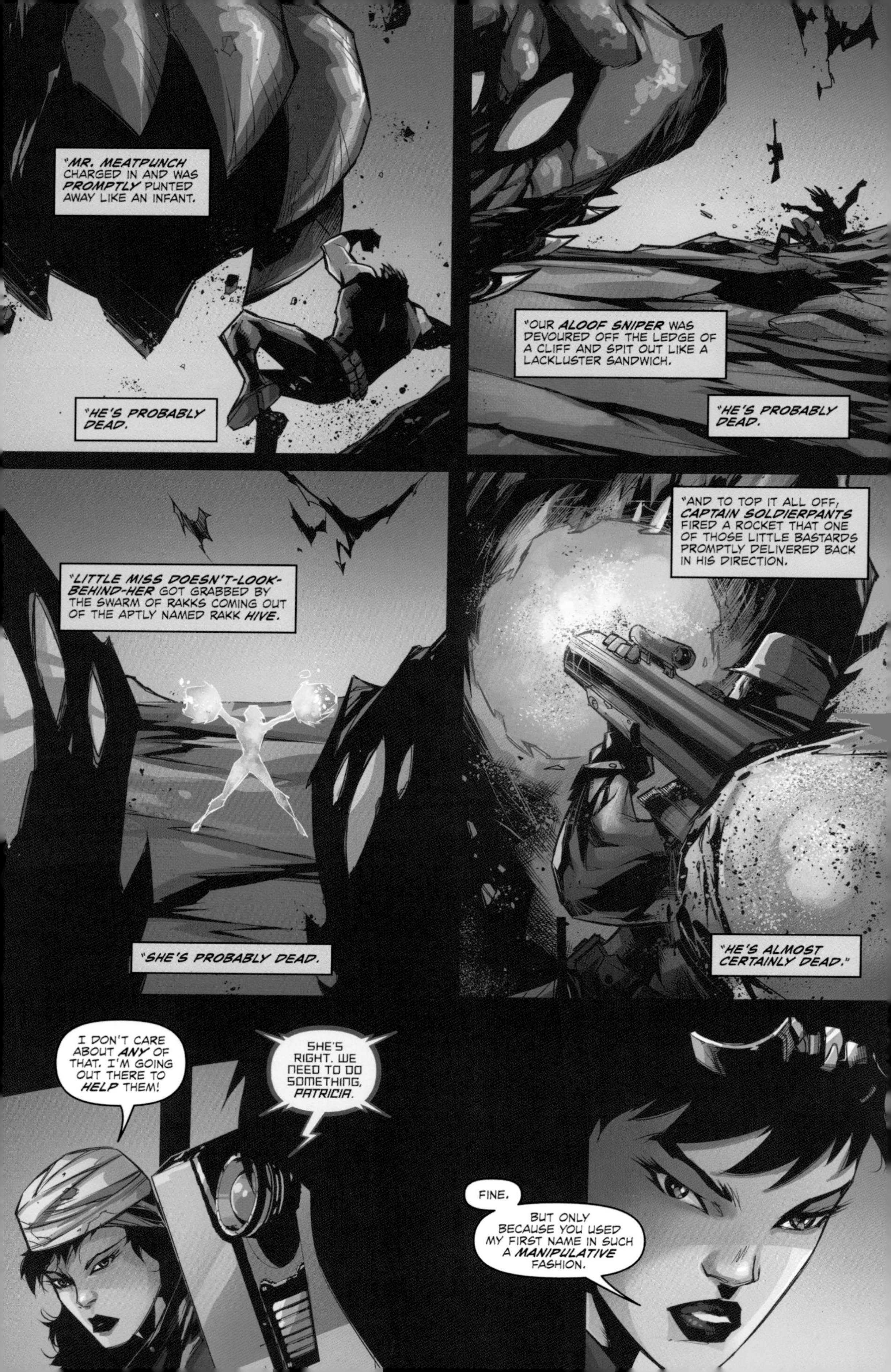
"MR. MEATPUNCH CHARGED IN AND WAS PROMPTLY PUNTED AWAY LIKE AN INFANT.
"HE'S PROBABLY DEAD.
"OUR ALOOF SNIPER WAS DEVOURED OFF THE LEDGE OF A CLIFF AND SPIT OUT LIKE A LACKLUSTER SANDWICH.
"HE'S PROBABLY DEAD.
"LITTLE MISS DOESN'T-LOOK-BEHIND-HER GOT GRABBED BY THE SWARM OF RAKKS COMING OUT OF THE APTLY NAMED RAKK HIVE.
"SHE'S PROBABLY DEAD.
"AND TO TOP IT ALL OFF, CAPTAIN SOLDIERPANTS FIRED A ROCKET THAT ONE OF THOSE LITTLE BASTARDS PROMPTLY DELIVERED BACK IN HIS DIRECTION.
"HE'S ALMOST CERTAINLY DEAD."
I DON'T CARE ABOUT ANY OF THAT. I'M GOING OUT THERE TO HELP THEM!
SHE'S RIGHT. WE NEED TO DO SOMETHING, PATRICIA.
FINE.
BUT ONLY BECAUSE YOU USED MY FIRST NAME IN SUCH A MANIPULATIVE FASHION.

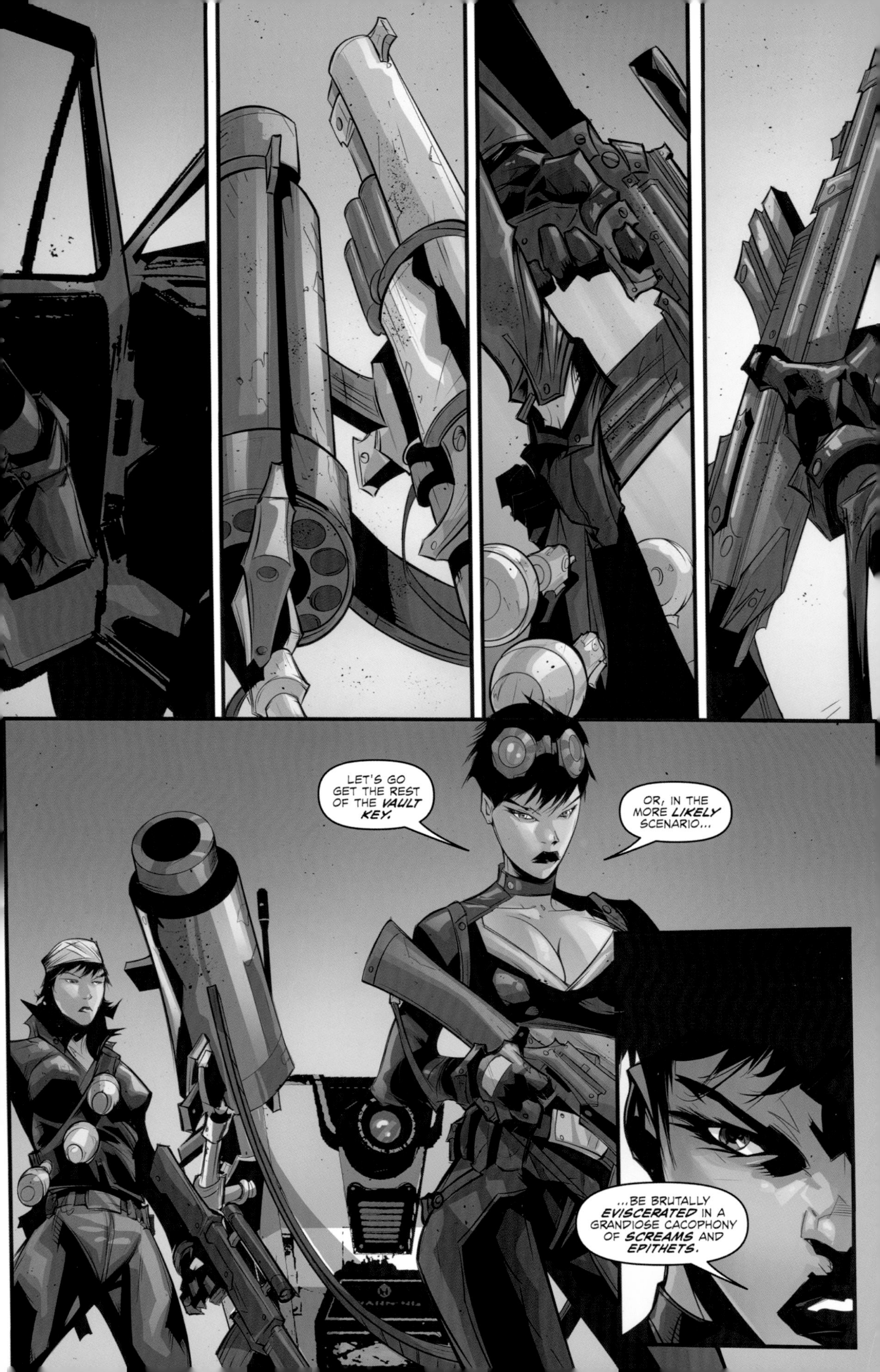

LET'S GO GET THE REST OF THE *VAULT KEY.*
OR, IN THE MORE *LIKELY* SCENARIO...
...BE BRUTALLY *EVISCERATED* IN A GRANDIOSE CACOPHONY OF *SCREAMS* AND *EPITHETS*.

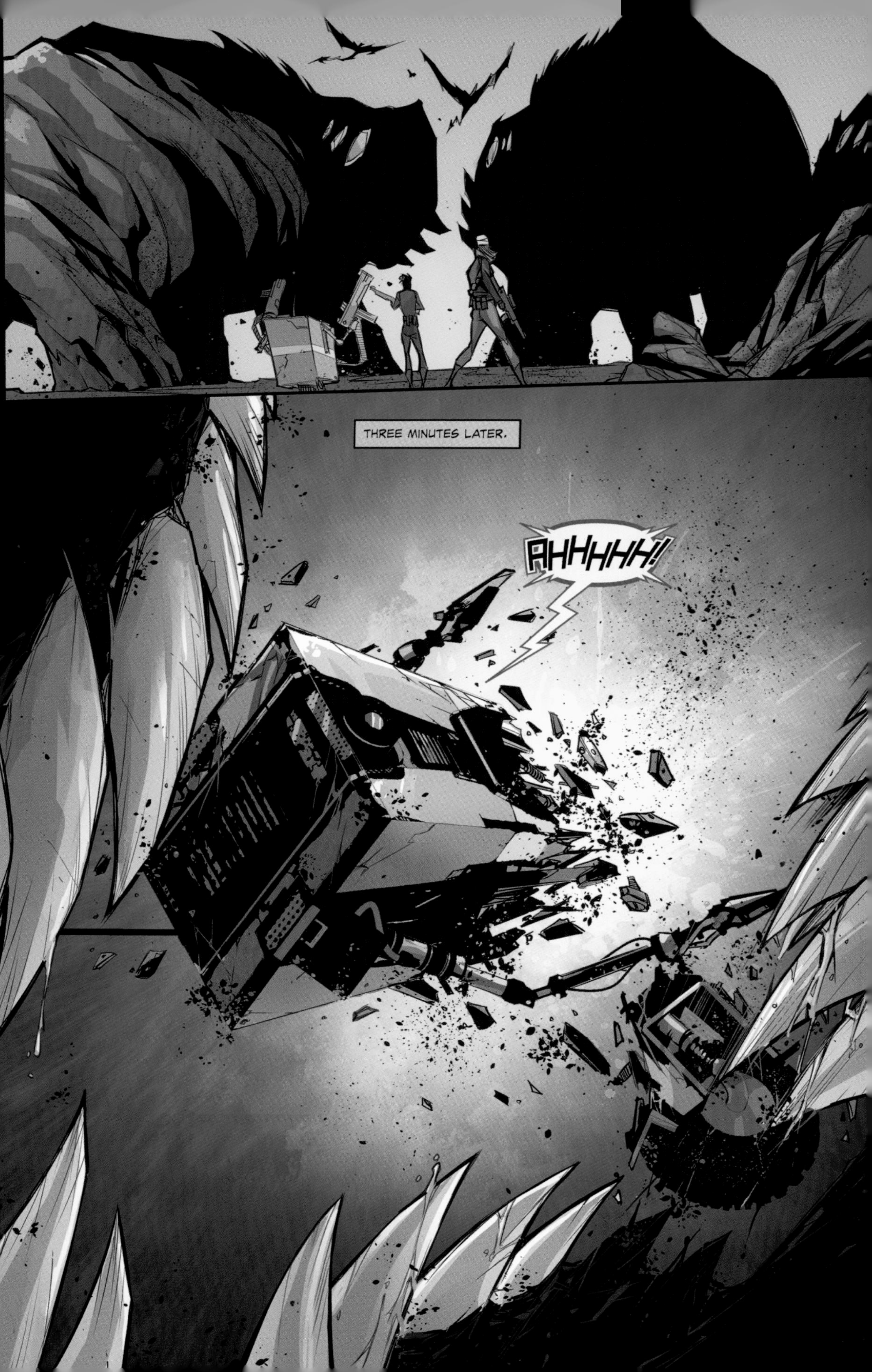
THREE MINUTES LATER.
AHHHHH!

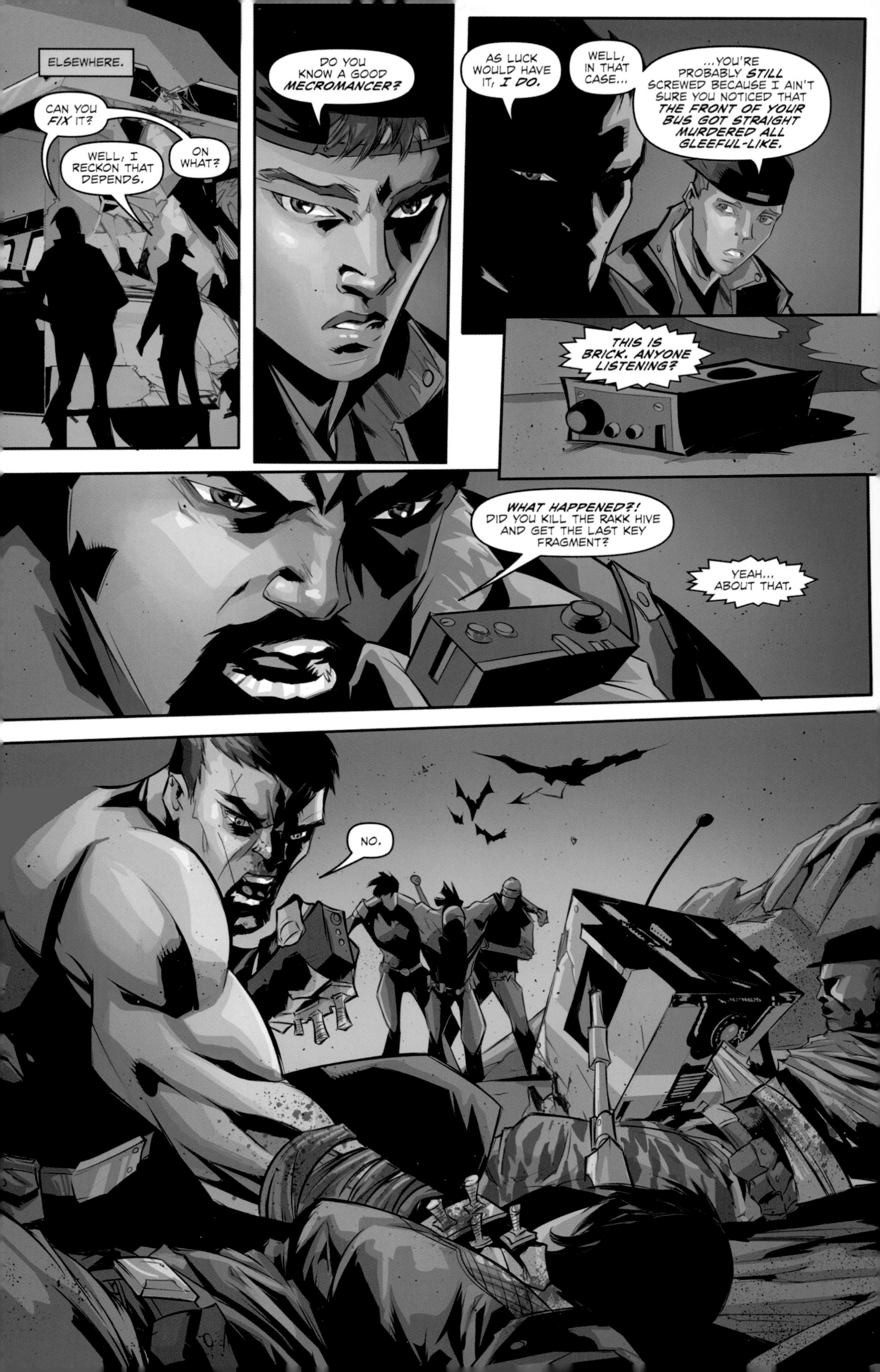

ELSEWHERE.
CAN YOU FIX IT?
WELL, I RECKON THAT DEPENDS.
ON WHAT?
DO YOU KNOW A GOOD MECROMANCER?
AS LUCK WOULD HAVE IT, I DO.
WELL, IN THAT CASE...
...YOU'RE PROBABLY STILL SCREWED BECAUSE I AIN'T SURE YOU NOTICED THAT THE FRONT OF YOUR BUS GOT STRAIGHT MURDERED ALL GLEEFUL-LIKE.
THIS IS BRICK. ANYONE LISTENING?
WHAT HAPPENED?! DID YOU KILL THE RAKK HIVE AND GET THE LAST KEY FRAGMENT?
YEAH... ABOUT THAT.
NO.

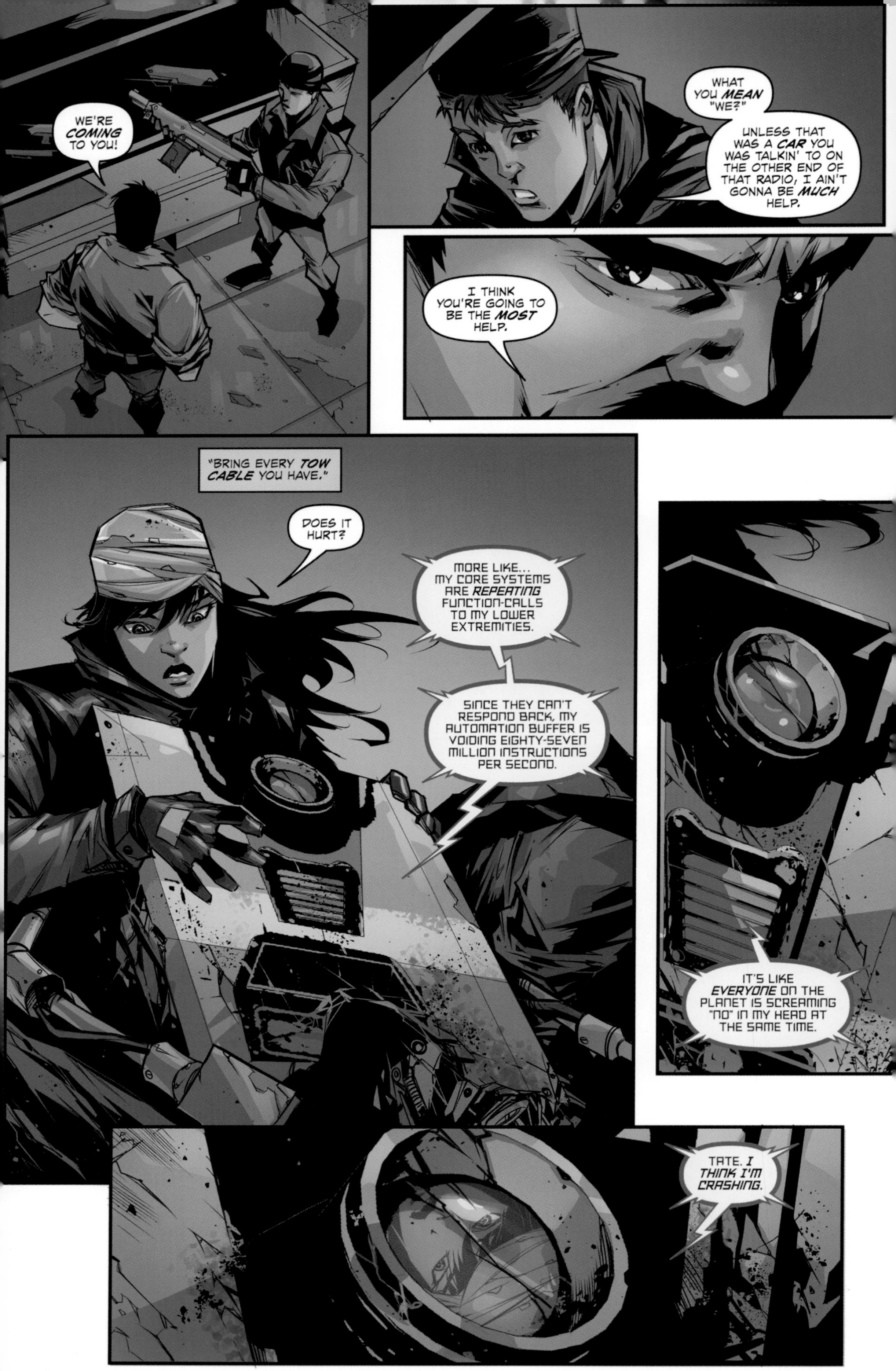
WE'RE COMING TO YOU!
WHAT YOU MEAN "WE?"
UNLESS THAT WAS A CAR YOU WAS TALKIN' TO ON THE OTHER END OF THAT RADIO, I AIN'T GONNA BE MUCH HELP.
I THINK YOU'RE GOING TO BE THE MOST HELP.
"BRING EVERY TOW CABLE YOU HAVE."
DOES IT HURT?
MORE LIKE... MY CORE SYSTEMS ARE REPEATING FUNCTION-CALLS TO MY LOWER EXTREMITIES.
SINCE THEY CAN'T RESPOND BACK, MY AUTOMATION BUFFER IS VOIDING EIGHTY-SEVEN MILLION INSTRUCTIONS PER SECOND.
IT'S LIKE EVERYONE ON THE PLANET IS SCREAMING "NO" IN MY HEAD AT THE SAME TIME.
TATE. I THINK I'M CRASHING.

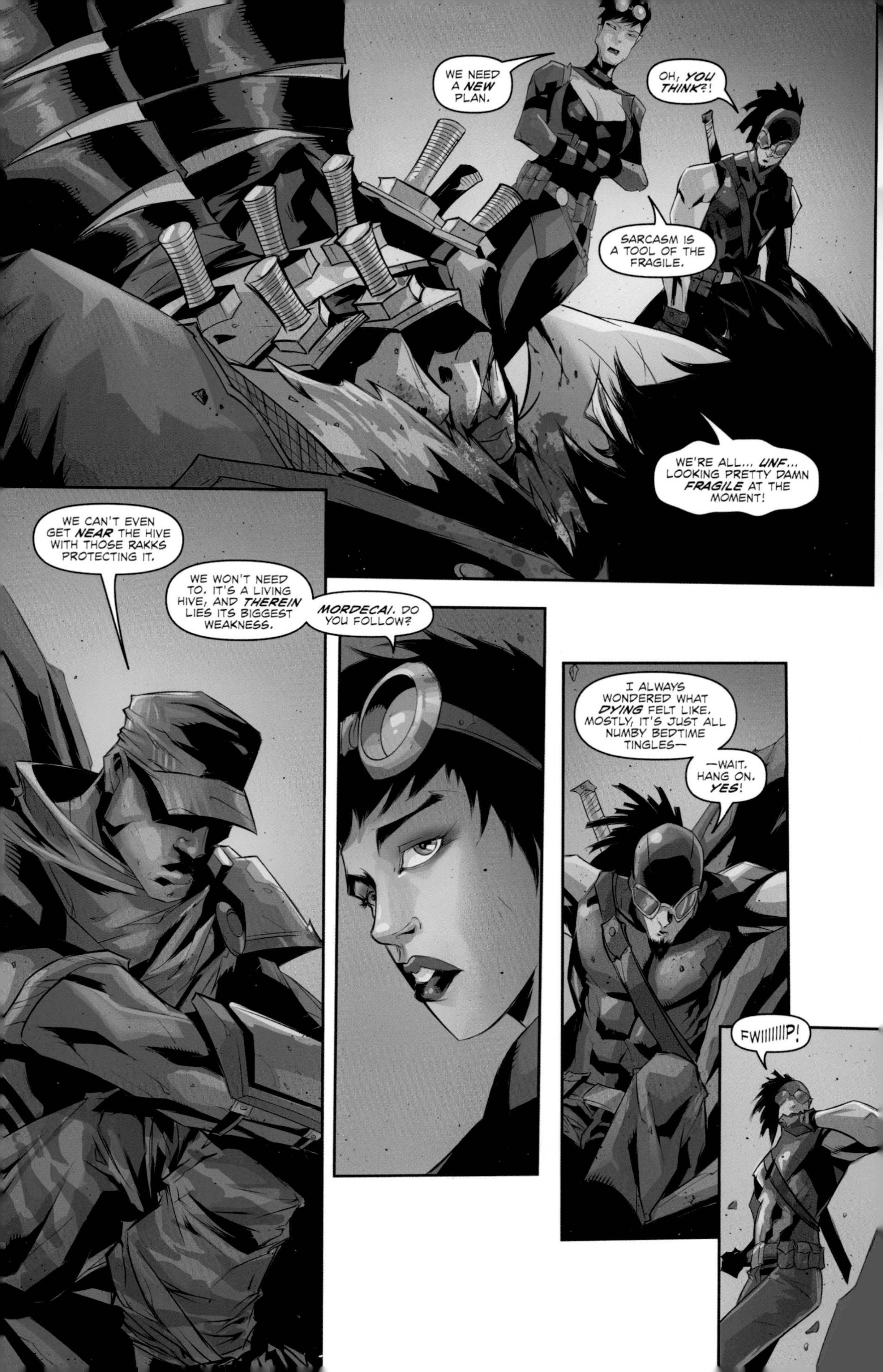
WE NEED A NEW PLAN.
OH, YOU THINK?!
SARCASM IS A TOOL OF THE FRAGILE.
WE'RE ALL... UNF... LOOKING PRETTY DAMN FRAGILE AT THE MOMENT!
WE CAN'T EVEN GET NEAR THE HIVE WITH THOSE RAKKS PROTECTING IT.
WE WON'T NEED TO. IT'S A LIVING HIVE, AND THEREIN LIES ITS BIGGEST WEAKNESS.
MORDECAI. DO YOU FOLLOW?
I ALWAYS WONDERED WHAT DYING FELT LIKE. MOSTLY, IT'S JUST ALL NUMBY BEDTIME TINGLES—
—WAIT. HANG ON. YES!
FWIIIIIIP!

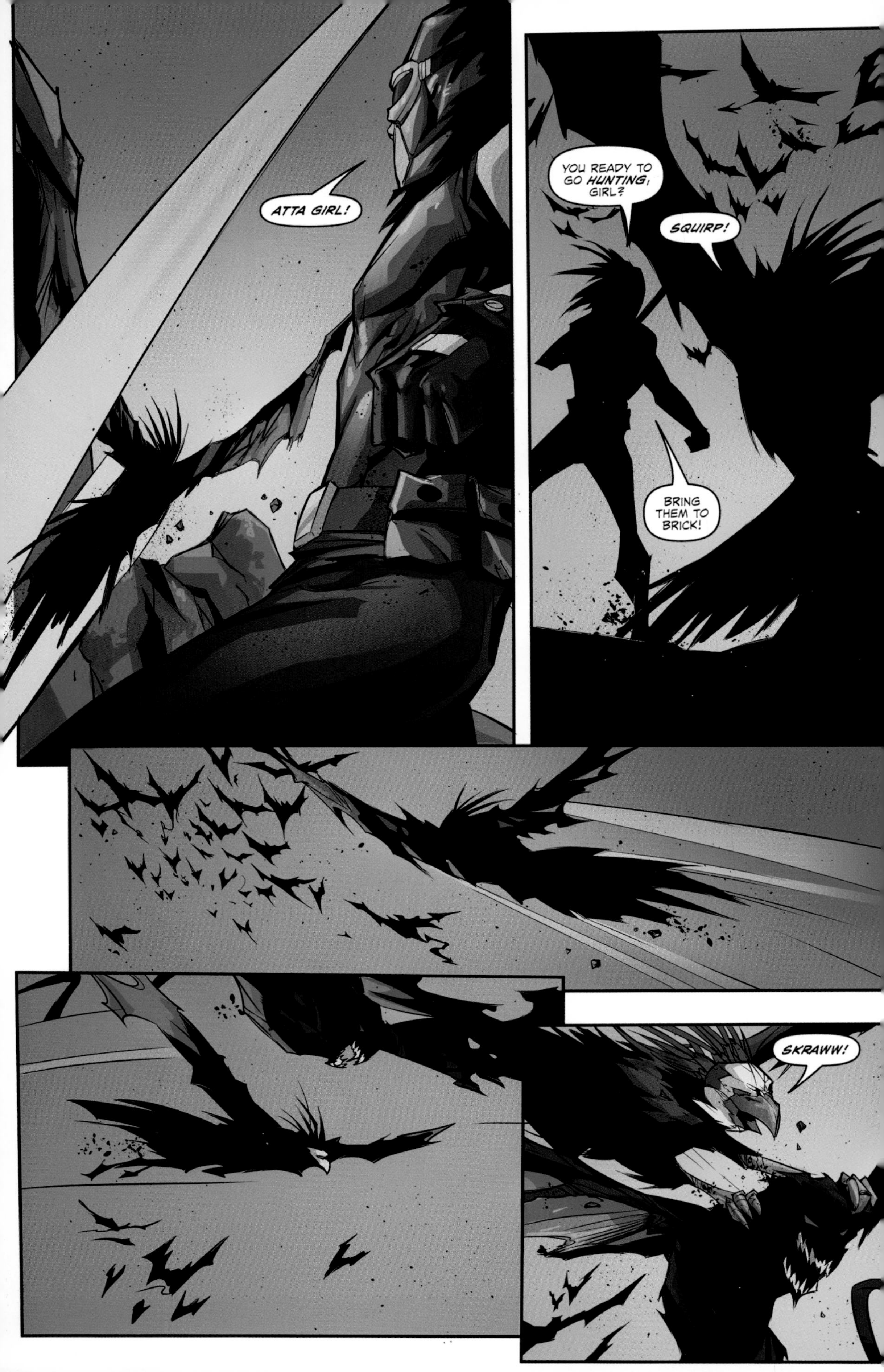
ATTA GIRL!
YOU READY TO GO HUNTING, GIRL?
SQUIRP!
BRING THEM TO BRICK!
SKRAWW!

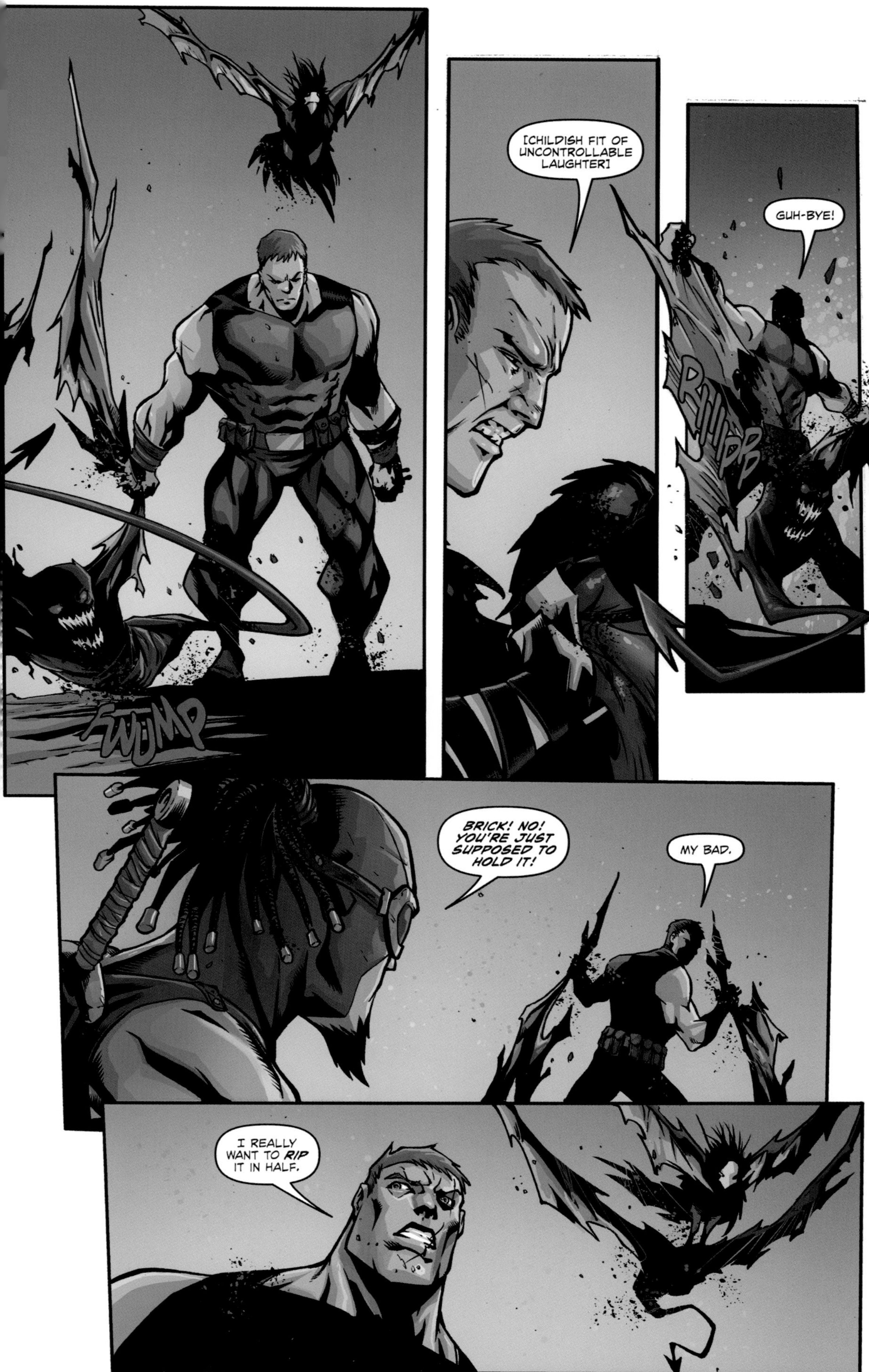
FWUMP
[CHILDISH FIT OF UNCONTROLLABLE LAUGHTER]
GUH-BYE!
RHIPP
BRICK! NO! YOU'RE JUST SUPPOSED TO HOLD IT!
MY BAD.
I REALLY WANT TO *RIP* IT IN HALF.

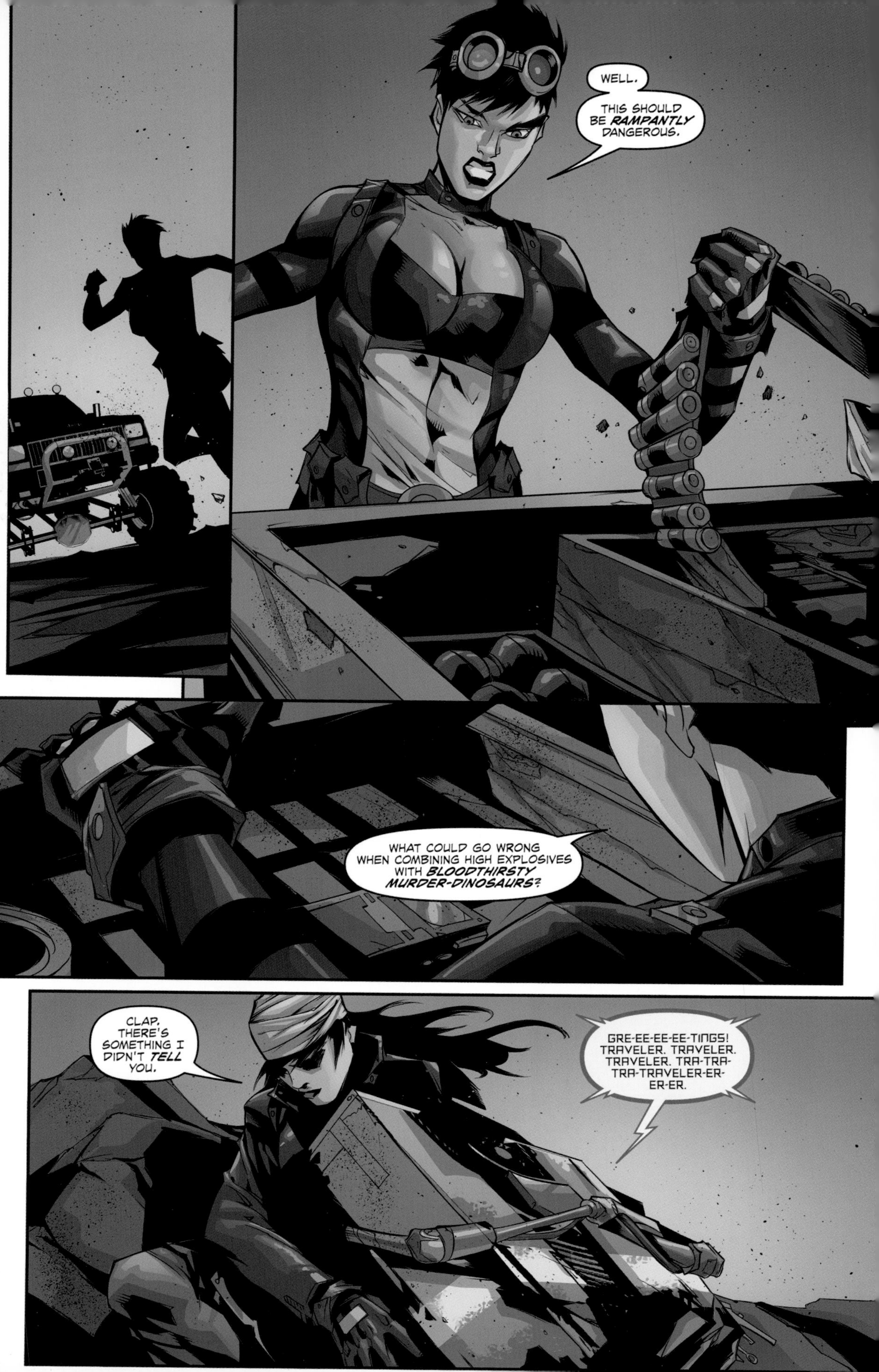
WELL.
THIS SHOULD BE *RAMPANTLY* DANGEROUS.
WHAT COULD GO WRONG WHEN COMBINING HIGH EXPLOSIVES WITH *BLOODTHIRSTY MURDER-DINOSAURS*?
CLAP. THERE'S SOMETHING I DIDN'T *TELL* YOU.
GRE-EE-EE-EE-TINGS! TRAVELER. TRAVELER. TRAVELER. TRA-TRA-TRA-TRAVELER-ER-ER-ER.

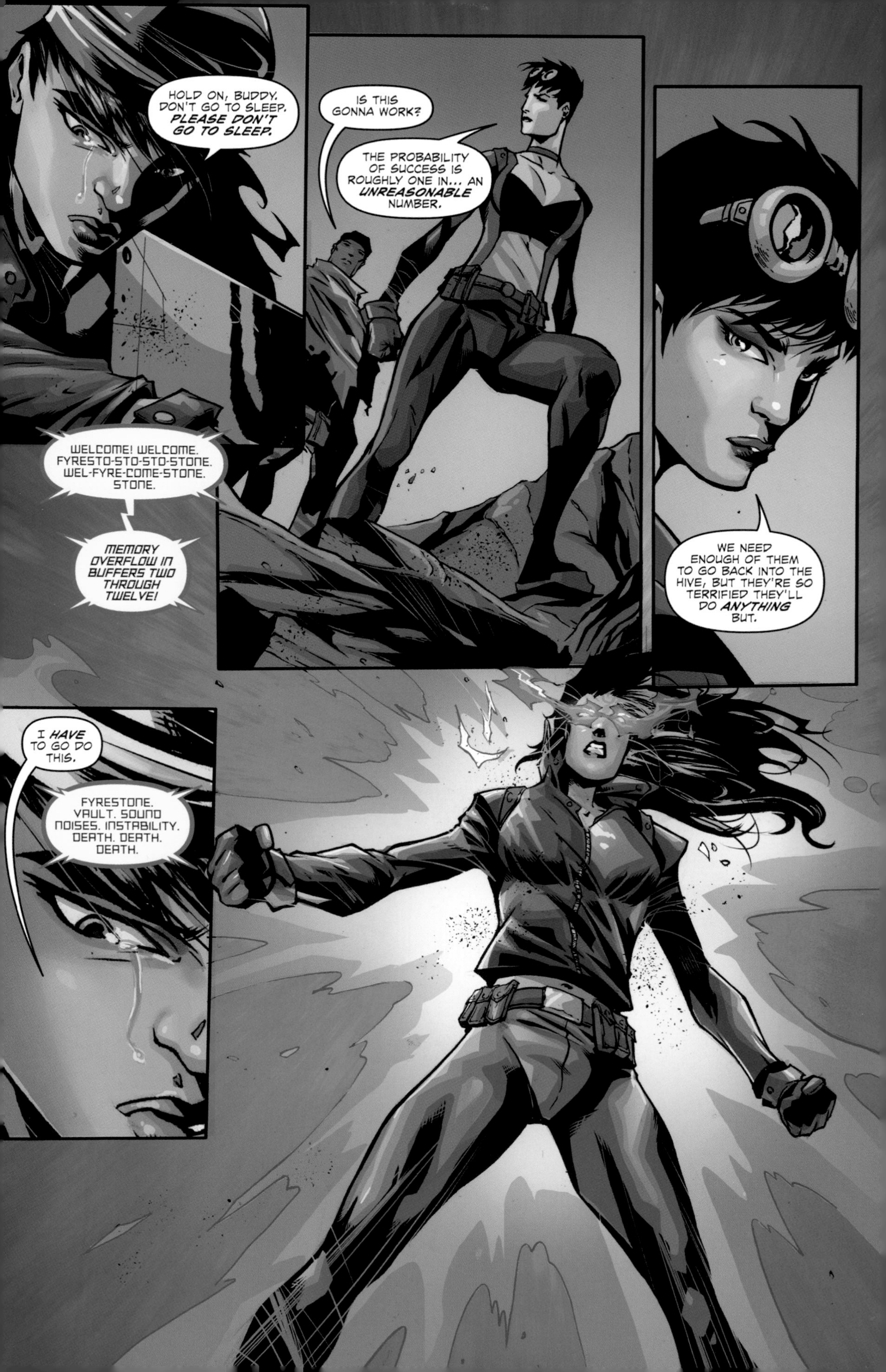
HOLD ON, BUDDY. DON'T GO TO SLEEP. PLEASE DON'T GO TO SLEEP.
IS THIS GONNA WORK?
THE PROBABILITY OF SUCCESS IS ROUGHLY ONE IN... AN UNREASONABLE NUMBER.
WELCOME! WELCOME. FYRESTO-STO-STO-STONE. WEL-FYRE-COME-STONE. STONE.
MEMORY OVERFLOW IN BUFFERS TWO THROUGH TWELVE!
WE NEED ENOUGH OF THEM TO GO BACK INTO THE HIVE, BUT THEY'RE SO TERRIFIED THEY'LL DO ANYTHING BUT.
I HAVE TO GO DO THIS.
FYRESTONE. VAULT. SOUND NOISES. INSTABILITY. DEATH. DEATH. DEATH.

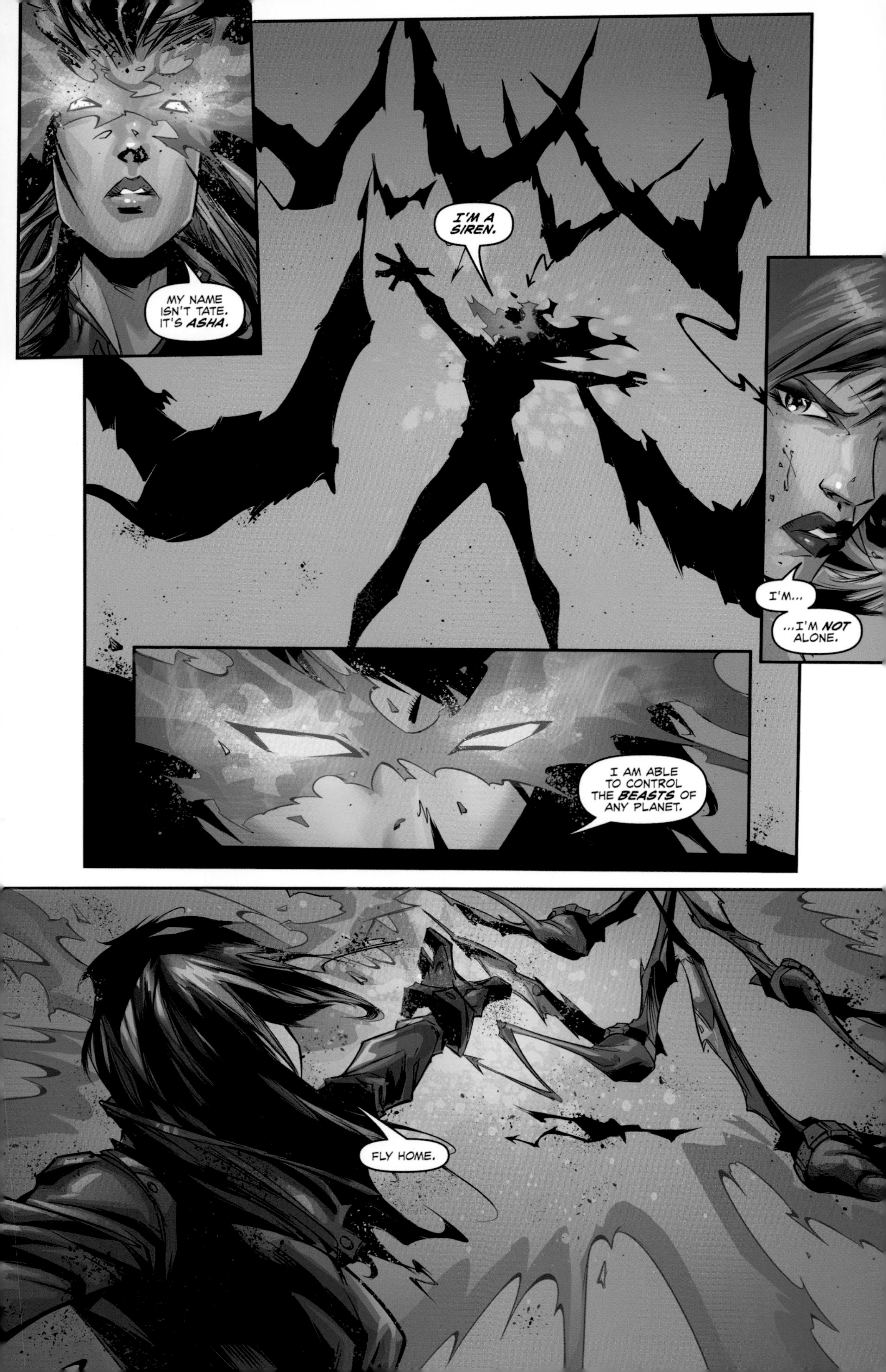
MY NAME ISN'T TATE. IT'S ASHA.
I'M A SIREN.
I'M...
...I'M NOT ALONE.
I AM ABLE TO CONTROL THE BEASTS OF ANY PLANET.
FLY HOME.

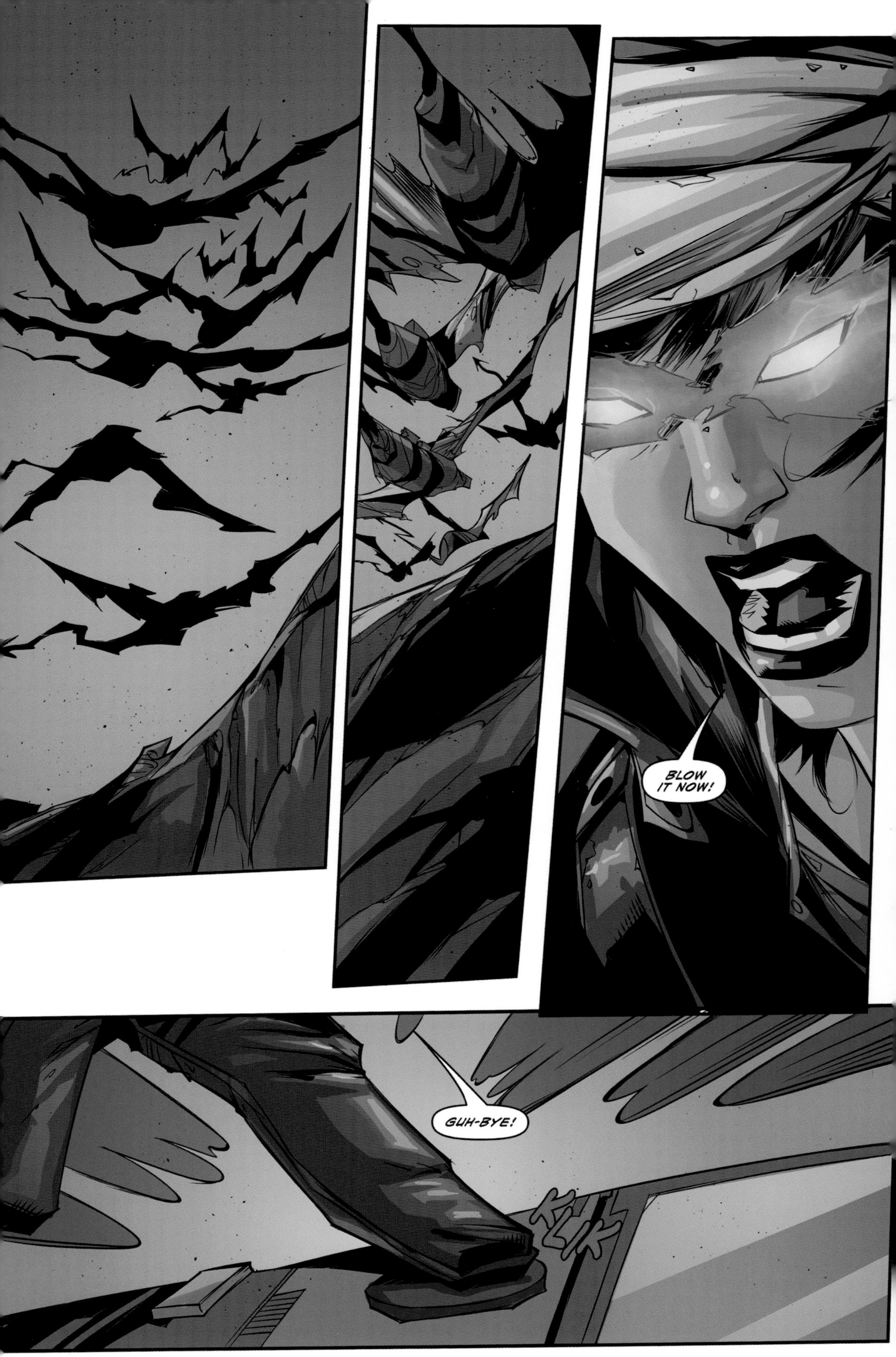
BLOW IT NOW!
GUH-BYE!
KLIK

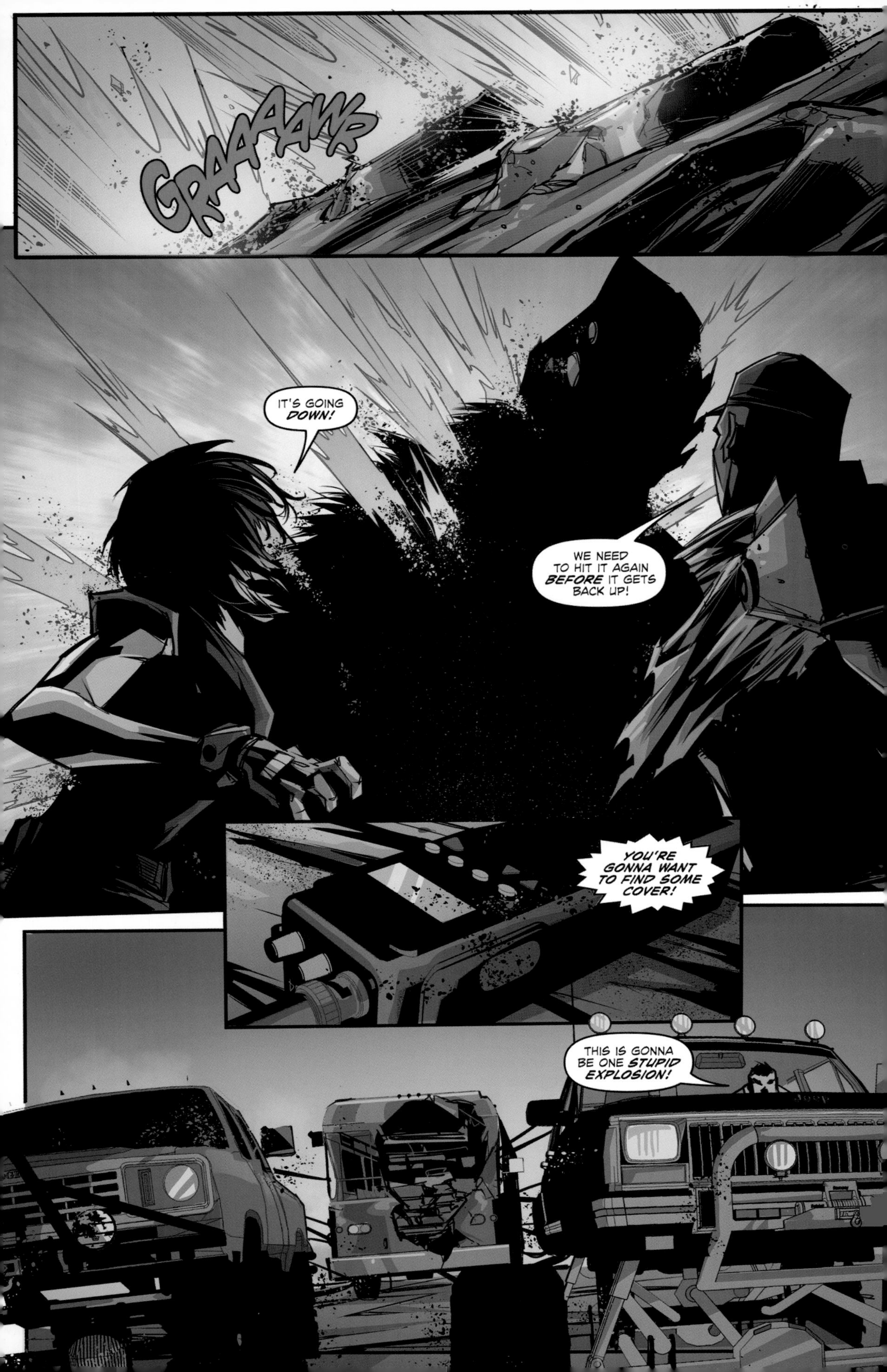
GRAAAAWR
IT'S GOING DOWN!
WE NEED TO HIT IT AGAIN BEFORE IT GETS BACK UP!
YOU'RE GONNA WANT TO FIND SOME COVER!
THIS IS GONNA BE ONE STUPID EXPLOSION!

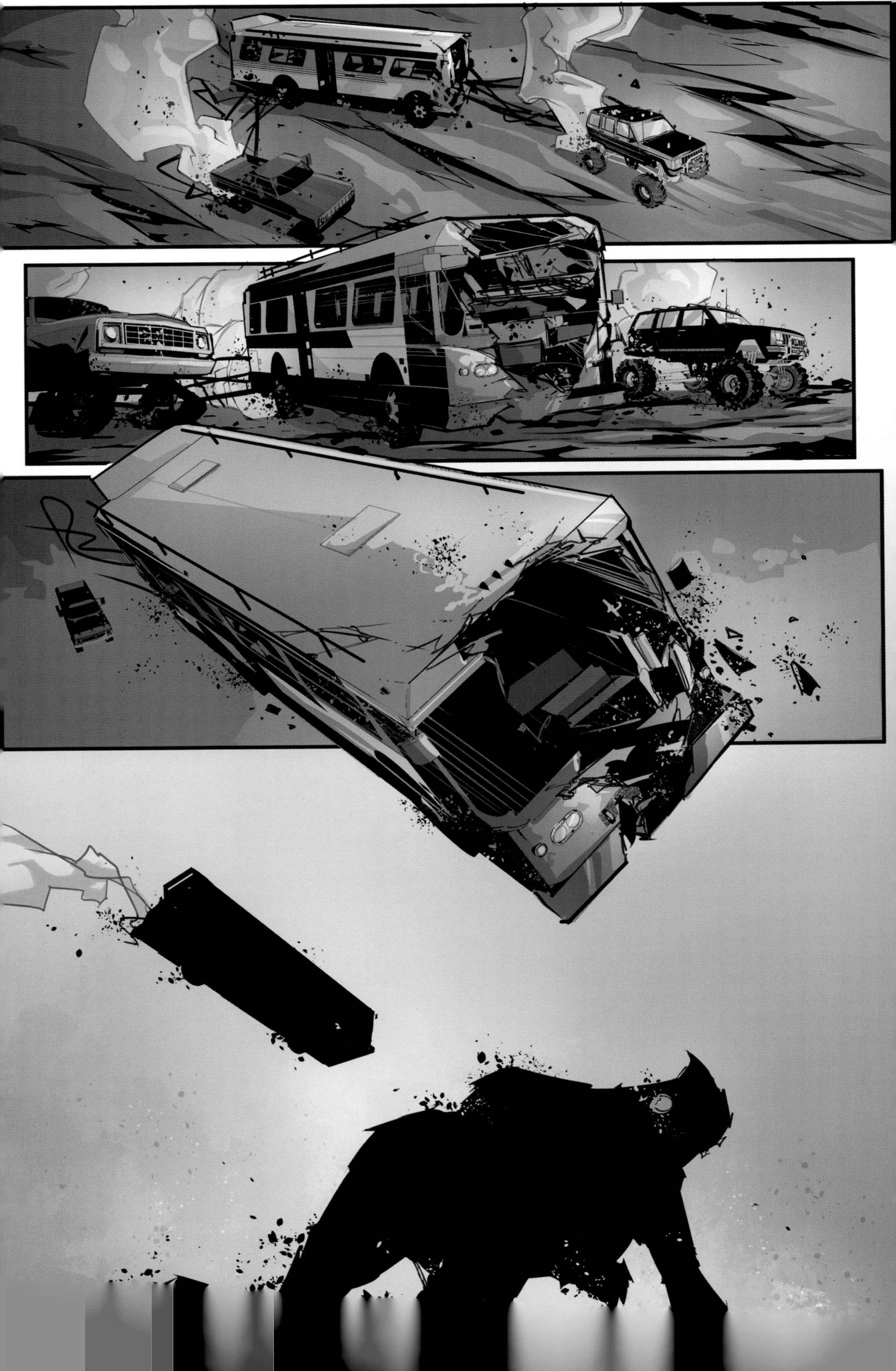

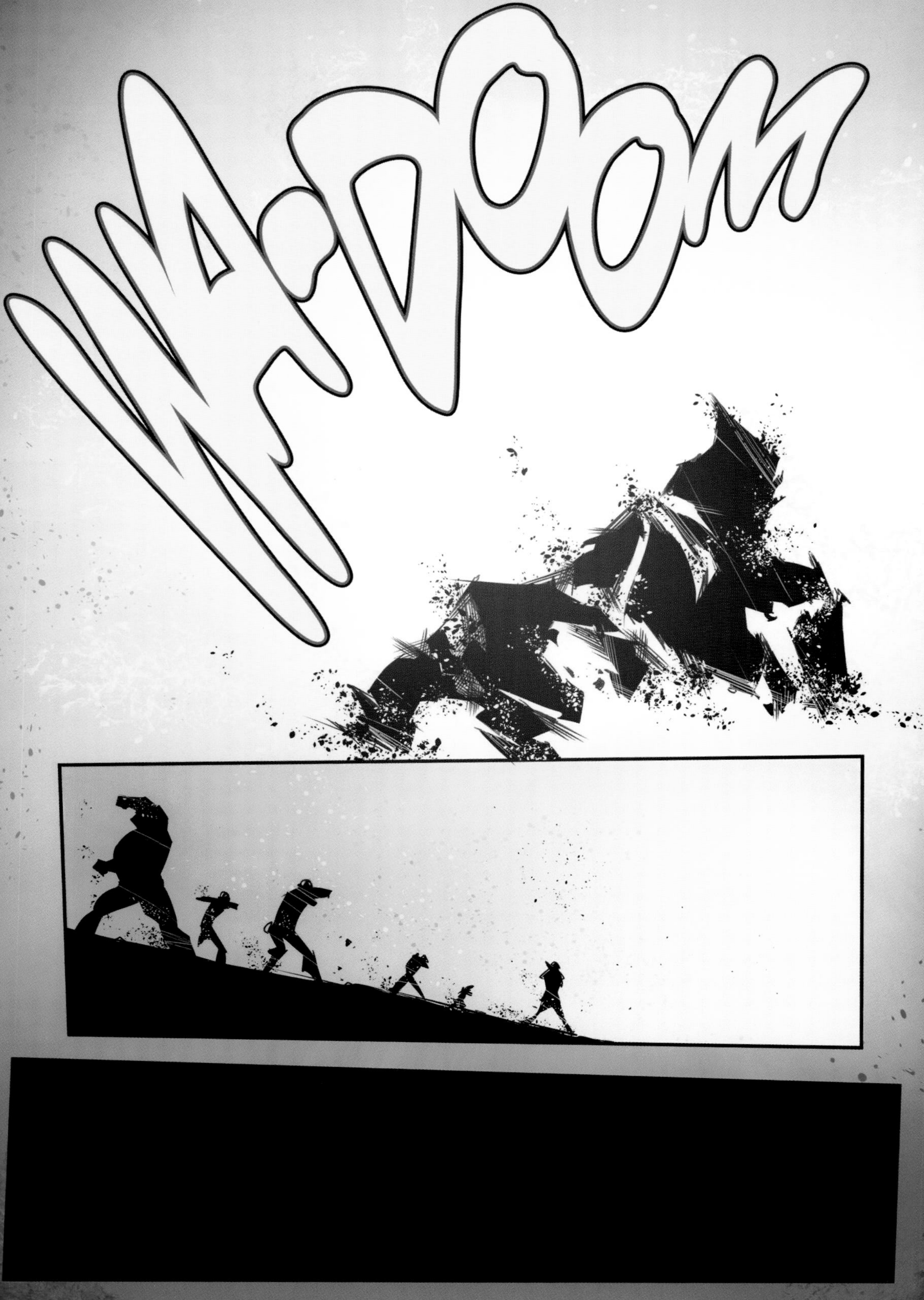
WA-DOOM

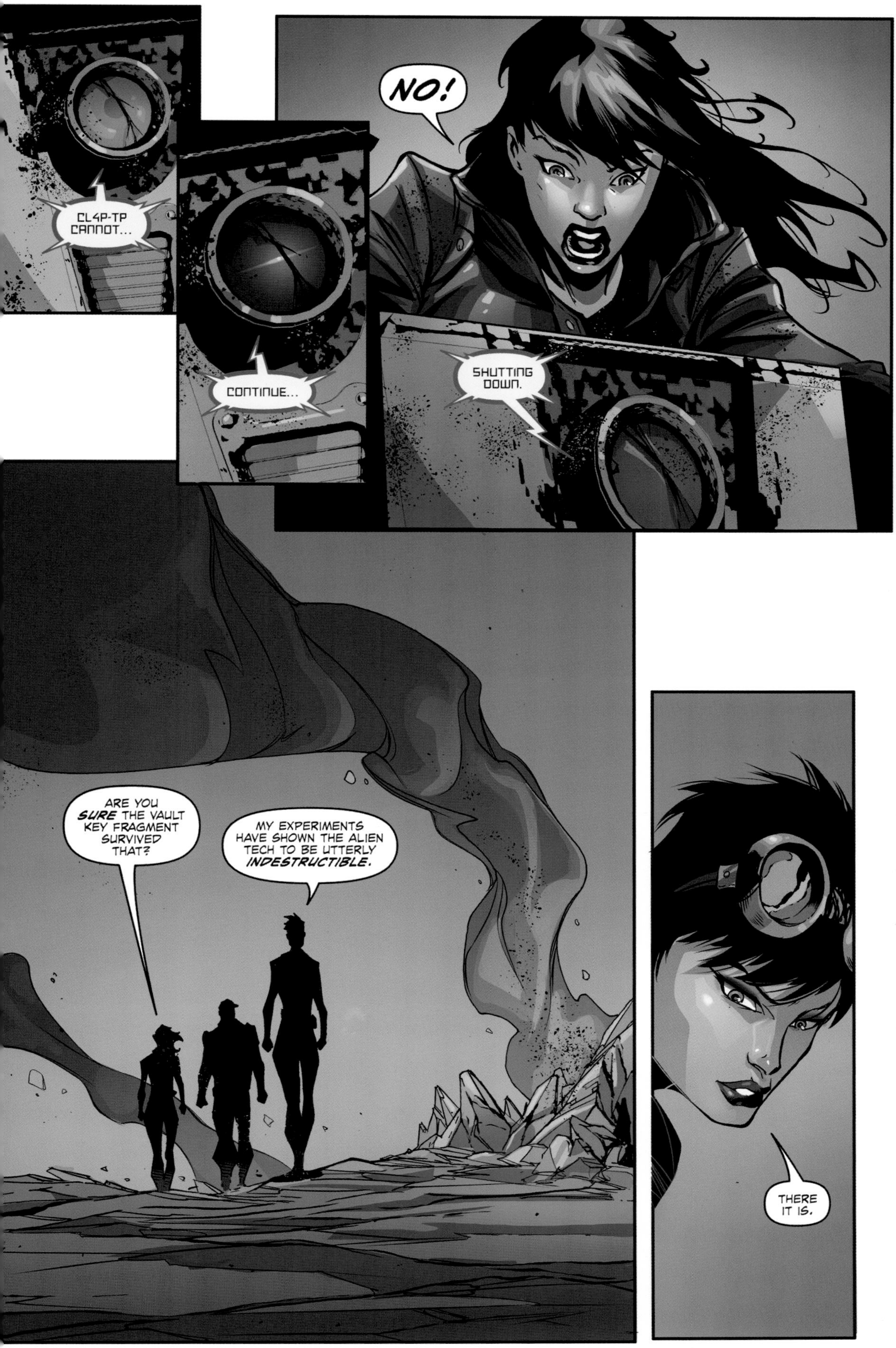
CL4P-TP CANNOT...
CONTINUE...
NO!
SHUTTING DOWN.
ARE YOU SURE THE VAULT KEY FRAGMENT SURVIVED THAT?
MY EXPERIMENTS HAVE SHOWN THE ALIEN TECH TO BE UTTERLY INDESTRUCTIBLE.
THERE IT IS.

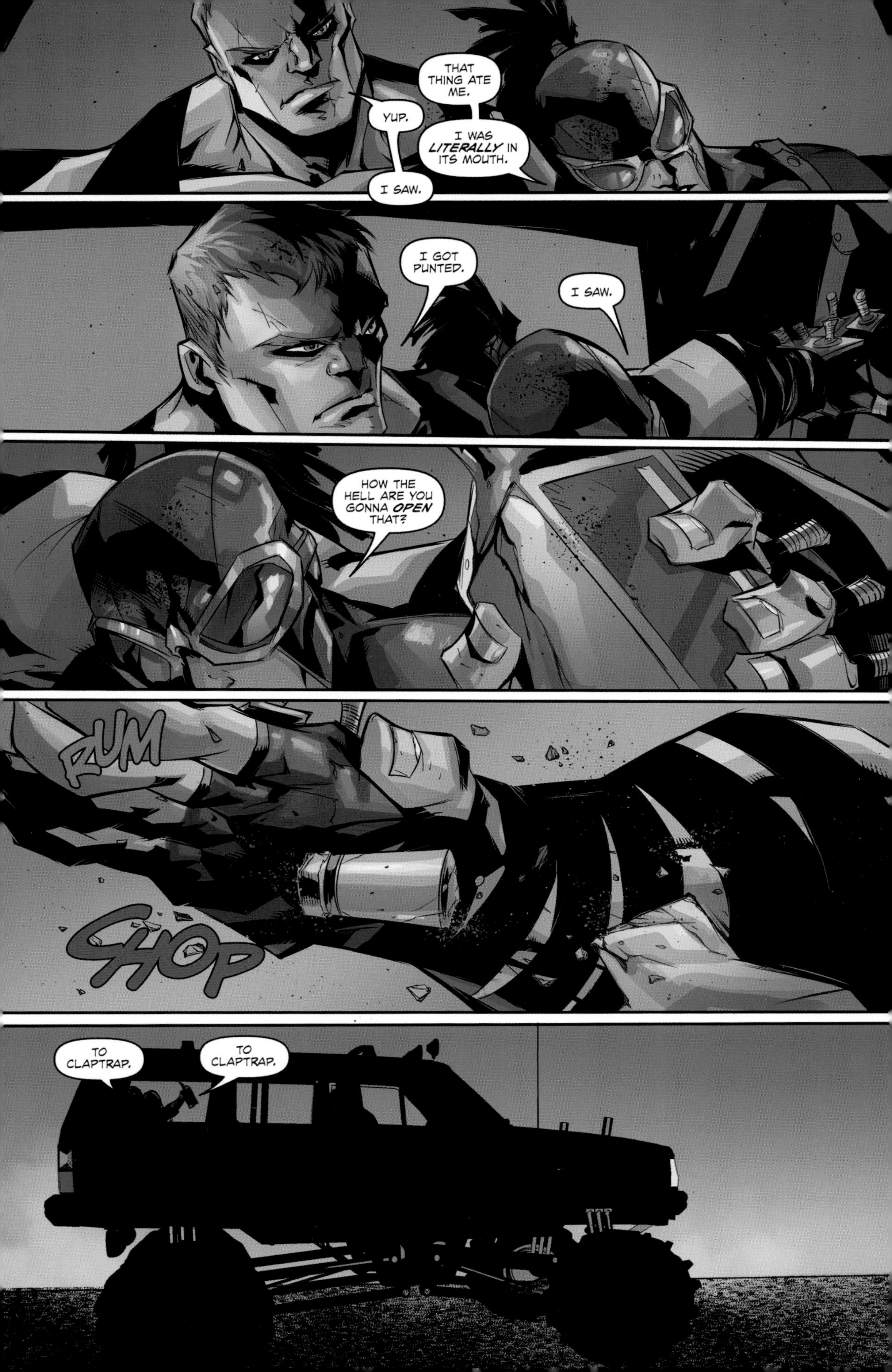
THAT THING ATE ME.
YUP.
I WAS LITERALLY IN ITS MOUTH.
I SAW.
I GOT PUNTED.
I SAW.
HOW THE HELL ARE YOU GONNA OPEN THAT?
RUM
CHOP
TO CLAPTRAP.
TO CLAPTRAP.

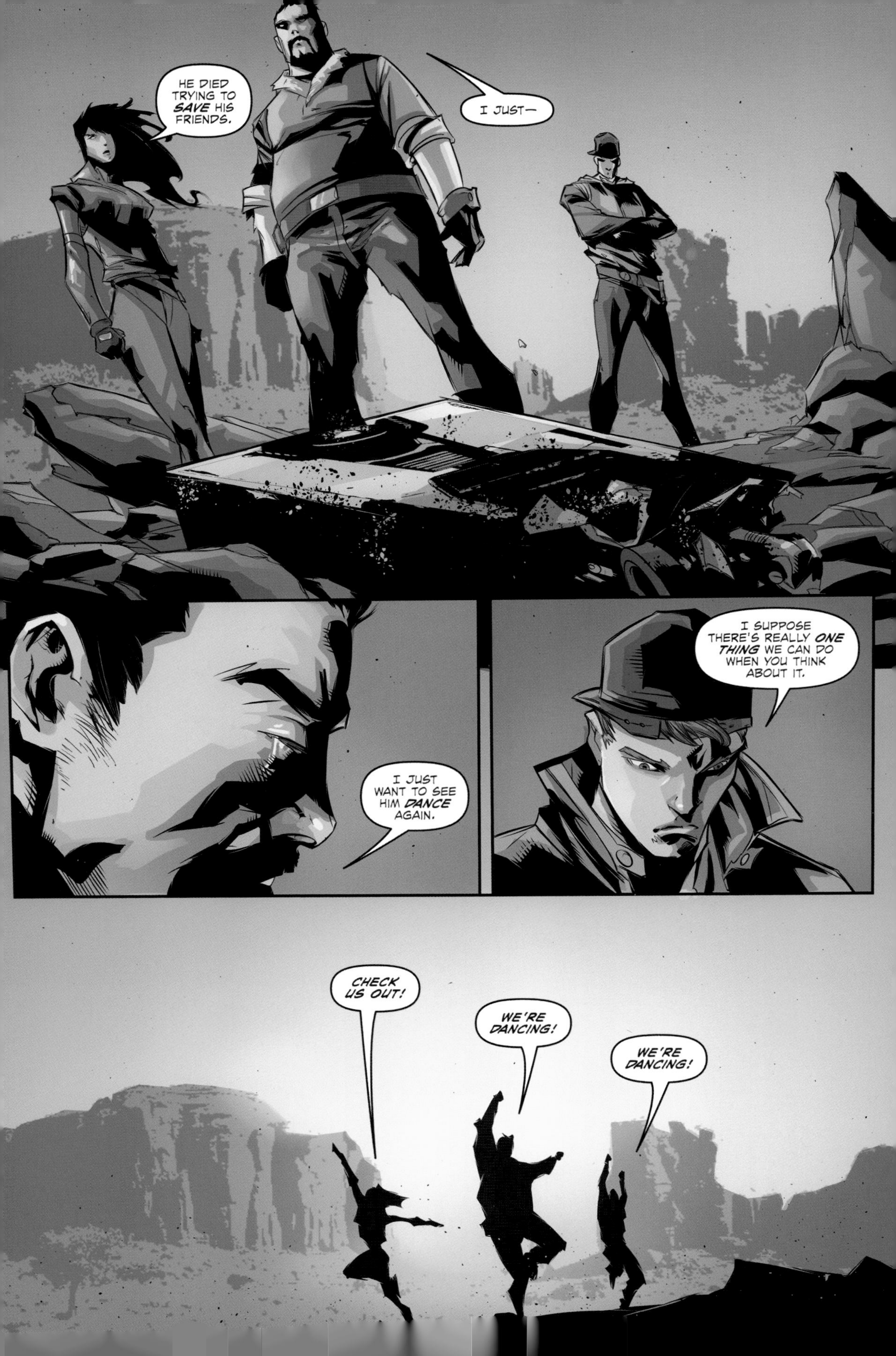
HE DIED TRYING TO *SAVE* HIS FRIENDS.
I JUST—
I JUST WANT TO SEE HIM *DANCE* AGAIN.
I SUPPOSE THERE'S REALLY *ONE THING* WE CAN DO WHEN YOU THINK ABOUT IT.
CHECK US OUT!
WE'RE DANCING!
WE'RE DANCING!

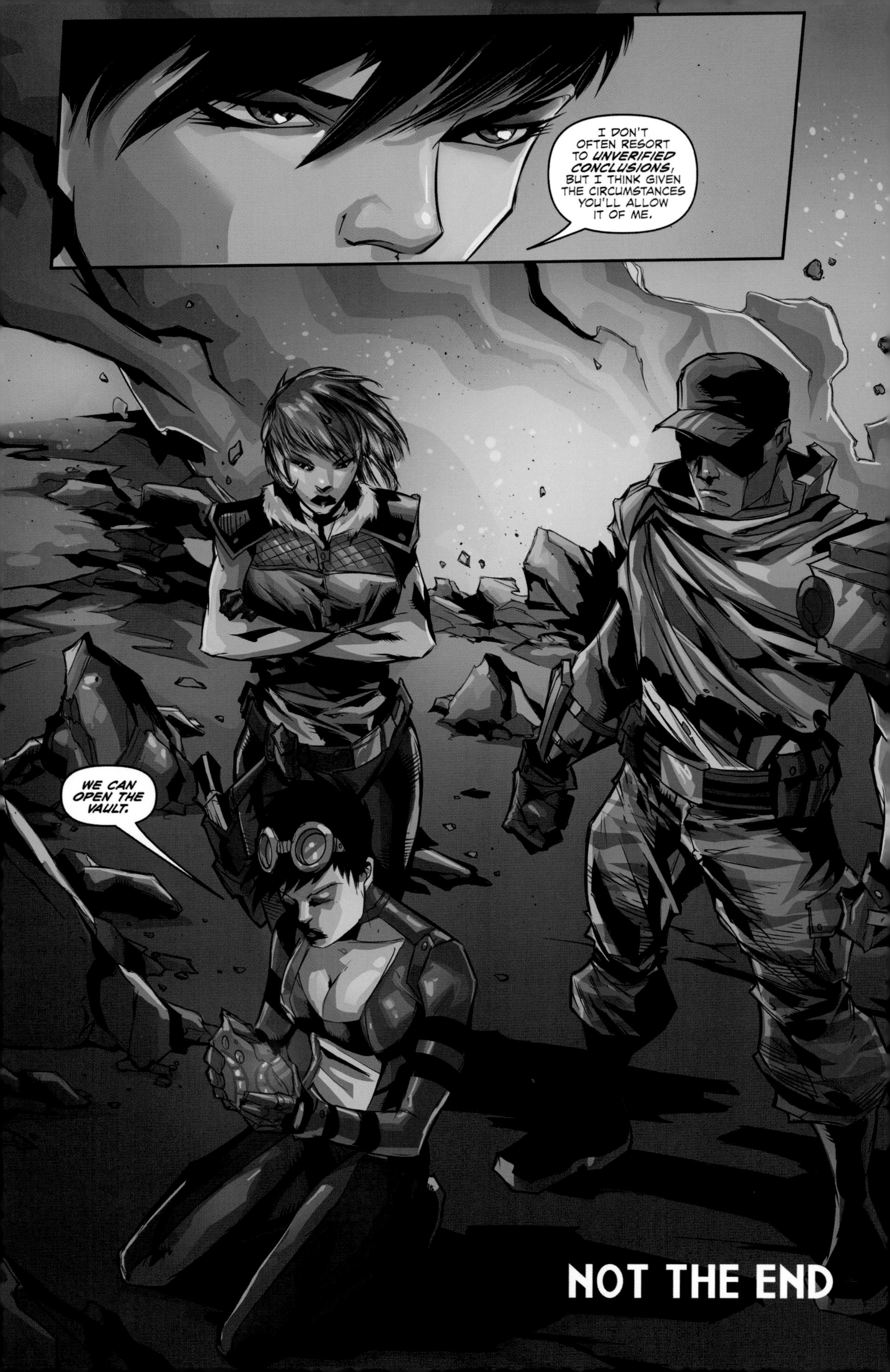
I DON'T OFTEN RESORT TO *UNVERIFIED CONCLUSIONS*, BUT I THINK GIVEN THE CIRCUMSTANCES YOU'LL ALLOW IT OF ME.
WE CAN OPEN THE VAULT.
NOT THE END

Art Gallery

ARTIST'S EDITION COVER

ORGANICAL — GREEN

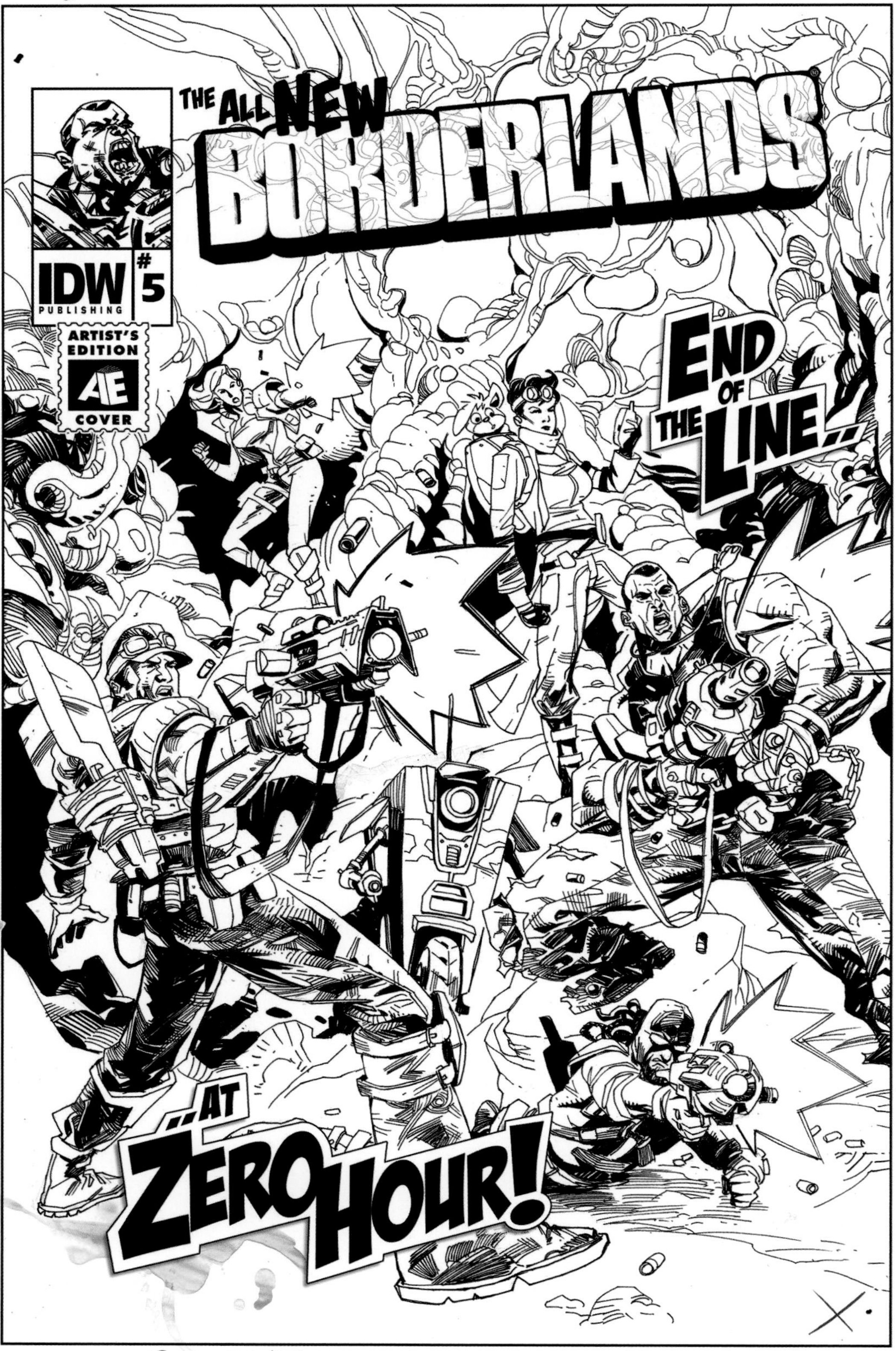

THE ALL NEW
BORDERLANDS
IDW PUBLISHING
#5
ARTIST'S EDITION
AE
COVER
END OF THE LINE..
..AT
ZERO HOUR!

YELLOW TS

BLACK TS

GREY GREEN ROCKS

MEMBRANE — BLUEISH

RED TS

BLUE TS

TITLE NO. BORDERLANDS #1

SCHEDULE

by JOSE HOLDER

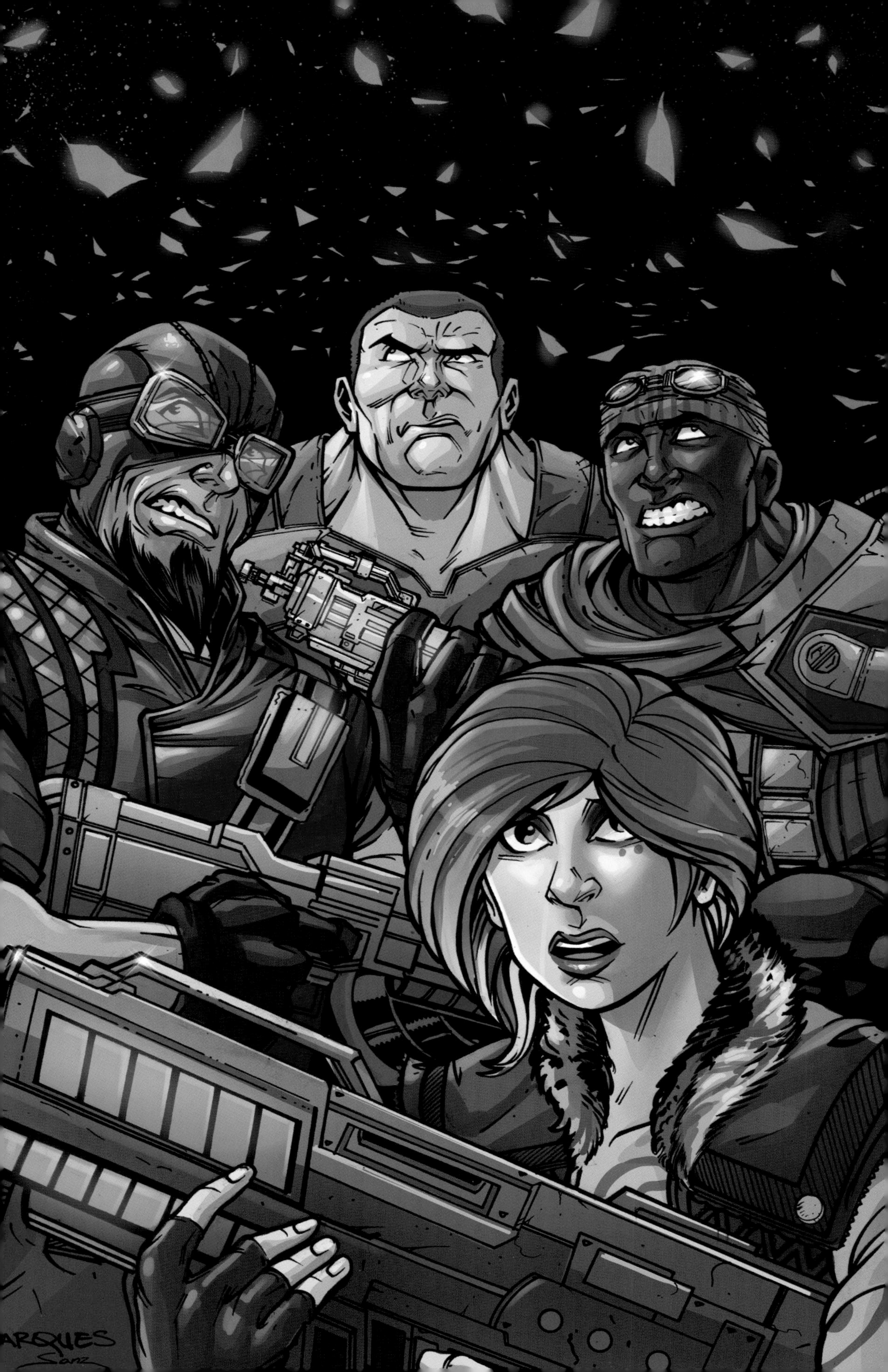
ARQUES
Sanz

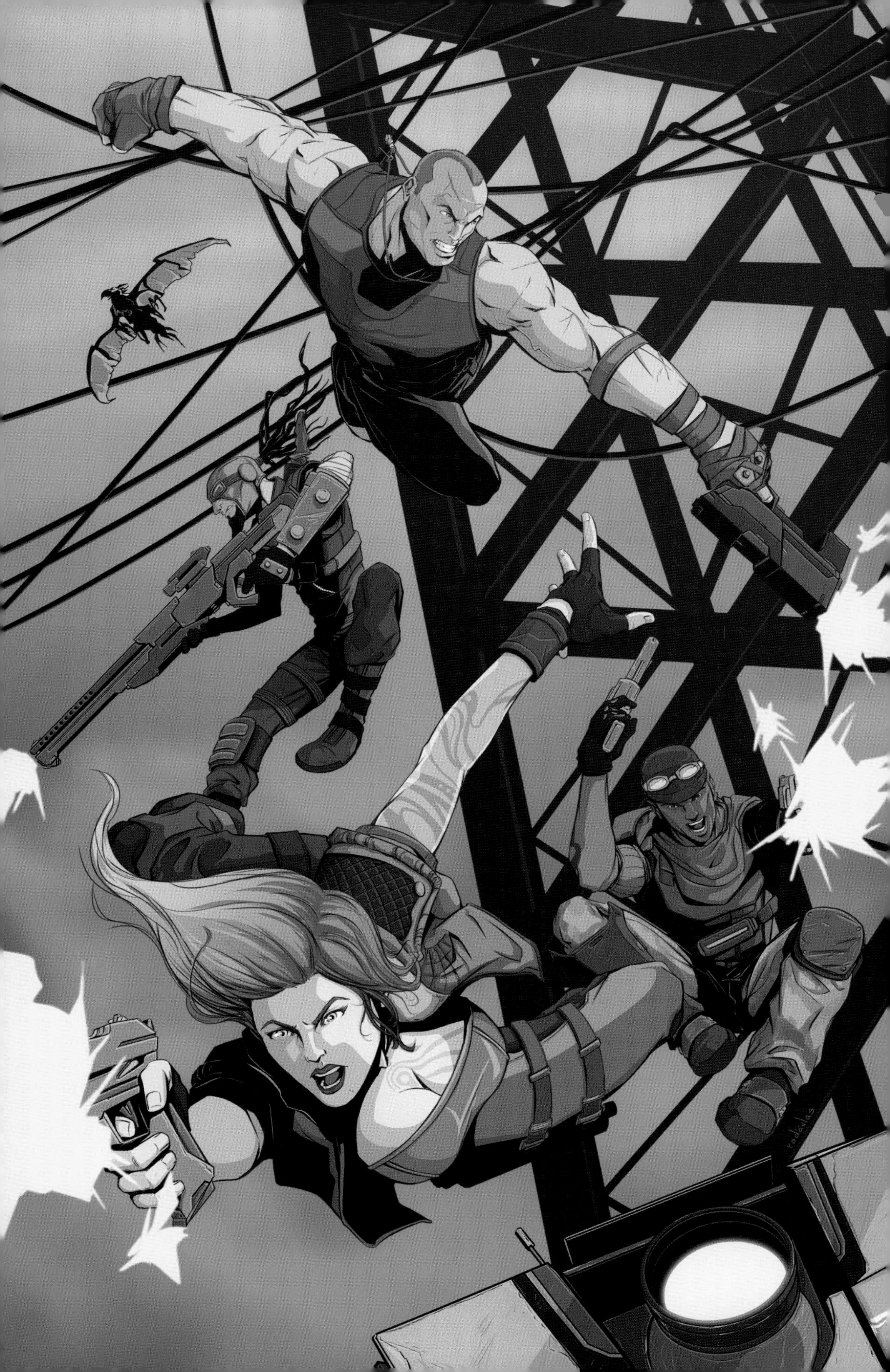

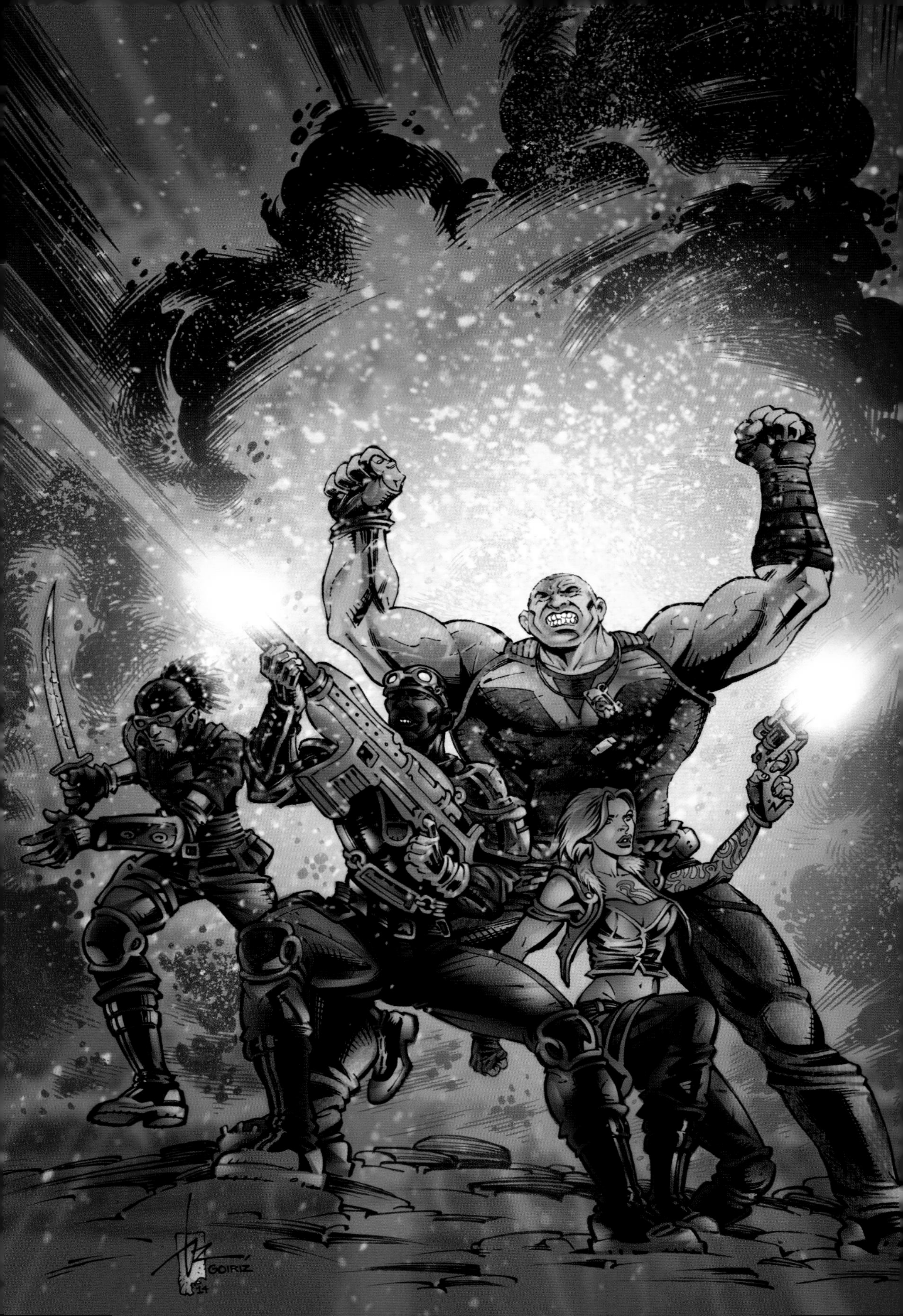
GOIRIZ

SITE PAGE: art by SAL

GE: art by ROBERTO

BORDERLANDS®

TANNIS and the VAULT

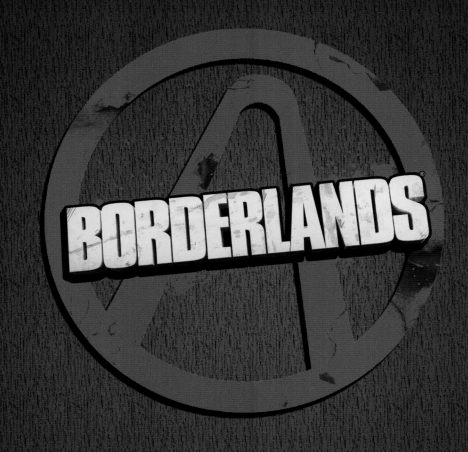